Contents

Preface

An Overture to Social Anthropology was written as a general introduction to social and cultural anthropology. Like most such volumes, it was born out of the author's dissatisfaction with the coverage, emphases and modes of presentation of similar books. The introductory text is too often a series of definitions of terms followed by ethnographic examples, all pretense to unity lost in narrow compartmentalization. Its style tends to the didactic, explanation is substituted by oversimplification and condescension, and memorization passes for understanding. It seeks its audience at the level of the least common denominator and, in the process, loses intellectual content. I intend to avoid these failings.

The book covers the main topical divisions of the usual one semester course in social anthropology in four-year undergraduate colleges. The field of social anthropology is broad and diverse, but it has an underlying unity of orientation and purpose which I have attempted to preserve and convey to the reader. In doing so, I have tried to avoid misleadingly tidy definitions in favor of theoretical explanations shorn of professional jargon. This allows each chapter, and the entire volume, to be developed around a series of central and interconnected themes; the chapters thus synthesize their subject matter rather than dicing it up into poorly related sub-sections. In the same way, the various chapters are brought together in an organic unity that bespeaks the interrelatedness of all aspects of social life to each other.

The scope of the book is consistent with the breadth of the standard textbook, but its style differs. It is my intent that *An Overture to Social Anthropology* will be suitable as an introductory text in social and cultural anthropology, but it is also my hope that the layman interested in obtaining an overview of the field will find the book readable as well as instructive. To this end, I have shunned narrow parochialism and have sought to relate anthropological thought to some of the main intellectual

An Overture

to

Social Anthropology

ROBERT F. MURPHY

Columbia University

PRENTICE-HALL, INC., Englewood Cliffs, New Jersey 07632

Library of Congress Cataloging in Publication Data

Murphy, Robert Francis,
   An overture to social anthropology.

   Bibliography: p.
   Includes index.
   1. Ethnology. I. Title.
GN316.M87   301.2   78-14544
ISBN 0-13-647461-6

TO MY STUDENTS
each and every one

Prentice-Hall Anthropology Series
David M. Schneider, Editor

Printed in the United States of America

10 9 8 7 6 5 4 3 2

Cover Photograph by
PAUL BYERS

PRENTICE-HALL INTERNATIONAL, INC., *London*
PRENTICE-HALL OF AUSTRALIA PTY. LIMITED, *Sydney*
PRENTICE-HALL OF CANADA, LTD., *Toronto*
PRENTICE-HALL OF INDIA PRIVATE LIMITED, *New Delhi*
PRENTICE-HALL OF JAPAN, INC., *Tokyo*
PRENTICE-HALL OF SOUTHEAST ASIA PTE. LTD., *Singapore*
WHITEHALL BOOKS LIMITED, *Wellington, New Zealand*

currents of Western culture, especially in social theory and psychoanalysis. And I have rejected an encyclopedic approach to social anthropology in order to focus on its principle directions and contributions. This has promoted the integration of the book while preserving an economy of size.

Teachers of anthropology have in recent years favored a diversity of readings rather than the older pattern of drawing all assignments from one large textbook, a change that is in part due to the increased availability of less expensive paperback books. The compact size of this volume allows it to be used to give an overview and introduction to the field in combination with supplementary assignments of monographic descriptions of cultures, collections of articles, and short works on special topics. Coupled with lectures and classroom discussions, the yield should be a well-rounded course which will also be as engrossing as anthropology truly is.

Finally, I have sought to communicate the sense of excitement and wonder that are the hallmark of the anthropological experience. In a specializing and secular age, anthropology is one of the last avenues of inquiry into the condition and fate of humanity and the only discipline to pose the general question "What is man?" In studying the bewildering kaleidoscope of human expression, anthropology thus becomes an inquest upon ourselves, and we travel to the most remote parts of the world only to confront our inner being.

Acknowledgements

An Overture to Social Anthropology is the product of almost twenty-five years of teaching introductory anthropology to undergraduate students at the University of California, Berkeley and Columbia University. Students past and present will recognize familiar passages within its pages, and they will also find their own comments and ideas interwoven in its development. A book so general as this is the result of multiple influences, and those of my students have ranked with the most important. I am grateful for their contribution to my education. At the same time, I must apologize to about half of them for recurrent references to "mankind" and "man" when speaking of *homo sapiens* in general, and for using "he" and "him" as genderless personal pronouns. English does not have neuter categories, and the alternatives to sex-linked terms are few and grammatically woeful. Our language is inadequate in this respect, but it is the substance and not the lexicon of sex statuses that should be our first concern.

Over the years, I have drawn upon the thought and writings of many people; it would be impossible to trace these links and it would be boorish to mention some names to the exclusion of others. I must, however, single out the imprint of a great teacher, Charles Wagley, who was over thirty years ago my first instructor in anthropology and who has been my mentor, colleague, and friend ever since. Other students and associates contributed directly to the making of this volume, and I list them with gratitude. Morton Fried read the manuscript and made many helpful suggestions; he deserves much credit for whatever merits the book may have, and a bit of the blame for its shortcomings. Joel Wallman made a detailed critique of the manuscript that served as a basis for its revision; I am grateful for his expert evaluation. Four anonymous readers retained by the publisher made valuable constructive criticisms; I do not know their identities, but I appreciate their interest and labors. David Schneider and Brian Burkhalter also read the manuscript and gave support and encouragement, for which my thanks. And Virginia Brown prepared the final manuscript for publication; the only flaws were my own doing.

Both the book and the author owe much to Columbia University. I have profited greatly from the stimulation of a remarkable group of colleagues in its Department of Anthropology, and I owe the very physical capacity to write the volume to two members of its medical faculty, Professors Daniel Sciarra and Edward Schlesinger. Beyond my indebtedness to my colleagues for both ideas and limbs, Columbia University granted me a sabbatical leave in the Spring of 1977, during which most of the book was written, and it has always provided an atmosphere of intellectual freedom and encouragement of excellence.

Finally, my wife, Yolanda, has been my fellow student, my collaborator, my mainstay and support. She encouraged me to write this book, just as she has joined me in all our undertakings. Our lives have become so entwined that to thank her would be a redundancy, and the debt must remain unspoken for the inadequacy of words.

Prologue to Anthropology

Many millions of years ago, in an age so remote that we can only perceive its dim outlines, a population of ground-dwelling, apelike creatures started on a unique evolutionary road. During a time span that covered hundreds of thousands of years, they gradually acquired livelihoods that required upright posture and found their key to survival in a burgeoning intelligence rather than in sinew and claw. These brutes, shambling and with knuckles dragging along the ground, went on to become humanity, the master of the planet and nature's most splendid work.

All animals are, in a sense, the authors of their own evolution, for success in food getting and reproductive activities is the major force in the adaptation through natural selection of creatures to their environments. The animals, including we humans, do not plan or even foresee their destinies, of course, but it is through their restless movements and their attempts to perpetuate their own existence that genetic variation in the short run becomes converted into biological evolution in the long run. It is also through these mechanisms that the animate world undergoes specialization and differentiation of populations and the proliferation of new species.

1

Humans evolved and are presumably still evolving through these processes, but the ultimate triumph of our species is that high intelligence, and with it language and the ability to pass knowledge from generation to generation and from society to society, has allowed us to partially escape from biological evolution. Whereas other animals adapt and survive through the progressive modification of their physical features, man's adaptation to other humans and to his natural milieu is accomplished largely through his creations, be they tools, houses, clothing, or ideas, the entire range of customary social practices which we call "culture." Lower forms of life adapt to their environments by changes in their bodies. Man adapts to his environment by creating artificial extensions of the body and thereby changing the environment.

The history of humanity is a history of the growth of man's attempt to control his surroundings. This can occur on the grand scale of our own industrial civilization, or it may manifest itself in the simple material inventory of primitive or nonliterate peoples. Our own society's victory over the environment has been so complete that we now threaten it with destruction. Massive road-building machinery rips swathes through the Amazon jungles; a pipeline cuts across Arctic tundra and mountains in Alaska; energy is drawn from fossil deposits of organic material or from the splitting of the atom. But our oceans are being plundered of fish, we breathe air that is used as a garbage dump for automobiles and factories, and we are assured that we will run out of oil by the end of this century. Those who maintain that we have adequate oil are often heard to say that it will last another century, as if this were eternity. One hundred years in the future will see all those now living dead, but one hundred years is a mere moment in the life of mankind, which spans more than a million years.

Our civilization is the purest example of man's triumph over nature, though it may well have begotten nature's revenge upon our descendants. But it is well to remember the recency of this modern technological revolution. If we date the dawn of humanity as over one million years ago, then the invention of agriculture, which occurred about ten to fifteen thousand years ago, affected only 1.5 percent of human history. That is, at least 98.5 percent of our past saw economies based only on hunting, fishing, and the gathering of wild vegetable foods! Similarly, the industrial age dating from the invention of the steam engine covers only .02 percent of human existence. Since most of the spoilation of the planet has taken place during this period, it is clear that our species is rapidly approaching a point at which it may cease to exist.

Technological progress, and with it the growth of populations and

increased social complexity, has had an uneven course. The seats of the earliest civilizations were in Asia and Africa, but industrialism arose in Europe, spreading to North America in the nineteenth century and to the rest of the world in our own age. Until very recently, substantial sections of the world remained untouched or hardly affected by the machine age. It is only a little over a century ago that the Sioux peoples defeated the Seventh Cavalry at Little Big Horn, a victory which did not stem the tide of invasion of their lands by European aliens. American Indian life had been seriously disturbed by this intrusion from its onset, but most of the western United States was peopled by autonomous Indian tribes through the first half of the nineteenth century. The penetration of sub-Saharan Africa by Europeans is also a recent phenomenon. The depredations of slave traders had repercussions far inland, but the whites seldom traveled more than a few miles from the coast. Indeed, it was not until the explorations of Mungo Park between 1795 and 1797 that we first learned the direction of flow of the Niger River. Similarly, large areas of the Amazon rain forests remained uncharted and unexplored until this century, and there are still a few Indian groups that have the wisdom to shun contact with the whites and that thus remain unknown to us. Most of the Pacific was colonized during the latter part of the nineteenth century and the island societies were drastically modified, but Australian patrols were still encountering uncontacted peoples in Papuan New Guinea until the 1950s.

The peoples found in these regions were radically different from the European explorers, traders, missionaries, and officials who were to plague them and change their lives. The newly found societies were vastly simpler than those of Europe. All but a few lacked any system of writing, and their histories, religions, laws, and knowledge were transmitted by oral tradition. Agriculture had spread to most of them, but it was generally of a rudimentary sort, using digging sticks or hoes rather than animal-drawn plows to break the soil. Production was generally for subsistence, though in some areas surplus produce was traded in local markets. Other groups in this rediscovered world existed by animal herding, sometimes with a bit of supplementary farming, sometimes in an uneasy symbiosis with agricultural communities. Finally, a number of groups, especially in semiarid or arctic zones, lived completely by foraging off the natural flora and fauna. They include the hunting and fishing Eskimo, the California seed gatherers, the aborigines of Australia, the bison-hunting Indians of our own Great Plains, rhea and guanaco hunters of southern South America, and scattered hunting peoples in Africa, Malaysia, and southern India.

The multitudinous and ingenious ways by which man manages to

wring a living out of all kinds of landscapes, no matter how forbidding, are eloquent testimony to his ability to adjust to the rigors of environment through traditionally learned behavior. Even with the simplest of technologies, the Eskimo has survived the Arctic through superbly wrought clothing, through that architectural masterpiece the igloo, and through a range of weapons that have made him equally effective in hunting whales at sea as in hunting polar bears on the land. Survival depends in the first instance on a full stomach, but it does not end there. There are also a host of social and psychological needs that must be satisfied if we are to effectively perpetuate ourselves and relate to each other. The ways in which people handle their social environments—the central topic of this book—are even more varied than their economic adaptations. To the Western observer, these ways are also more bizarre and exotic. There are peoples who grind up the bones of their own dead and drink them in a gruel. There is a New Guinea tribe in which young men perform fellatio on their uncles as part of the initiation ceremony. There are groups throughout the world that practice genital mutilation upon their young, including circumcision, subincision (cutting the underside of the penis through to the urethra) and clitoridectomy (excision of the clitoris). There are societies in which one woman may have several husbands at one time, just as there are others in which a man may have many wives. One could go on and on, for the panorama of human societies presents us with a wild profusion—a panoply and a feast—of modes of human behavior. And it must be remembered that what seems to us to be strange is everyday, common-sense, and rational conduct to the people who follow these practices. Moreover, they look upon our behavior as odd, sometimes inhuman and barbaric, and often childlike.

It is the purpose of social anthropology* to understand the human situation by the study of all its manifestations and variations. Ideally, anthropology teaches us how to comprehend the internal logic of the cultures of alien and different societies. If the lesson is learned well, then what seems irrational, quixotic, immoral, or just plain senseless in other groups can be seen as logical, even useful. At the very least, we learn to refrain from judging strange customs on the basis of our own preconceptions, an error called "ethnocentrism" by anthropologists.

---

*I use the term "social anthropology" interchangeably with "cultural anthropology," though many anthropologists make a distinction between the two on methodological grounds. I also take as synonymous the word "ethnology," which means the science of custom. This term is ·to be distinguished from "ethnography," which refers to the description and cataloguing of customs.

The same process by which we come to understand the inner workings of other societies estranges us from our own—not deeply, perhaps, but just enough so that we can look at our particular mundane, everyday reality and say "how wondrous!" Through the study of ways of life that are different from ours, we come to understand that customary ways of behaving and believing, or cultures, are intelligible mainly in terms of their contexts and not by some abstract and absolute standards. Whatever our private views might be on the practice of taking human heads as trophies, the only insight that we can obtain into the custom is through seeing in what ways it relates to the religious and family life of the people, to their political order, to the peculiarities of their environment. The realization that ours is only one among thousands of societies, past and present, and that the customs of each find meaning only in the internal logic of that particular society, leads inevitably to the conclusion that standards of behavior and expression are relativistic and arbitrary. They are rooted neither in god nor in nature, and like all other things human, they are transient. We would like to feel that we live in a world of order, certitude, and a rationality based on ultimate truths, for this allows us to act with confidence and within a stable frame of reference. But this is not the way the world really is. It is changeable, shifting, and composed of hollow meanings—a truth that has been gradually gaining acceptance in the Western world, and which is at once a symptom and a source of the failure of confidence of our times.

Anthropology is a view of the human condition and a means toward gaining some removal from and perspective on our own lives. As such, it is one of the humanities. But it is also a social science, for it attempts to explain the ways in which various societies are organized and to analyze their institutions. Anthropology is not one of the more exact sciences, for its subjects are thinking, sentient beings—their behavior is determined, but it is also to some degree self-determined. Moreover, the scientific study of society is made difficult by the enormous complexity of even the simplest of societies and by the fact that experimentation is almost impossible.

The scientific experiment sets up an unnatural condition. That is, it takes the matter or problem to be studied out of the natural realm and studies it in the artificially closed and limited environment of the laboratory. The number of variables within the experimental situation is sharply decreased, and these few variables are then changed and manipulated to ascertain their effects upon the others. Both ethics and expediency prevent the social scientist from doing this. In only a few types of social situations is it possible to set up an experiment, and these are often small matters, such as a contrived problem in decision making.

Even in these few instances, it is difficult to extrapolate the results back into real social life. It would clearly be impossible or undesirable to place people in, for example, new and different family forms or types of marriage solely for scientific purposes. There are inherent limits to our inquiry, for few anthropologists would wish to tamper with the living arrangements of other humans.

Lacking the means, or the wish, to carry out experimentation—the commonest means of testing hypotheses—anthropology turns instead to its enormous inventory of data on several hundred societies. Our information is striking in two ways. First, there is an amazing diversity of accepted and sanctioned behavior and belief in the social universe. Second, in all this array of diversity, there is a pronounced tendency for institutions and practices to recur across social boundaries. This is sometimes an outcome of geographical proximity, allowing one group to learn from another. In many cases, however, no such contact can be assumed and we are led to conclude that the practice appeared independently in each place due to similar governing conditions. If we can demonstrate this with facts, then we have made a scientifically verifiable statement. By showing a necessary interdependence between variables, we have effectively explained a part of the social order. We cannot study the interrelation between variables X, Y, and Z in a test tube, but we can look at all societies that are characterized by X, Y, and Z and see what they have in common. We can then go on to examine groups that have X and Y, but not Z, to see how they differ. In this way we can impose a scientific control—a kind of mental discipline—over our hypotheses. The procedure, called the comparative method, is central to social anthropology and explains the anthropologist's passion for gathering information on as many societies as possible.

The first systematic explication of the comparative method was given to us by the nineteenth-century English anthropologist Sir Edward Tylor. Tylor noted that certain customs recurred in different societies in association with other practices. The phenomenon of two or more traits sticking together in this way was termed an "adhesion" by Tylor. Taking as an example the practice by which a man systematically avoids his mother-in-law, he surveyed all societies following the custom and found that a percentage of them well above the level of chance and random association required a married couple to live in the natal household of the bride. Tylor reasoned that the built-in problems of living with one's in-laws can be eased by minimizing interaction with them. At the same time, he showed us that the delicacy of the mother-in-law relationship is universal and not merely a pet theme of American humorists.

An American anthropologist, the late Julian Steward, used the comparative method in illuminating the deep relations that exist between social systems and their ecological settings. He noted that societies in which small bands of hunters, which were held together through kin ties between their men, and owned delimited territories, frequently had a subsistence economy based on the hunting of nongregarious and nonmigratory animals. On the other hand, hunters of large, gregarious, and migratory animals, such as the bison, were more commonly ordered into what he called "composite bands," or larger aggregates of people who could be related in either the mother's or father's line. Presumably, the first type of organization allowed a group of cooperating and related men to continue to hunt a limited area that they knew well and that could yield a fairly reliable subsistence; the second, or composite band, drew together people from a wide territory into a single group that ranged over long distances in pursuit of herd animals. Steward also demonstrated that there was a profound association between the rise of the earliest civilizations and the practice of irrigation agriculture in arid zones. According to this argument, first advanced by the historian Karl Wittfogel, the controls needed to organize labor for the building of large waterworks and to then allocate the water would lead inevitably to class stratification and centralized organization. Moreover, the high yield from this form of agriculture would provide the means for supporting specialized governing and artisan classes. We will expand upon this theme in Chapter 6.

There are pitfalls to the comparative method, of course, and one can be sure that, if he finds a 100 percent correspondence between two institutions, with one always accompanied by the other, they are in actuality part of a single larger phenomenon. One must also be cautious in inferring causality. A correlation may be found between societies that have indoor plumbing and those with atomic energy, though neither one explains the other. And one can fall into the classic fallacy illustrated by the experimenter who drinks scotch and soda, bourbon and soda, and brandy and soda. Finding that all three make him drunk, he concludes that it must be due to the soda, the one variable common to each experiment. Above all, the practitioner of the comparative method cannot expect a neat and invariant correspondence between social institutions. Social life is far too complex and varied for this. We must be satisfied instead with strains toward consistency. In the final analysis we are talking about probabilities and gambler's odds, expressed in elegant statistical terms.

Our literature on primitive, or simple and nonliterate, societies is the raw material of the comparative method, for we have rich data on several hundreds of such groups. A word is in order on anthropology's seeming obsession with the "primitive." First, as we have seen, such peoples provide the variety and the recurrent social institutions and practices for the comparative study of society. Second, they are usually fairly simple in organization and have small populations, making them easy to study in their entireties, as wholes. This is another hallmark of the anthropological method; it attempts to see societies in their totalities, to analyze and describe their parts, and to understand the relation of the parts to each other and to the whole organization. The student of industrial society is ambitious if he undertakes the study of a factory, a city block, or a church, but the student of the primitive can see and grasp an entire way of life.

Anthropology fell into the rich legacy of the study of primitive society almost by accident. Or it might be more correct to say that anthropology grew up around the study of primitives because the other disciplines ignored them. When the modern-day academic fields emerged in the English and European universities during the late nineteenth century, the nascent social sciences devoted their attentions to the study of Euro-American society. Economists focused on price movements within a market structure, historians dealt largely with the United States and Europe, and sociologists set out to understand industrial society and the city. Anthropology, which had been a catchall field for antiquarians, students of the American Indian, artifact collectors, and the like, became the residuary legatee of everything that the other sciences excluded from their ken.

Anthropology inherited much more than an interest in primitive customs. The early anthropologists and their forerunners encountered unwritten and unknown languages, which they catalogued and analyzed. From their efforts issued dictionaries and grammars—and modern anthropological linguistics. The native peoples investigated were commonly different in appearance from Europeans, and the researchers diligently set about describing their anatomical characteristics, measuring head shape, examining teeth, and so forth. From this effort and an interest in human origins arose the study of physical anthropology, the science of human variation and evolution. Finally, lacking written records, the histories of the simpler peoples could only be reconstructed by unearthing and analyzing their material remains. Pieces of pottery, arrow points, house remains, old campfire sites, and almost everything else discarded or left behind by ancient peoples were dug out of the ground. From these data the records of lost ways of life were reclaimed. Today, the science of prehistoric archeology is a burgeoning subdiscipline, second in size only to social anthropology.

The circumstances by which anthropologists became sociologists, linguists, anatomists, and historians to primitive peoples may have been fortuitous in part, but the result of this conjunction was the birth of a broad-based science of man. The four fields of anthropology—social or cultural anthropology, anthropological linguistics, physical anthropology, and archeology—provide a quite general overview of the human situation, and especially of that part of the human condition that is directly related to life in society. Anthropology is hardly a complete and comprehensive study of man, but its goals and scope are nonetheless so sweeping as to require Renaissance people for their realization. In the early years of the discipline—from the late nineteenth century into the early twentieth—there were indeed scholars of such breadth. As the science grew, however, it became increasingly compartmentalized and fractionated. Despite this splitting, the perspective of anthropology remains broad. We study ancient ruins for information on the social systems of the past; we investigate the ways in which tradition, language, and thought interrelate; we muse on the relationship between human anatomy and physiology and certain social institutions. Individual anthropologists may have narrowed and focused their interests, but those of the discipline as a whole have expanded.

When the other social sciences elected to restrict their inquiries to Western civilization, they left to anthropology more than just the primitive peoples, for they also excluded most of the complex civilizations of the rest of the world. By the 1930s anthropologists were already studying peasant populations in India, China, South and Middle America, Africa, and even Europe. They directed their attention at first to small agrarian communities, for anthropologists prefer to study all of something small rather than a tiny sliver of something big. With the realization that the whole, in this case the whole of a civilization, was greater than the sum of its parts, they next turned their eyes toward the cities of the non-Western world and to entire regions and nations. The next logical step was the repatriation of anthropology and the study of communities in modern Europe and the United States. The expansion of our geographical range has brought us into closer conjunction with the other social sciences at just the time when they, in turn, have broadened their own scope to include the nonindustrial world.

Today, most anthropologists do not conduct research in primitive societies, but it is where the discipline was born and where its fascination still lies. Anthropology blends the spirits of both romanticism and the Enlightenment. It derives from romanticism its historicity, its absorption with the bizarre and different, while the Enlightenment contributed to its search for order and internal rationality in this riot of human expression. We learn to find the sensible and the useful in what is manifestly, to us, odd, and we learn to regard our own mundane surroundings with the same surprise and sense of discovery that our primitive friends arouse in us.

Beyond the scientific mission, a knowledge of primitive societies is an aesthetic experience. We are exposed to different styles of expression and relating, each of which has its own unique structure, just as does a work of art. The tapestry of experience encapsulated by these small societies, isolated and bypassed in the more remote and inaccessible parts of the earth, is also hauntingly evocative of something long past, lost to us, never to be recaptured. No society is changeless, and this is certainly as true of simple ones as of our own complex social organism. The primitive ones, however, have changed at a much slower pace than our own, leaving them with economies that civilized society has long since transcended. If we trace our own origins to the great Mediterranean and Near Eastern civilizations—admittedly a cultural and nongenetic ancestry—we left hunting and gathering behind almost fifteen thousand years ago and we went beyond hoe agriculture over six thousand years in the past. Modern primitives are not unchanged replicas of life in these ancient times, but they provide us with an approximation of what archaic societies were like. We cannot retrodict the past on the basis of our knowledge of contemporary primitives, but we can indeed discover in them what were the limitations imposed on past societies by their rude technologies.

It is for this reason that a sojourn among primitives is much like a long step backward into a past condition of man. I remember vividly the entrance of my wife and me into a village of Mundurucú Indians, far up a southern tributary of the Amazon River, close to the geographic center of Brazil. The village was situated on a grassy rise of land, commanding a view of forest and savannah stretching out toward the southeast. Some seven hundred miles in that direction were Brazilian frontier communities, but everything in between was either populated by other Indian tribes or had no human inhabitants at all. The village consisted of five bark-walled, thatch-roofed houses, arranged in a circle around a central plaza. A sixth structure was an openside lean-to affair. This was the men's house, where all males over puberty slept. It was like no other settlement we had ever seen before, except in the kinds of books we had studied, but which had always had a never-never land quality until we saw it ourselves.

In my memories of the village, I can still smell the wood smoke from the household fires, which soon diffused and dissipated in clear, uncontaminated skies. On a moonlit night, the outlines of houses and trees were softly blurred by the haze, providing the visual backdrop for the deep vibrant sounds of the musical instruments that the Mundurucú men kept from the sight of their women and which, they believed, contained the spirits of their ancestors. The tempo of life was slow and muted. Other than the soft voices of the people, the only sounds came from a passing parrot or the chattering of a band of monkeys in the nearby forest. During several months in the village, we heard a motor only once, an airplane that appeared as a distant speck in the sky for a moment and then was gone.

We lived without money, credit card, checkbook, or identification cards during this time, a virtual impossibility in our own flawed civilization. And we also lived without police or any other presence of outside government. The Indians knew about Brazil, but to them it was a distant and faraway country, like "Amerikó-be," where the anthropologists came from. Problems of maintaining public order were rare and handled by the people according to traditional means. Their livelihood derived completely from the yield of their gardens, the fish of the rivers, and the game animals of the forest, and they shared their food freely with us.

Our village had less than one hundred people, and we soon came to know each and every one as an individual. It must be remembered that in groups of this scale, everybody is famous. The people did not much value privacy and they gave us very little. This was personally irksome, sometimes embarrassing, but it also allowed us to see almost everything that was happening and to enter their houses as freely as they entered ours. We were thus able to find out through interview and conversation what the Mundurucú believed to be right, decent, moral, or proper in certain situations and then to check these behavioral standards against what they actually did. Not surprisingly, the two differed, but they differed in systematic ways. The small size also enabled us to describe the main outlines of Mundurucú social life, a task that was further facilitated by the fact that they were unsegmented by differences of wealth, creed, race, and all the other divisive goblins of modern man. We learned many things, but beyond our research we had left behind the reality of our own world, from which we became progressively more remote, and entered another. It was a new world of different meanings, which at first eluded us, and a measure of our studies was the degree to which these strange meanings became commonplace and common sense. We had stepped through a looking glass.

It was a different universe, and those lucky few who have known these sights and experienced these modes of existence have seen something that will never be observed again. Each year sees the survival of fewer autonomous primitive societies. From the time of colonial exploration onward, primitives have been hunted and killed by Europeans or have fallen victim to newly imported diseases, such as smallpox, tubercu-

losis, measles, and whooping cough. Those that have been spared have
become increasingly absorbed by Euro-American society. The North
American Indians survive, but they are no longer "primitives." They
drive cars, vote, go to school, shop in supermarkets, and do many of the
things that white Americans do. They are indeed different from white
Americans, but they are also just as different from their forefathers. Much
the same thing has happened in New Guinea, now an independent nation.
Groups that were practicing cannibalism only twenty-five years ago are
now forming coffee-marketing cooperatives or sending their brightest
young men to the legislature. In South America, new roads into the
Amazon are funneling in hordes of land-hungry settlers and ranchers,
who now threaten to push the Indians off the lands remaining to them
and to exterminate them culturally if not physically.

There is little doubt that by the year 2000 there will no longer be
primitive societies. With the expansion of trade and technology into
the remaining fastnesses of the planet, the spread of the tools, knowledge,
and ways of the industrial world will make people less different, more
the same, and the human panorama will become arid and dull. Perhaps the
most important accomplishment of anthropology will be the documenta-
tion of this splendor before it disappeared forever. Alexander Pope was
right in saying that the proper study of mankind is man, and we have
done this. But the anthropologist Claude Lévi-Strauss tells us that we
have also done something else—we have borne witness to these peoples
and to their dying cultures.

It is largely to these societies that we will turn our attention in our
attempt to understand the human situation. We will, moreover, make
reference to non-Western peasant societies and to the contemporary
United States, for we too are splendid grist for the anthropological mill.
This will be an exploration of human "culture," or "traditions," "ways of
life," "customs," and "social practices," to cite the synonymous terms
I used in the foregoing pages. We will have much more to say about this
concept, one of the important unifying ideas in the social sciences, and
I wish only to define it as a setting for what follows. Culture means the
total body of tradition borne by a society and transmitted from generation
to generation. It thus refers to the norms, values, and standards by which
people act, and it includes the ways distinctive in each society of ordering
the world and rendering it intelligible. Culture is, as we have said, a
set of mechanisms for survival, but it provides us also with a definition
of reality. It is the matrix into which we are born, it is the anvil upon
which our persons and destinies are forged. To grasp human cultures and
their workings is at once a venture out into the social universe and an
investigation into ourselves.

Karl Marx once wrote that if everything were exactly as it seemed, there would be no need for science. This statement is applicable to the physical sciences, but it is even more germane to the study of man. The inquiry is made troublesome by the complexity of the subject matter and by the contrariness of the individual subjects, who never seem to do what they are supposed to do. But it is made doubly difficult by the faulty perceptions of both the anthropologists and the people they study, for both parties are defining their "real world" by culturally given mental constructs. And even when we manage to break through this wall of mutual misunderstanding, we find that behind every conscious motive there is a hidden agenda, behind every social practice or institution there lies a covert and undetected function, and after every great plan there follows a series of wholly unintended and unanticipated consequences. We must look, then, behind the façade of appearances and the reality of common-sense experience in order to reach the organization and flow of social life that goes on beneath the surface. Our task is to describe and analyze other modes of experience, but, even more important, it is to look at the known and familiar and discover something totally new.

The Human
Situation

There are a multitude of views on what humans are really deep down like, but they distill out into two main types. This dichotomy was best expressed by the writer Samuel Beckett in his novel *Murphy*. The hero, it may be recalled, devoted his time to total, studied idleness, in the hope that it would prolong his life. His girlfriend would have preferred that he go out to work, freeing her from her profession of streetwalker and admitting her into the world of respectability, no matter how shabby. One day, when Murphy was sitting naked and motionless in his chair, his lady friend urged that people should be up and about. "I am what I do!" she exclaimed. "No," Murphy replied, "you do what you are, you do a fraction of what you are, you suffer a dreary ooze of your being into doing."

One view of man states that the human personality and the human mind are plastic, malleable, and almost wholly molded by the life experience of the individual. Since this experience takes place within a cultural context, the resultant personality is largely explainable by social factors. Humans, then, are tabula rasa upon which the imprint of their social environment is indelibly printed. This school allows that there are certain innate drives, such as sex and hunger, but regards them as diffuse in form and few in number. Granted that some human institutions serve these biological needs of man, there are no other propensities of the psyche that seem to much influence culture. Rather, the determinism goes the other way. Culture is not an expression of mind, but mind is a product of culture and social activity. You are what you do.

The position taken by Murphy's girlfriend is the majority view among social anthropologists. Moreover, it is a fairly consistent interpretation of what humans are like, for it attributes little to man as such, stressing the negative and passive aspect of people vis-à-vis culture. On the other hand, Murphy's interpretation—Beckett's Murphy, not this one—is a catchall for a veritable Pandora's box of views on man, ranging from gross notions that attribute most behavior to instinct or race to highly sophisticated theories on the structure of language. All of them, however, advance the thesis that human beings are not just lumps of clay, to be shaped in any way that culture dictates. Rather, they maintain that mankind is constituted, has certain unrefractory and enduring characteristics, and has an innateness and integrity of its own. Culture may modify these traits, but it cannot get rid of them altogether. Culture must take account of these human bents and accommodate them in its own functioning. Culture may indeed become imbedded in the individual, according to this perspective, but at the same time ineradicable needs and dispositions of people become imbedded in culture.

Murphy and his girlfriend represent one expression of the so-called "nature vs. nurture" or "heredity vs. environment," controversy. I do not intend to bog us down in this issue, for it is irresolvable, given the present state of our knowledge. First of all, since all humans are subject to environmental influences from the prenatal period onward, there is no possibility that the hereditary can be factored out. Second, our knowledge of human genetics, especially of inheritance of behavioral characteristics, is still both sparse in depth and spotty in coverage. For all the ambitious claims of the biological determinists, there is little hard genetic evidence to back their positions.

Our discussion is not, however, restricted to the nature–nurture argument, for people have been advancing views of human nature long before genetics was thought of. Aristotle believed that man was a social animal, a political one at that, and few would disagree with this characterization, given the manifest and involved interdependencies among people. The social-contract philosophers of the Enlightenment period based their theories of society on interpretations of the essential, irreducible nature of man. This hard kernel of humanity could be reached, they believed, by seeing man free of the influence of organized civil society and alone—in a state of nature, so to speak. Thomas Hobbes, a seventeenth-century philosopher, imagined such a pristine human condition and deduced that life at that time was short and brutish, and society a state of anarchy in which every man was against all others. The state and other apparatus for the maintenance of the social order were developed as a contract among men by which they gave up their original freedom to gain protection. The theory was at once Hobbes's way of endowing the state with legitimacy and of justifying its use of coercion and oppression. Man was evil, society good.

The opposite stance was taken by the eighteenth-century French philosopher Jean-Jacques Rousseau. Rousseau derived his insight into the primeval state of man through acquaintance with a group of Tupinamba Indians who had been brought from Brazil to France by explorers. Here, certainly, was humanity in the raw, man in nature, thought Rousseau, making the same essential mistake about primitives that is still repeated by well-intentioned idealists of our own time—and also by a few uninformed social scientists. His knowledge of the Indians convinced him of their essential goodness and rationality and we owe the term "noble savage" to him. It was society, particularly the modern form of the nation-state, that had corrupted mankind, Rousseau concluded, and it was the task of philosophy to design a social order that would be in conformity with human character and rationality.

It is clear from the examples of Hobbes and Rousseau that a view of human nature is in large part a political doctrine. Hobbes used his view to justify the established order, while Rousseau launched a critique of his society. This is equally true of contemporary theories of human nature. The idea that human thought and activity are largely the result of learning within a certain social environment would seem at first glance to have only negative political connotations, but it contains the hidden message that if we transform society, we can transform man. This might be a hopeful view, for it offers promise for the possibility of a more just society and a more righteous populace. But the notion of human plasticity also contains the germ of the idea that we can condition people to anything. If they can be made more gentle, then they can be made more cruel; if they can be taught to share freely, then they can be taught selfishness. If man is not constituted in a specific way, then he can be remade any way. Latent in this oversocialized image of man is the premise that he cannot effectively fight society. But he can and does.

Whatever its possible drawbacks, there is a flexibility in the stress upon human plasticity that is lacking in those theories that emphasize the innate and hereditary. As was noted, these have a considerable range and enjoy varying degrees of intellectual respectability. At the bottom of the pit are the various theories that explain cultural differences by ascribing them to inequalities of biological heredity. The noted anthropologist Morton Fried once said of such notions, "You can't kill a bad idea," a comment that is unfortunately true of racism. Racist thought has told us that Italians are inherently libidinous, Jews greedy by nature, blacks given to rhythmic movement, and Germans innately superior to just about everybody. Most of these mirages have been consigned to oblivion, but they have a tendency to rise from the dead like Lazarus. "And Lord, he stinketh" (John 4:39) is a comment that applies to racism as well as to Lazarus.

The latest revival of the notion that there are inherent mental differences between the races comes from the work of Arthur Jensen, an educational psychologist, who cited the results of intelligence tests to argue that blacks have a lower inherited ability for abstract thought than whites. It would be a useless digression to discuss his ideas at length, and I refer the reader to the excellent critique by Alexander Alland in his book *The Human Imperative*. It must be said, however, that although American blacks generally tend to score lower than whites on intelligence tests, the results do not point to an inferior black mentality when consideration of urbanism and class structure is introduced. The intelligence tests are constructed by and for middle-class whites and reflect cultural differences more than native intelligence. An anthropologist, Roy D'Andrade, found that a group of Hausa boys in northern Nigeria did woefully on a part of a test designed to measure abstract conceptual ability. D'Andrade, realizing that white American children actually if not purposefully train intensely for these tests through the toys they play with, gave the boys less than two hours training in the conceptualization of geometric designs, the subject of the test. At the end of that time, he tested them again and found that their scores had more than doubled. It was clear that innate capacity had little to do with the group scores.

In reality, it would be a genetic miracle if it were true that there are racial differences in intelligence. Homo sapiens is one unitary species to which all living humans belong. There are indeed physical differences among the people of certain global areas, but the differences between groups in the same area may be of even greater magnitude. Thus, the Watutsi, the tallest people on earth, and the Pygmies, the shortest, live within a few hundred miles of each other. Both have black skin, which seems to be the sine qua non of race for those who think the concept "race" has any significance. The observable and demonstrable anatomical differences among the races, as conventionally defined, are few in number and anatomically unimportant. These are differences of skin and hair color, which vary with the amount of the pigment melanin in the body surface, hair shape, nose shape, and broadness of the head. The races are by no means internally uniform, nor are the racial traits strictly confined to the groups they supposedly typify. The physical characteristics of adjacent groups tend to shade off into each other, and trade, travel, and warfare have spread chromosomes far beyond what is thought to be their home territory. The result is that it is impossible to delineate the boundaries of a race and equally impossible to list a neat, uniform catalogue of the traits of any race. Scientifically, our popular racial classifications make as much sense as would a taxonomy of black-haired, white-haired, and brown-haired dogs. Many anthropologists think we should extirpate the concept, root and branch.

There is no evidence whatsoever that innate mental or emotional traits are linked to the superficial characteristics of race. In fact, the thesis that lighter-skinned people are more intelligent than darker ones flies in the face of both biological and historical knowledge. Evolutionary changes in intelligence have taken many, many millennia to come about; yet the primacy of the northern European peoples dates only from about the sixteenth century A.D. Back when Europe was floundering in the Dark Ages, the Arabs had built a brilliant civilization in North Africa and the Near East. Empires and great cities flourished in sub-Saharan Africa at a time when Paris was a rude town and European monks were using their literacy in copying scrolls. And long before the trappings of civilization reached northward from Rome, complex societies existed in China, India, Iraq, and Egypt. The time spans in which the ebb and flow of history took place were far too short to have been influenced by evolutionary changes in intelligence. Moreover, the immense social changes that have occurred in populations throughout the world prove that a single people can switch from one culture to another in a surprisingly short time; there seems to be no link between biological inheritance and a particular way of life.

Beliefs in inborn mental characteristics typifying races or groups have no support in fact, no matter how much they attract the fancy of those who find them politically expedient. There is another approach to the question of the nature of man, however, that is more defensible. This starts from the position that humanity is psychologically unitary—there are inherited mental and behavioral differences among individuals but not among populations. That is, every populace includes the bright, the dull, and the in-between, and in roughly the same proportions. Thus far, this is the stance of those who attribute all our predispositions to learning—the school of Murphy's girlfriend. It differs from this persuasion, however, in stating that there is indeed *a* human nature consisting of certain positive characteristics that must be taken into account if we are to understand man or his societies. There are a sea of such theories, of course, for every adherent seems to have a different catalogue of traits for this panhuman nature. There are those who see it as highly sexualized and others who view libidity as a minor theme. There are those who believe man to be naturally selfish and those who think him to be essentially altruistic. There are the theorists of innate aggression and others who look upon man as pacific. And all of them seem to have written books.

There are problems in these ideas of hereditary and panhuman psychological characteristics. Many years ago, there was a psychologist who had a syndicated newspaper column that gave out free psychological advice to those who wrote to him. A good portion of his correspondents had marital problems, frequently involving unfaithful mates. When a husband wrote about his wife's infidelity, the psychologist's indignation could hardly be concealed. But in the case of a cheating husband, he would reassure the wife that it was in the nature of males to want more than one woman; they were naturally polygynous. Now there are certainly enough cheating husbands to lend an air of credibility to this claim, but the psychologist's belief that women just as naturally stick with one man is shaken by the equally impressive number of cheating wives. Moreover, most men seem to find one woman at a time to be either quite enough or more than they can handle. One can cite the frequency of the custom of allowing the marriage of one man to more than one woman, but the truth is that the overwhelming majority of unions in this world are monogamous. In short, our newspaper therapist had made a fundamental, yet common, scientific error. He had explained the particular by the general, attributing a phenomenon occurring among a minority of people to a trait that is supposedly panhuman. We should ask of such reasoning, "why does everybody not act according to his nature and how do we explain the exceptions?"

I have chosen a rather gross example to illustrate the fallacy of "reductionism," which in the social sciences usually takes the form of explaining cultural and social facts by inherited biological causes. There are a number of such theories, and we will mention only a few of the more pervasive ones. Recent years have seen a substantial growth in ethology, the science of animal behavior. Specialists in the field have produced splendid work on animals, but few have been able to resist the temptation to apply their results to human behavior. One ethologist, Konrad Lorenz, wrote on the basis of work in the field that mankind inherited from its nonhuman ancestry a predisposition toward aggression, manifesting itself in forms of violent behavior ranging from common brawls to modern warfare. Granted man's capacity—not bent—for aggression, the theory does not begin to explain the enormous differences in levels of violence among different societies or the militarism of some groups as compared to the pacifism of others. These are clearly the result of social circumstance and historical process. Human passions may be captured and used in the vicissitudes of war and strife, but they do not explain their occurrence. The idea that man is impelled by his biology toward violence has proved attractive, as shown by Lorenz's extensive readership. First, the theory tells us that the curse of Cain is genetic and inescapable, leaving very little that one can do about it. Second, it provides an easy, single cause explanation of very involved social phenomena. In actuality, the single cause, a genetic disposition toward aggression, is totally hypothetical, as we do not know the genetics of such behavior, or even if there are any. As long as we are explaining human behavior by the unknown, it would be just as valid to say that God made us that way—which is, of course, exactly what millions of people do say.

There are political overtones to Lorenz's ideas, but these are not at all as pronounced as in the writings of Robert Ardrey, a playwright and writer of popular anthropology. Ardrey champions Lorenz's work, adding the notion that the special qualities of human aggressiveness were part of the adaptation of our forebears, the australopithecine man apes, to hunting on the African savannahs. Not content with making warfare and homicide natural, Ardrey used the work of zoologists and anthropological researchers on primates to state that we have an instinctive drive to hold and defend territories. It has long been known that many species of animals, including birds, stake out territories. Since a similar territoriality was found among baboons, it took only a bit of imagination to find that tribal boundaries and the nation-state were products of a general biological tendency toward territoriality. The problem with this reasoning is that territoriality is by no means universal among humans, or among baboons for that matter. Nor is territoriality all of one piece, a unitary phenomenon. The resemblances between human institutions and animal behavior are often no more than analogies, and the ethologists make the common error of interpreting the actions of animals in human terms. Indeed, what is territoriality? Is it territoriality when animals or humans defend their food resources and nests, or is this simply a manifestation of the rage of all organisms to survive? The study of animal behavior promises a great intellectual yield, but in the final analysis its results will tell us a great deal about animals and little about people. But, then, what's wrong with that?

Those human-nature theorists who preach our inborn imperatives for certain customary practices enjoy an understandable popularity. The theories are extremely simple, even simplistic, and one can understand them without even knowing genetics; though based on genetics, the genes are always hypothetical. These notions also tend to support the status quo. We learn from Lorenz that warfare is programmed into us, and Ardrey tells us that private property and nationhood are equally natural. The theories allow us to avoid all the hard questions of anthropology and history, short-circuiting thought itself. They comfort us by the reassurance that things may look bad, but at least they are normal and in keeping with man's essential nature.

The attribution of character to heredity is of great antiquity in European culture, and we Americans have absorbed the belief fully. The English especially were great believers in hereditary insanity, inheritance of the noble traits of the aristocracy, and the eternal inferiority of colonial peoples. In the United States people are still wont to justify their racism by quite nonsensical folk biology, and our ideas on inherited sexual characteristics form a mythology in itself. The concept of a biologically given human nature serves to justify the world as it is, firming up our perceptions of reality and endowing our own behavior with an absolute justification. If you ask a South American Indian why a particular practice is followed, he will probably say, "Because our grandfathers did it," which is a sound cultural explanation. Ask an American, and he will commonly tell you, "Why, it's human nature to act that way." It is human nature for men to dominate women, just as it is human nature to covet your neighbor's goods, or wife. In the popular imagination, human nature becomes an inventory of original sin. Paradoxically, it is also used at the same time and by the same people to rationalize what they consider good.

Biological explanations of socially accepted and articulated behavior should be treated with suspicion, at best. At the same time, the idea that all of human experience and formation is culturally determined has its own problems. It tells us that all of Homo sapiens has a common humanity, but it does not tell us what that humanity is. It would be facile to say that it derives completely from our conditioning within a specific culture, for the fact is that cultures differ far more from each other than do the personalities, hopes, aspirations, and fears of their bearers. As an anthropologist, I have lived with groups whose cultures were sharply at variance with my own; yet as soon as I was able to overcome the barriers of language and expression, I saw in the people types I had known all my life. I could empathize with their values and perspectives, share their emotions, and understand their problems. I could not, of course, understand them completely and thoroughly, for the gaps were too great and I was always an alien. But, then, not one of us completely understands all others, or his own self.

We do have a recognizable and positive humanity that unites all mankind into a family, but its study has been made difficult by the either/or choice of opting between hereditary and environmental factors. There is a common belief among anthropologists of all persuasions that human behavioral characteristics that are universal, or nearly so, are biological in origin. What is completely overlooked is that there is a middle ground between nature and nurture, which recognizes that general attributes of man may well derive from a common human experience and from living in the same kind of body. Specifically, our preoccupation with cultural differences has led us to neglect the similarities of our experience. We document the ways that infants are breast-fed and weaned, and we emphasize the culturally standardized ways of holding the child, scheduling the feedings, withdrawing it from the breast, and shifting to other foods. What we forget, or take for granted, is that in all societies the burden of infant care falls on women, that the child develops a primary or primal relationship with the mother, and that the fact of whether the child is a girl or boy has great effect on the impact of that relationship upon the maturing personality. Cultural differences are not all that vast to the infant, whose effective environment is initially the mother's body. Obviously, that women bear and nurse children are biological facts. Men cannot do it, women can. Beyond this bit of practical, common-sense knowledge, there is little more that biology can tell us about the mother-child bond. One could bring up that old chestnut, the "maternal instinct," but he would then be hard put to explain the sharp wane of this urge during the past decade in the United States and Europe.

I would argue, then, that many of the universals of human behavior derive from universals of the human situation. If biological factors enter into this situation, they are not questions of instinct, or inherited dispositions to specific behaviors, but a matter of the body as an instrument, in all its capabilities and limitations. The human personality is indeed largely a product of experience, of learning and socialization in certain milieus, but there are similarities in these milieus that account for the unity of mankind. There is such a thing as being a Navaho, or an Eskimo, or a Frenchman, but there is also such a thing as being human.

The most important single attribute of man is his intelligence. Other animals are capable of some learning, but man is unique in that the overwhelming bulk of his behavior is learned. Moreover, it is through the socialization process that this acquired behavior becomes organized into a coherent, consistent personality. Man is also distinctive in the possession of language, a statement that will be roundly disputed by everybody who has seen a television special on talking chimpanzees. It would not slight the intelligence of the chimps, or the patience of their trainers, to say that what often passes for language in these cases are rather elaborate sign systems. The Russian psychologist Pavlov conditioned a dog to salivate at the ringing of a bell, but he never claimed that "ding" was the dog's word for "food." The animal experiments are, however, too intriguing to be dismissed out of hand, though I will only become convinced of their linguistic abilities when one chimp teaches another how to speak.

The signal outcome of human intelligence is culture. Human cultures were defined in the last chapter as distinctive life-styles characteristic of different societies. Culture includes designs or models for behavior—norms for what is considered proper, or moral, or even sane. These are modes for acting that are learned, rather than biological, in origin and that are shared to at least some extent by other members of the society. Culture is a body of knowledge and tools by which we adapt to the physical environment; it is a set of rules by which we relate to each other; it is a storehouse of knowledge, beliefs, and formulae through which we try to understand the universe and man's place in it. Culture is preeminently a means of communicating with others, a tautology in the linguistic aspect of culture but equally true of manners and etiquette and the language of gesture and expression. It is culture that stabilizes the social environment and makes it possible for man to associate with his fellows. The sociologist Georg Simmel once said that every social encounter is an immanent disaster. Cues get mixed, signals scrambled, and people become angry, embarrassed, or reduced to inaction by the failure of scenarios to come off as planned. Interaction is not always a smooth process. Culture minimizes this uncertainty by setting the rules on how one should behave in a given situation. It is in this sense that the sociologist Talcott Parsons's definition of culture as a "set of expectations" is most instructive. Culture not only tells us how we should act, but it also tells us what we can expect of the other person. Behavior is thus rendered predictable, often within broad limits, and we gain a degree of mastery and confidence in social situations.

Culture, as the anthropologist Leslie White wrote some decades ago, consists of a system of symbols, or signs endowed with general and more abstract meaning. A simple sign is some visual or auditory stimulus that has a single and narrowly defined connotation. The red-and-green traffic signals designate only stop and go and nothing more. Similarly, Pavlov's dog had learned to make a simple bell–food identification and was thus responding to a sign. Symbols, on the other hand, are signs to which more general meaning has been attributed. They refer less to single objects or phenomena than to classes of objects and phenomena. Your dog Fido may come when he is called by that name or sign, but the word "dog" is a true symbol, for it generalizes a whole category of life forms under one rubric.

Our symbol systems, especially words, are veritable taxonomies of experience. They lump parts of the universe sharing some common characteristics under one class and split them off from others. By carving our perceptions into different domains in this way, our symbols organize and define our apprehension of reality itself. One other important property of symbols is that the relationship between what is signified and the word or image that is doing the signifying is wholly arbitrary. There is no inherent or necessary connection between the word dog and any property of canines, and different languages even imitate the sound of barking differently. Our symbol systems are historical products, not scientifically verifiable maps of the real world, and the ways they classify reality are just as arbitrary as the word labels placed on the classes. Cultures are not rooted in absolutes. They are the products of human activity and thinking and, as such, are man-made. The elements of culture are artificial, contrived, and changeable and, enduring though they may seem, they are, like their bearers, mortal.

Symbols let us communicate our notions of the real and the good to each other. They also endow experience with meaning by placing every event or object in juxtaposition with others. The arbitrariness of the symbols, then, extends to an equal arbitrariness of our view of reality and of all meanings. Culture indeed bestows meaning in and upon our lives, giving us our identities and reducing the chaos of events to order. But the order and the meanings have no basis except in reference to each other, and everyone's reality rests on shifting sands. The Jívaro Indians of Ecuador believe that the everyday world is false and chimerical, and the real world is the one they enter after taking the hallucinogen *ayahuasca*. I think they are wrong, but I am not sure why.

I am not suggesting that there is no real world out there, for we keep bumping into it, often painfully, all the time. Nor am I taking the extreme position that we do not at all grasp this reality but see instead a wholly manufactured cultural mirage. Rather, it is through culture that we organize reality and endow it with meaning. It is a view through a special kind of filter that warps and alters the real world without counterfeiting it completely. And it is a view of life, as we will see, that has certain quite useful purposes—useful, that is, to society, not to the individual. The arbitrariness of cultural symbols does not mean that they are whimsical, capricious, or without rhyme or reason. It only means that the meanings of symbols are humanly imposed and not absolute or natural. Arbitrary though they may be, symbols are the glue of social life and the grist of our thought processes. They have profound meanings and important purposes, which are intelligible only in their social contexts.

The capacity for culture, for the coining and use of symbols, is simultaneously the capacity for abstract thought, and this is a peculiarly human attribute. One answer, then, to the question of what kind of animal man is would be that he is sapient and cultural, the gifts of a large brain and a highly complex central nervous system. One of the byproducts of the large brain—besides abstract thinking processes and the use of language—is the self-awareness of humans. We are not, of course, sure of whether other animals may or may not have a notion of themselves as independent entities, for they cannot tell us, but humans do indeed universally conceptualize the self and distinguish this ego from all others. This introduces a primary dichotomy between the "I" and the "Thou" that serves as a template and model for other forms of classification. The ego–other separation is important for social interaction in that we all operate with some kind of idea of what we as individuals are like, a self-image, as it is popularly called. We also have broad, generalized notions of what other people are like. The two preconceptions are conditioning factors for almost all social behavior. The contents of the images of self and other are, however, neither God-given nor idiosyncratic, for ample models are presented to us within our cultural traditions. The sociologist George Herbert Mead wrote that everybody's idea of the self was ultimately a product of how he was treated by others. Similarly, there are cultural norms and standards in every society that tell us what all humans are like and what certain classes of humans are like. Even our most closely guarded and private domains of the mind are invaded by society, which from the time we are at mother's breast extends threads of culture into our every sense of being.

Another product of intelligent self-awareness is that we have the knowledge of life and death. Other animals struggle just as we do to defend their bodies and prolong their lives, but it is doubtful whether any animals know that they, too, must inevitably die. This we do know from childhood and it poses a paradox. Mankind has a sense of "life" and "being" that is directly related to his keen apprehension of death. Death is the counterpoint of life, and the zest and joy of living are accented by human transiency. Life and death create each other as categories of experience, but each one negates the other in the passage of time. Knowledge of the certainty of death and the uncertainty of its time of arrival introduces a deep note of anxiety in all human existence. Most people do not sit around in fearful brooding over their mortality, but for all it is a background motif in their thoughts and actions and a precondition of how they approach themselves and the world. It is an existential fear, one that is too pervasive to be isolated and too interwoven with other assumptions about life to reach awareness. It is infrequent in our conscious thoughts, but never absent in the underground realms of the unconscious mind, whence so much of our consciousness wells.

The knowledge and fear of death are an accompaniment of our understanding of life and ourselves, but we have a difficult time accepting its inevitability. The struggle to survive is a common property of all organisms. It is man's strongest impulse, from which many other drives and urges are derived. The human battle to sustain life is given a distinctive coloration, however, by the foreknowledge that we can only delay the death of the body, not thwart it. Fortunately, mankind has an enormous talent for self-delusion and some of its more imaginative creations are devices for the denial of death. Beliefs in an immortal soul, or an afterlife or reincarnation are obvious ways for reconciling the fact of biological death with the fond wish for a continuation of the conscious self. We will explore these concepts in the chapter on religion. There are, however, more fundamental means of suppressing death that are more subtle and elusive than hopes for salvation.

The passage of every day leaves us with a day less of life, and if we do one thing with certainty it is to age. Time and life are opposed to each other, for time erodes everything human and we are survived only by our creations. These products, which outlast ordinary lives, consist of material objects and the less-material realms of culture. Objects, be they tools, jewels, or houses, are seized upon as extensions of the self, vehicles for investing the personality outside of the body, embedding the ego in what may outlive us. This is not why the objects are made, of course, but they are among the secondary and covert meanings that people attach to many items of their experience. Culture itself transcends time, binding it together, and providing a stable shell of form and meaning for the chaotic and transient events of everyday life. People are born and die, events transpire and are forgotten, but societies are enduring, as are the symbols by which we live. The overriding of time through the relative stability of cultural forms is a denial of death. I would venture to say that it is a principal source of the conservatism of the old. Finally, the immortality project is epitomized by the relation between the generations, which starts with the infantile assertion of mastery over and oneness with the universe, a sort of immortality, and ends with the investment of our lives in the continuity of our offspring. The mind has a lonely journey in the finitude of the body, and it finds life in its outward connections and in the relationships of society.

Homo sapiens is by birth and nature an intelligent animal, but is he also a rational one? Is the organization of the mind, the means by which one thinks consecutively and analytically, inherent and uniform for all humanity, or is all of logic something we absorb with the rest of our culture? Until the last twenty years or so, most anthropologists would have chosen the latter proposition and taken the view propounded by the psychologist B. F. Skinner that logic is the outcome of conditioning and the adjustment of learned reflexes to each other. Recently, however, there has been reintroduced into social thought the idea that certain structures, or modes of organization, of the mind are hereditary and common to all mankind. These structures do not by any means account for all of human rationality, but rather are the basic armature upon which this rationality is built. It is an idea very reminiscent of Immanuel Kant's "categorical imperatives" of the mind, and it shares the same intellectual ancestry.

The reintroduction of Kantian, and Hegelian, thought into anthropology has come from a number of directions. First, the Swiss psychologist Jean Piaget has for many years been expounding the view that there are regular and inherent pathways for the development of reason that are ascertainable at various levels of child development. A second strand comes from linguistics, and particularly from the work of Noam Chomsky. Working mainly on the English language, Chomsky found certain grammatical regularities that suggested to him that deep below the surface organization of conventional grammar there lies an infrastructure that is the hidden organizer of the grammar—a structure of structures, so to speak. Grammar, then, is not something that is totally learned. Rather, one learns it, but only because one has a predisposition to it; the acquisition of the formal rules of a language is made possible by the human possession of deep mental structures, and the grammars, no matter how varied, must conform to the deep structure. Inasmuch as a grammar is also a form of logic, the postulation of latent grammatical structures also hypothesizes an inherent rationality, an idea that is more fully developed in the work of the French anthropologist Claude Lévi-Strauss.

In 1912, the great French sociologist Emile Durkheim wrote a book entitled *The Elementary Forms of the Religious Life*, which advanced a theory on the social origins of religion. Central to his ideas was the premise that man organizes his experience into the categories of "sacred" and "profane," or the awesome and the mundane, the remarkable and the ordinary, the holy and the base. He went on from his discussion of religion per se to the more inclusive argument that the sacred–profane opposition was humanity's first and primary attempt at classification. As such, it was man's initial step toward the development of rationality, which would thereafter remain rooted in this basic dualism. The idea that human reason proceeds by organizing the world and experience into paired categories, each element of which dyad is conceived of as opposite in meaning to the other, dates back to the Greek philosophers and was carried into European thought by the early church fathers. The theme runs through the work of the German idealist philosophers, and from them into the writings of Karl Marx. Through the influence of Durkheim and Marx, Claude Lévi-Strauss developed his theory of mind and society, a school of thought known as "structuralism."

In structural theory, the structure of the psyche is universally the same, and the working of the mind involves a continual process of sorting one's perceptions into paired opposites, which are then reconciled. In short, the mind works in a dialectical fashion. In the first place, the stream of consciousness becomes broken up into discrete events and things, which are usually reducible to words. We chop up and distort the flow of reality in this process, but words and language are the only ways in which we can think of our world and by which we can communicate these thoughts to others. We fracture and break up our perceptions, but we have no choice. How we do this is where the dualism of thought comes in. Fundamentally, we arrive at our delineation and definition of objects, which we express in words and symbols, by defining what an object is not, as well as what it is. The category of "night" is defined by darkness, but this only infers the absence of sunlight. Night, then, is the absence of day. It is nonday or antiday. In much the same way, a man is a human creature that is not a woman; and if the Democrats did not have the Republicans, they would have to invent them. Words and symbols, the very substance of our thought, are given definition by their otherness. This allows us to break up reality and reduce it to the hard, objective status of the word. At the same time, it does a certain violence to the human grasp on reality.

Lévi-Strauss continues his theme of dualism by asserting that the same human mind that sets up these oppositions is also continually trying to mend them, to reconcile them, and to synthesize their antitheses. The antithesis between life and death is healed by belief in the immortality of the soul, and the opposition of the sexes is sealed by marriage. Lévi-Strauss feels that one of the great dualities, one from which others are spawned, is that between nature and culture, between the nonhuman part of the environment and the artificial and man-created order of culture. Man has the peculiarity of being both an animal, and therefore part of nature, and the creator of culture, an ambiguity that Lévi-Strauss finds hidden within the symbolism of mythology. Humans reconcile this duality and set themselves off from the animal world by many ways, including dress and adornment. The South American Indian practices of body painting are not, then, an attempt to imitate the plumage and colors of the animal world, but rather set man apart from it through arbitrary and artificial decorations—through culture. Similarly, marriage bridges nature and culture, for it involves the natural functions of sex and procreation but is carried out through culturally imposed law.

Dualism finds expression in culture, for the same basic logic is found in all mankind and must, therefore, be accommodated by all cultures. In his monumental work *The Elementary Structures of Kinship*, Lévi-Strauss attempts to show how the dualism of opposition, and the triadic relations created when a mediating factor is introduced, are expressed in the institutions of marriage and kinship. In a four-volume analysis of the mythology of South and North American Indians, he finds these structures of the mind to be faithfully reproduced by the structure of myth. He has also suggested that these elemental and underlying structures are inherent within music, art, and literature.

Structuralism is a controversial theory, but its extreme complexity does not permit further discussion at this early phase of my narrative.

I believe, however, that Lévi-Strauss has correctly identified a panhuman logic. In doing so, he has told us not only that all the varieties of mankind are rational, but that they are rational in the same way. The universality of human binary, dialectical reasoning has led Lévi-Strauss to speculate that the structure is rooted in the neurophysiology of the brain. This is entirely a guess on his part, but it is a hypothesis that may be totally superfluous. The very fact that we speak in words and that these words are not only inclusive of certain meanings but exclusive of others, as previously discussed, would predispose us to binary expression and thought. Moreover, there is much that is dual in our experience. The body is fundamentally symmetrical—we have two eyes, two ears, two arms, and so forth—and there are two types of body, male and female. Binary structures may exist in the brain, but human speech and human experience are sufficient in themselves to account for this characteristic.

Just as there is a basic human rationality, there is also a set of emotional predispositions that is common to all our species. In addition to being naturally endowed with superior intelligence, humans also have a long period of infantile and childhood dependency relative to their total life spans. The average life expectancy in the United States today is about seventy years, of which at least the first seventeen or eighteen are spent in learning and play, dependent for sustenance on the older generation. The dependency period for those entering certain professions may extend to the age of twenty-five or more, or over one-third of a lifetime. In simpler societies than our own, the lack of a formal schooling period may allow a boy to assume adult functions by fifteen or sixteen and a girl at thirteen or fourteen, but the life span is also much shorter. Primitives, too, must support their young for more than 25 percent of their lives.

Prolonged dependency is related to a number of important learning factors. We are born with a group of drives and physical requirements, such as hunger, thirst, sex, rest and sleep, play, elimination, and bodily warmth, but these are very limited in number and are felt as diffuse, broad, and nonspecific urges. They are not "instincts" in the sense we use the term for animal behavior; in the latter context the urge is seen as specific, and a part of the instinct is a set of innate behaviors for gratifying the urge. Except for the smiling and sucking reflexes in infants, this is not true of human behavior. We have to learn a good deal of our drive satisfying activity.

Nature provides us with certain needs, but culture tells us how to fulfill them. Reminiscent of Lévi-Strauss's words on the separation of nature from culture, almost all of our natural functions are heavily governed by culture, including some highly formal rules of etiquette and a frequent sense of shame. Among many peoples bodily elimination is done in private, and among the Arabs and other Moslem groups, one uses only the left hand to clean himself after defecation; the right is considered sacred, the left profane. This is reminiscent of our own custom of washing the hands after urination, a practice that many men follow only in public restrooms, and neglect at home. Similarly, sex is natural enough, but its satisfaction is surrounded by taboos, sanctions, secrecy, and that most reliable of indicators of a sensitive area, false information. Similarly, everybody needs food, but we follow cultural dictates on what to eat, when and how much to eat, and whom to eat with. The act of eating, too, is heavily colored by manners and rules of propriety. We do not talk with our mouths full, and we have to learn how to use our cutlery. A Yurok Indian of California learns to eat with serious countenance while thinking of wealth, and a Brazilian Mundurucú does not engage in boisterous behavior while eating game meat lest he offend the spirit mothers of the animals. We engage in the same life-sustaining activities as lower animals do, but it is exactly while doing these things that we are enjoined not to "act like animals." If somebody wolfs his food in our society, we say that "he eats like an animal" (and note the use of the metaphor wolf). And when asked whether incest occurred among them, a Mundurucú Indian told me "only animals do that."

The period of prolonged dependency is a time in which we learn to satisfy our needs in socially approved ways and, since we are not equipped by nature to survive on our own, it is a period in which we learn to cope with the environment and gain subsistence from it. We mature slowly, but it is time well spent. The dependency of the young on their parents is also an important source of man's social nature. We cannot survive as adults without the cooperation of others in gaining self-defense and livelihood, and we certainly require the nurturance of our elders when children. It is during this time that we establish close ties, which become the models of other relationships we acquire in life, and it is during this time that we learn to love.

Contemporary views of human nature have been greatly influenced by the writings of Sigmund Freud, the founder of psychoanalysis. I should enter the note that, though I am by no means orthodox in my advocacy, I attribute more significance to Freudian theory than do most anthropologists. Freud was one of the great geniuses of the modern period, and his ideas have proven peculiarly congenial to anthropology for their focus upon the emotional life, especially human sexuality, and for a theory of symbolism. Moreover his vision of mankind had a grandeur and sweep that is appropriate to the human panorama presented by anthropology.

Freud's theory of human nature was founded on the dependency of the child and the unique sexuality of mankind. The latter had three principal features: the libido theory, infantile sexuality and polymorphous perversity. I would add a fourth that Freud took for granted, but we cannot. This is that there is no human estrus cycle, or periods of female heat. We humans are in heat all the time—or seldom, depending on individual bent and point of view. Some people think the year-around urges of our species account for marriage, a canard that fails to treat adultery and premarital sexuality seriously. What human sexuality does do, however, is require that people, particularly male and female people, live together. Familiarity breeds! It is thus a part of the impulse that makes us preeminently social animals.

Freud believed that our life forces, including sexuality, are propelled by a source of energy he termed "libido." Too often confused with the highly specific and object-oriented activity of adult heterosexuality, libido was conceived of as a quite broad force; libido is sexualized energy, but it is more than just sex. It is also the energy behind the more Platonic forms of love, altruism, and family relations; and when channelled into creative activity, it is a wellspring of art. One of the more shocking aspects of Freud's new psychoanalysis in the post-Victorian era in which he did much of his early writing was his notion of infantile sexuality. That very little children play with their genitalia and their feces and that baby boys often have erections should be obvious to anybody who has ever reared a child. These were things that one did not talk about in Europe, however, and suppression of the fact had turned into denial. Part of the horror was due to gross misunderstanding of what Freud was saying. He hardly had in mind little Don Juans of the nursery, for the sexuality of the child was part of its general libidinal energies and therefore ill defined. Indeed, it is this very diffuseness and amorphousness of the sex urges that characterizes polymorphous perversity, or the multiple outlets, objects, and activities humans resort to in the satisfaction of their sexual impulses.

Far from being sex as adults know it, infantile sexuality is initially expressed in self-love, or narcissism. The earliest stages of infancy see the child living almost wholly inside of himself. His environment, small as it is, is probably felt to be an extension or part of his self, and this unity with the rest of the world produces a sense of mastery and control at a time when, paradoxically, the child is most dependent. The child begins to separate himself from the outer world through his relation with the mother, who is from the time of birth the focal point of the infantile universe. It is the mother who loves him, makes him comfortable, and feeds him, and it is the mother who is the first external object of his affections. A piece of the narcissistic libido is detached, so to speak, and is transferred to the mother. The relationship with the mother serves as the model for all other close, affective relationships, especially those we term "love."

The child's love for the mother is highly eroticized and finds expression in the desire to monopolize her affections and her person. This desire is continually frustrated by the vicissitudes of life, for the child must face the competition of other siblings, especially younger ones, and also that of the father. The mother, herself, frustrates the strivings toward her of her young, for though she gives, she also denies; she rewards, but she punishes; she is at the command of the infant, but she sometimes does not respond. This dualism in maternal care introduces an important element—one that invades all intense relationships—the attitude of ambivalence. The mother is in time seen as both a positive and negative figure, as the giver of life, but a potential destroyer of the child's emergent sense of self. The child loses its infantile sense of mastery early and its subsequent battle to regain autonomy and control is ever threatened by a return to dependence and passivity. Indeed, such a regression is doubly menacing for being inviting, for it promises a return to wholeness and indivision.

The course of maturation is measured by the progressive division of the psyche into specialized parts and by a gradual expansion of the social universe, with an accompanying differentiation of this universe into different human categories. Socialization is a process of growing up from and away from the self, but its residue is a loss of psychic wholeness and a feeling of alienation that I would speculate is universal. Part of this growing up and out is the escape of the child from the totality of the maternal bond, an episode known as the "Oedipus complex." In early Freudian theory, it was thought that the Oedipus complex was precipitated by the fact that the father's sexual relationship with the mother thwarted the libidinal strivings of the child toward her. In more recent writings, the role of the father as frustrater of the child is emphasized less, and it is believed that the negative and threatening aspect of the ambivalent mother figure is sufficient to discourage the child from his urges to possess her. Whether in the form of the father-mother relationship or in the mother's role as socializer and disciplinarian, the child learns that society requires that he give up the infantile claim upon the mother and transfer both his identification and eroticism to others.

The onset of the Oedipal complex is much the same for girls and boys, but its resolution is different. Boys find a rival in the father, but they must wrench themselves away from overattachment to the mother, and forge a new sense of identity with the father. And while they must renounce an erotic attachment to the mother, they transfer these longings to other persons of the same sex as the mother. The girl, too, renounces the mother, but she maintains her identity with her as fellow females. On the other hand, and unlike the boy, she must switch her erotic attentions away from members of the mother's sex. Freud also saw psychosexual differentiation to arise from envy of the male organ by little girls.

The notion of "penis envy"—an idea that annoys most women—can best be looked on as an early recognition by girls of their secondary position in the power politics and prestige hierarchy of the family. The upshot of the Oedipal period is that females are more secure in their sexual identities and in their continuing maternal attachments. They do not lose the mother as decisively as does the boy. Boys, on the other hand, are less secure in their identities and very often relive their ambivalence toward the mother in a need for power and domination over women. The masculine overprotest is motivated by fear and insecurity about male powers and is not a statement of strength. We will see that the residue of this anxiety over a return to passivity can be found expressed in many cultures. Freud regarded the Oedipal phase as the most critical juncture in personality development. It is a primary renunciation of a wish and a turning of desire toward the larger world. Repression is at the root of socialization, and with it deferral and displacement of urges. This is also, in his view, the origin of culture.

Many anthropologists maintain that the Oedipal syndrome is specific to Euro-American culture and is the product of a certain kind of family. Thus, the Polish anthropologist Bronislaw Malinowski wrote that the Oedipal complex is absent in the Trobriand Islands of Melanesia. The Trobrianders reckon certain important rights and responsibilities through the mother's line, and the mother's brother is, therefore, the primary authority figure in the kin group. The result of this, said Malinowski, is that the uncle replaces the father of the Western family. Moreover, the boy's repressed and unconscious sexual attentions are directed toward the sister rather than the mother, for, as a future mother's brother himself, he has a vital interest in the sister's sexuality. The problem with Malinowski's argument is that all these things take place too late to be relevant to the Oedipal situation. The Oedipal transition usually occurs at any time from four to seven years of age, but the Trobriand boy does not come under his uncle's authority until he is about twelve. Granted that variant family structures can alter the Oedipal syndrome somewhat or produce differences in its intensity, it is doubtful that it is absent in the Trobriands, or anywhere else for that matter. The essentials of the Oedipus complex are that a woman gives birth to and nurtures a child, who comes to love the mother. He or she must, however, partially relinquish the mother and redirect his or her interests and loves beyond the family, a wrench which leaves scars in the psyche. This is the pan-human situation reduced to its rudiments; it is universal and so also are its psychic products. And from this situation is formed the human capacity for love, loyalty, and sacrifice. The mother-child tie is more than one relationship among many; it is the breakout from the self, the template upon which all other relations are modeled.

Just as the Oedipal period is never navigated unscathed, so also is man never fully socialized. One matures within a social context and absorbs social norms, but this is in part accomplished by opposing the very system one is adjusting to. The Oedipal transition, so necessary to the formation of our sex identities and our capacities for stable social relationships, is a time of struggle between the child and his parents, and within himself. The child protests every discipline inflicted on him, be it toilet training, weaning, or studying, and every jump in his maturation is made by leaping hurdles. The society can shape a person to its ways, but it still must cope with an unrefractory part of the self, which tends to be selfish and asocial. And to the extent that a single kind of human being emerges from the constancies of the human situation, so also is this human nature often resistant to the varieties of society.

Our picture of mankind is incomplete and hastily drawn. We have seen the cardinal characteristic of man to be his high intelligence, and a resultant capacity for abstract thought. This equips him for the use of language and symbol, and for the governing of his activities by learned tradition, or culture. Man is rational as well as intelligent, and human logic everywhere follows the same underlying structure. The hallmark of this rationality is binary thought, or thinking in terms of conceptual opposites. Our rationality is, however, a faulty one, for the crowning achievements of our intelligence, culture and language, are means by which we shape and articulate reality and filter and screen our perceptions; the real world is to a great extent a cultural world.

There are basic similarities in the emotional life of all peoples due to the fact that there are universals in childhood experience, and also because the psychic life of all mankind is highly eroticized. Out of this common experience comes the capacity for love and attachment and an orientation outward to the wider social world. The differences between the sexes are not completely fixed by heredity, and mechanisms exist within the parent-child relationship for establishing sexual identity and the development of full heterosexuality. The human career is indeed fraught with perils and every phase of our development involves a struggle that leaves an aftermath of anxiety and ambivalence. Freud traced both neurosis and culture to the human propensity for repression, and I suspect that we are by definition highly neurotic animals. But we are neurotic in socially useful ways; we are troubled to great creativity.

Social
Systems

Man is by need and by nature a social animal. Man, of course, is also antisocial at times and always estranged to some degree from others; he thinks of himself in separation from his fellows, and his consciousness exists entrapped in a weak and mortal body. This is the ambivalence of all things human, but in the final analysis our species can only survive and perpetuate itself through social life. The needs of subsistence, pro- creation, child rearing, and mutual defense bind us perforce into organized social aggregates. Man may be imagined as living outside of ordered society, as in the social contract philosophies or William Golding's novel *Lord of the Flies*, but he has never been discovered in a nonsocial state. Even the hermit's life may be understood only in reference to the society from which he seeks to escape.

For our present purposes, the term "society" will refer to aggregates of people that enjoy some degree of economic and political autonomy, and which recruit most new members through the procreation of their own people. In this respect, we can speak of the society of the United States or of a tribal group in New Guinea, but we cannot treat a club, an association, or a business firm as a society. Societies are also generally understood by definition to be *organized* aggregates. That is, they are internally divided into specialized parts whose operations are related to each other, usually in a complementary way. The terms "social structure," "social organization," and "social system" arose in the language of anthropology and sociology treatises, but they can be found now in popular newspapers and magazines. We all know roughly what is meant by them, but we have not, perhaps, thought too hard about the implications of their meanings.

Simple though it is, the idea that societies are systematized is central to the social sciences. The systematization occurs through the mutual adjustment of norms, ideas, values, aesthetics, and other things cultural, and it takes place as well in the closely related arena of practical, everyday activity, in the adaptation and accommodation to each other of ways of behaving. In the first case, cultures can be looked upon as symbolic systems in which the meanings of the various symbols of culture are adjusted and related to each other. The various norms of conduct given in culture together form an ethical code, just as the several forms of creative expression add up to an art style. In the case of the norms, coherence among these standards of conduct is obtained by their logical fit with each other, whereas the art forms are unified into a whole by aesthetic criteria, or canons of form and beauty. The most famous anthropological attempt to discover the stylistic unity of cultures was Ruth Benedict's *Patterns of Culture*. Through an analysis of the Zuñi Indians of Arizona and the Kwakiutl of British Columbia, Benedict found that certain principal themes or "patterns" characterized entire cultural systems. She described the Zuñis as "Apollonian," the philosopher Oswald Spengler's metaphor for a balanced, moderate, and even way of life, as opposed to the "Dionysian" Kwakiutl, who were supposedly given to excess and a quest for the extremes of experience. Many anthropologists have found Benedict's categorical assignment of an entire culture to a particular pattern to be a gross simplification, leading to distortion of the data, but a less-sweeping idea of pattern has proved useful in our search for internal consistency in life-styles. A culture may not be reducible to a single theme, but it is still more than a catchall of diverse customs. Rather, any culture is a set of meanings, understandings, and perceptions that are related to each other as an entire web of mutual expectations.

The second mode of systematization in human society lies in the adjustment and accommodation to each other of our activities. These are rules of the road for social interaction that place people in a social situation or a task and schedule their acts relative to each other, ensuring that interaction goes off smoothly without people duplicating one another's tasks or interfering with them. Taking as an example a social system smaller than a whole society, a modern factory has a high level of conscious and deliberate system planning, or "rationalization" in the terms of the German sociologist Max Weber. The entire production process is split up into a number of departments. Within each of these it is further subdivided into a multitude of tasks, each of which can be done by one worker or a small team. Every worker's activities are complementary to the others', and the sum total of everybody's efforts is the finished product. A social system, though not perhaps consciously designed, first splits the totality of social life into a number of compartments, jobs, offices, or whatever and then relates these parts to each other to make a whole, working organism.

The notion of a social system does not imply that every part of a society or group is rigidly connected to each other and to the whole. Actually, in any society certain practices are only loosely related to the entirety of the social system, and there are also clusters of closely interwoven behaviors that are only weakly tied to the rest of the system. There are, then, subsystems within larger systems, just as one can speak of a system of community relations in our larger American society and of family systems within the community. Every social system also contains discordances and contradiction among the parts. As an example, any unity of either values or relationships that American society may aspire to founders on the racial situation. It is also evident that there is a profound contradiction between the capitalistic economic system and the need to husband our resources and curb population growth. These contradictions are vital agencies of change and are central to historic processes in all societies. They can be looked upon as symptoms of social pathology if one is of a conservative bent, or as promises of a bright future if one is more progressively inclined.

Whatever one's politics, contradiction and ambivalence invade all social relations. Every proposition about human affairs can be stood on its head with instructive results. Freud was a master at this. People thought infancy was the age of innocence, but Freud saw it fraught with libidity; men believed that they were entering women in the sex act, but Freud in his delineation of male "castration anxiety" suggested they were also being eaten. In this same manner, we should not accept on face value that the main problem of human association is establishing positive relations with people. We are essentially lonely in our outreach to others, but there is always the contrary danger that we may reach out too far, overidentify with others, and become estranged from ourselves. And we must also remember that every social tie is based on a social disjunction. A tie of friendship has meaning only when contrasted with a category of nonfriend. It can be further heightened and the friendship intensified if there is a category of enemy, giving a positive emotional tone that is in direct proportion to the degree of hostility. In just this way, the closest bonds of group membership are predicated on the exclusion of most others from the group, and the closest ties are jealously guarded and held in privacy. Every bridge that we throw out makes new gaps, every communication generates secrecy and silence.

Societies and groups are not tidily structured clockwork mechanisms, but they must allow the work of life to get done and, to accomplish this, they must guarantee some orderliness and predictability in social relations. There are indeed social systems. Social systems are composed of social groups and statuses, a concept we will discuss a bit later, that form the skeletons of society, frameworks within which social life takes place. The actual working out of this process is referred to by anthropologists and sociologists as its "functioning," or the operating relations of the parts of the system to each other and to the overall structure. The understanding of these processes and the explanation of the contribution of each part of the system to them is one of the main chores of social anthropology.

Emile Durkheim, the French founder of modern sociology, wrote that the task of our discipline is not to understand how a particular trait became part of a culture or why it has its peculiar form, for the origins of most cultural features are lost in the past. Our charge is rather, said Durkheim, to understand how the item works in its social context and to analyze its impact upon other elements of the society and on the whole social system. How is each part of a social system shaped and modified by other related parts, and how do these parts promote each other's existence? How, also, are the parts of a social system shaped and modified by the entire structure, and how do these parts serve to mold and perpetuate the system as a whole? These are questions of "function."

The notion of function must not be confused with conscious purpose, for the latter implies utility to the individual or a goal of individual or group effort. Function, on the other hand, refers to the social utility of a practice, a matter that usually is not pondered by anybody except social scientists and remains unknown to most people. These "latent functions" reveal hidden agendas. Parents whose conscious and honestly felt purpose is to provide the best education for their children may be trying on another level, of which they are unaware, to improve their own social standing in the community. A latent function of exclusive schools, then, is to maintain the class hierarchy. Pursuing this thought, most churchgoers will explain their attendance at services as a means of glorifying God or seeking salvation. On another level, however, they are promoting the cohesion of their religious community by common worship. Durkheim did not coin the tired old saw that "families that pray together stay together," but the idea was his. The function, then, of any practice or cluster of practices is not what people feel to be its purpose but what deeper analysis reveals to be the contribution it makes to the social system of which it is a part.

I have just outlined a view of society and culture known as "structural functionalism." Despite the overlap of terms, this is an entirely different school of thought from plain "structuralism," the branch of theory identified with Claude Lévi-Strauss; to avoid confusion, I will refer to the former persuasion simply as "functionalism." The major source of the functionalist tradition is the work of the turn-of-the-century French sociologist Emile Durkheim. His writings, in turn, influenced the English anthropologist A. R. Radcliffe-Brown and Bronislaw Malinowski, a Polish expatriate whose writing and teaching were largely carried out in London. Both anthropologists saw societies and cultures as whole, functioning systems. Both maintained that the parts of any system must be understood in terms of the total configuration in which they are lodged. Both saw these configurations in much more rigid terms than most anthropologists do today.

Malinowski's idea of function had three aspects. First, an item of culture could be understood by its operations within an overall social system, much as the term function has been used thus far in our discussion. Second, Malinowski saw many cultural traits or practices as having a psychological function, especially in the reduction of fear and anxiety. He argued, for example, that the function of magic was to assure people that they could control unknown or dangerous forces or circumstances, thus giving them the self-confidence to take more pragmatic actions to solve their problems. Finally, human customary behavior functions to satisfy the basic physiological needs for food, maintenance of body temperature, activity, play, growth, physical security, and reproduction. These requirements are satisfied, in the same order, by subsistence techniques and technology, houses and clothing, injunctions to work and movement, sports and humor, patterns of education, strategies for maintenance of internal order and external defense, and the family. These are hardly earthshaking ideas, but despite their self-evident nature Malinowski reminded us that cultures must first ensure the survival of the species.

A. R. Radcliffe-Brown hewed more closely to the Durkheimian tradition than did Malinowski. The reference of function to biological and psychological needs is absent in his work. He saw the function of any social practice to be its relation to the overall operation of the social system. Moreover, Radcliffe-Brown treated this relationship as one in which the social item in question contributed to the maintenance, or perpetuation, of the social system; function and the defense of the status quo became synonymous. Radcliffe-Brown was fond of organic analogies and compared his notion of structure or system to gross anatomy, while his idea of function was akin to physiology. But he went beyond analogy to assume that social systems, like physical organisms, have a tendency toward equilibrium, that is, they resist or minimize the effects of disturbing outside influences and have a natural tendency to return to a prior, steady state. This is not only inherent within agencies of social control dedicated to the public order, but it is a property of all social process. Needless to say, functionalist theory of this type has proved less than useful in the study of social change, and in a world where flux and change are normal one can doubt the entire validity of his assumptions. Most anthropologists now use the concept of equilibrium, or homeostasis, as an "as if" proposition in which balance is assumed in order to highlight and study relationships. But they know that all tendencies of real social life are toward the dissolution of old forms and their replacement with new ones.

"Structuralism" is based upon Lévi-Strauss's theory of the mind discussed in the last chapter. The French anthropologist, it will be remembered, postulated processes of binary thought that resolved the very contradictions they posed. In his theory of society this oppositional structure is mirrored in social relations. But just as the mental structures lie below the level of conscious thought, so also are those of society "infrastructures." As such, they do not exist on the surface of observable social relations but are deep and abstract principles that ultimately shape social forms. We will return to a closer examination of structuralism in later chapters, but we should stress at this juncture one of the cardinal principles of the theory. Lévi-Strauss starts from the premise that the fundamental act of human sociation is the deferral of one's own desires in order to meet the needs and desires of others, an assumption that has clear parallels with Freud's ideas on repression and sublimation. In this scheme, people refrain from using or enjoying things that pertain to them, giving them instead to others in the expectation that in the future they will be similarly rewarded. This act of reciprocity is fundamental in human relations, for on one level it is a statement of human interdependency, whereas on the more abstract level of structure the contradiction between the self and others is sealed by the exchange of gifts. Lévi-Strauss has spun an entire universe of kinship forms out of this bare principle, for, he says, the greatest gift, a total gift, is that of a wife. We will return to him, and to Freud, Radcliffe-Brown, and others, in later chapters.

The scope of anthropological inquiry ranges from the social systems of whole societies down to simple systems of interaction between two persons. Both pose problems on how we deal with people as individuals, for every human being is unique and in some ways different from all others. In studying even a small society, we are overwhelmed by this individual variation, by private idiosyncracies, and by seemingly capricious behavior. The problem, then, is how to reduce this kaleidoscope of unique personalities taking part in a series of events that will never again be exactly repeated into some orderly and coherent description. What do they all, or at least some of them, have in common? One way of reducing individual acts to least-common denominators of behavior is through reference to the norms that guide, or are supposed to guide, the activity. Our attention thus shifts from individual variation and style to the relation of the behavior to social expectation, to what is normally anticipated of people in a specific situation. Another way of avoiding randomness is by considering the people whom we study as "personages" or "social actors" rather than as private individuals. This in no way robs individuals of their uniqueness but only acknowledges that there are both private and public aspects to any person. As social scientists, we are best equipped to handle the public aspect, leaving the study of the total individual to psychology.

Every individual is an "office holder" of sorts, for we all occupy positions that carry with them certain rights and responsibilities. There are doctors and teachers, rich people and poor, men and women, old and young, mothers and daughters, and a host of other social categories that are recognized in society. Societies assort and classify people according to certain criteria that are considered significant, objectifying them, splitting them off from others, and even dividing their personalities into socially meaningful compartments.

These divisions into offices or positions were first reduced to systematic theory by the anthropologist Ralph Linton in his book *The Study of Man* (1936). Linton used the term "status" to refer to a position or office within a social system, and the associated word "role" was used to denote the behavior expected of the incumbent of a status. The choice of nomenclature was only partly a happy one. The term role is most apt, for it carries the connotation of lines and actions in a play, and a social role is indeed like a part. This was most neatly expressed by Shakespeare's line, "All the world's a stage," which carries the dramatic metaphor a step further, reminding us that we play our roles in front of audiences. The word status, however, has been a source of confusion due to its popular association with rank and prestige. Linton, to the contrary, used status in a neutral sense as a niche in life, whether or not it has reference to the esteem in which the status holder is regarded.

The concept of status and role is a relatively simple one, bearing the ambiguity of status in mind. As an example, a teacher has a recognized status in our society, though there are many societies in which instruction is part of the general responsibility of the older generations and is not a specialty; there is plenty of teaching, but there are no teachers. But in complex societies such as our own, the teacher occupies a clearly demarcated position, with special educational requirements, licensing in the status, and a specific roster of duties. In the broadest sense, teachers teach, and that's it. The person in a teacher status, however, is generally understood to do his teaching in the institutional setting of a school, where he follows a schedule, a syllabus, and where he is usually responsible for imparting a certain subject to his students. The teacher has a set of codified responsibilities and rights, which form his role. Part of the role is, of course, that he assures that the students learn and that he is effectively communicating with them. But he also must maintain order, and the disciplinarian aspect of the role sometimes makes him aloof or stern to the students. Teachers are also expected to maintain an even-handed attitude toward their students that admits neither favoritism nor the intrusion of other considerations into the relationship. In all these aspects of the teaching status, each teacher plays his role a bit differently, but all teachers tend to keep within the confines set both by statute and by customary usage. Radical departure from the behavior expected of the teacher can lead to negative sanctions, including official censure, loss of employment, ineffectiveness in the classroom, or just plain ridicule. However much he may fancy himself an individualist, the teacher, and every other role player, knows that there are limits beyond which personal style turns into eccentricity and deviancy.

There are some statuses that are bestowed on us at birth or are at least predictable from birth, and others that we attain or at least wander into in the vagaries of life. Linton called the latter type "achieved statuses" and the former category "ascribed statuses." Ascribed statuses are those that are largely unavoidable. One's status as a male or female and the orbit of family and kin we are born into are not matters of choice. One can change a sex status by transvestism or surgery, and hermaphrodites have a built-in indeterminacy of sex, but these are unusual cases. For the overwhelming majority of the population the sex status is ascribed. Similarly, one is ascribed a kin status at birth that will define a series of relations with one's kinfolk. One can choose his friends, but not his relatives, it is said, and the only way that one can avoid kin ties is by running away from home—which lots of people, young and old, do. In the same vein, one is born a baby by definition, and the only way to avoid being a teenager, a young person, middle-aged, and old is to die young. Sex, kinship, and age are all statuses that are found universally and that invade the social identities of every human being. It is next to impossible to change one's ascribed statuses, and the dissatisfied usually attempt instead to change the role. The women's movement seeks economic uplift and higher personal esteem for women as women, and the Gray Panthers lobby against compulsory retirement and for better Medicare and Social Security benefits and not for rejuvenation. The occasional success of their efforts tells us that the ascribed roles are not fixed by biology—not even the sex role—and that we can indeed escape some limits of the body imposed on us by society.

Age, sex, and kinship do not exhaust ascribed statuses, but they are the only ones found in every society. Skin color, or race, is an ascribed status in American society, which carries with it a broad spectrum of role behavior. It is not automatically dictated that a black American should also be poor, but if one is black there is a better chance of his being poor than if he were white. The status commonly assigns blacks to certain neighborhoods of American cities, disables them in their search for education and jobs, and even entails a distinctive dialect of American English.

The ascribed status of race is linked with a physical characteristic, but there are other, almost equally unescapable statuses that have no such demarcators. One of these is "caste," a kind of grouping best known in India but found in other parts of the world also. In traditional India, one was born into the caste of one's parents, married into the caste, and remained a member until death. Caste membership had certain religious attributes, but its most salient characteristic was occupational specialization. There were castes of priests, of goldsmiths, of warriors, of barbers, of farmers, and of almost every conceivable occupation. One could not change his caste, and if a person was mobile and ambitious, his only choice was to lobby for an improvement of the rank of the entire caste. The system still continues, though weakened, and most Indian fathers are still careful to check the ancestry of prospective sons-in-law; people can jump the confines of caste today more easily than in the past, but they get caught at it also. Finally, another type of ascribed status is that of inherited rank or office. One becomes an aristocrat in Britain by birth, and king or queen through direct descent; the oldest son of the monarch inherits the throne or, if there are no sons, the oldest daughter.

There are other ascribed statuses, but they are limited in number and vary from one society to another. On the other hand, the number of achieved statuses in a society can read like a laundry list of every occupation and activity in which the people are engaged. Most jobs, for example, are achieved statuses, and in a society as complex as our own there are tens of thousands of separate types of employment. There is also a vast and bewildering array of political and religious statuses and an entire lexicon of leisure statuses. Linton's choice of the word "achieved" was unfortunate, for it connotes striving and success, whereas an achieved status may be something that one has either fallen into or happened upon. A beggar has an achieved status just as much as a banker; it is a position that one wins, or is cursed with, through the chances of life.

One measure of the evolution of society is the growth in number of achieved statuses, in this country reaching the point at which they overshadow ascription. In the very simplest societies, there are few achieved statuses. Many groups are organized around the simple criteria of sex, age, and kinship. Political leadership roles may be few and weak and directly inherited. Even religious offices are commonly transmitted through the kinship network. Social groups in primitive societies are generally organized around criteria of kinship, and the principal division of labor is along lines of sex and age. Life presents few alternative paths, and choices are limited by the very simplicity of the society. The differentiation and proliferation of achieved statuses are functions of the progressive growth of technology and related social institutions, for achieved statuses mirror the division of labor.

Ascribed and achieved statuses are not mutually exclusive categories, and the ways in which ascription and achievement are interwoven is one of the more intriguing facets of role analysis. One can see some element of achievement in even the universally recognized ascriptive statuses. Leaving aside the fact that pure survival is an achievement of sorts, one may reach an age level appropriate to a particular status without assuming the social role. In some societies, people want to become elders, for the status brings respect and veneration. In American society, however, people routinely attempt to hide their age either by adornment or through their conduct. It matters little that they are looked upon as foolish by others, for being old is a greater sin than foolishness in our land. Sex roles, as we said, are not totally dictated by biology, and people achieve diverse levels of identity with their sex status. Male homosexuals, for example, have acquired a male identity, but their role behavior is considered to be a departure from the masculine norm. In short, we may indeed acquire, willy-nilly, our ascribed statuses, but the ways in which we play out the roles may define the status as being of a certain subtype.

The interpenetration of ascription and achievement is more pronounced in achieved statuses. A classic instance of this is the American presidency, which has only two constitutionally decreed qualifications: one must be thirty-five years of age and a native citizen of the United States. Other than this, the "American dream" is that anybody can become president, especially if he or she was born poor in a little log cabin. In actual fact, of course, there have been no female presidents, no nonwhite presidents, no Jewish presidents, and only one Catholic president. It may be suspected that there was a heavy anti-Catholic vote in the 1960 election of John F. Kennedy, but this is hard to determine, as people do not like to reveal their prejudices to political pollsters. These prejudicial attitudes have abated somewhat in recent years, but the United States is still a long way from electing a woman president, and a black incumbent is an even more unlikely prospect.

The influence of sex, age, and kinship on achieved statuses is found in every nook and cranny of American life. We like to think that our society is "universalistic," to use the terminology of the sociologist Talcott Parsons, in its treatment of people before the law and in the economy as well. That is, every member of the society should be offered equal treatment and opportunity and should be selected for certain positions on the basis of ability alone. Nonetheless, women have had to fight for equality of opportunity and reward throughout the twentieth century, and the battle has hardly been won. The situation has been even more severe for black Americans, who have been systematically discriminated against in every area of American society since Emancipation. They simply did not have legal status as human beings before 1863. The bias has been so pervasive that quota systems have been instituted for certain jobs or for admission to universities in an attempt to raise the level of opportunity for blacks. Ironically, these quotas are under attack by people who, though never vocal when informal quotas kept blacks out, cite the sacred tradition of American universalism against quota systems favoring the disadvantaged.

Americans, in both government and business, are not supposed to get jobs on the basis of kinship, but it happens all the time, though frowned on as "nepotism." Most would maintain that it is not quite nepotism when the owner of a small business passes it on to a son or son-in-law, but it is certainly nepotism when one advances in a large corporate or government bureaucracy through the "pull" of influential kinfolk. Given strong pressures today for equality of opportunity, it is conceivable that many of the covert ascriptive qualifications will diminish and gradually disappear. It is now possible for a black family to buy a house in a suburban neighborhood that had previously been closed to blacks. The family still needs enough money for the down payment, reenforcing the barrier of color with differences of wealth, but it is a small step away from ascription.

Many social statuses are a blend of achieved and ascribed, and we must keep in mind subtle and blatant ascriptive barriers to certain achieved statuses. The status of coal miner is an achieved one, but there are only a few female miners in the entire country. And as for the men, achievement need not infer free choice. When you are born in Harlan County, Kentucky, you either go into the mines or you migrate. The ascribed statuses have a powerful influence on all parts of the status system because they commonly involve the person's total sense of identity and are deeply imbedded with strongly held cultural values. One cannot speak of being a teacher or a plumber as roles comparable in importance to being a woman or a man. One thinks of him or herself in the first instance as a man or woman; it is a role for which each of us is trained from infancy, and it is etched into our personalities and our very sense of being. All other roles are predicated upon it. A woman can now become an officer of the law, but she will be thought of by her colleagues, the public, and herself, as a police *woman*. Similarly, one of the differences between American whites and blacks is that the whites think of themselves as white persons only in certain situations, whereas racial identity is a constant consideration in the consciousness of black people.

The ascribed criteria of sex and age, and race in the United States, make a total claim upon identities and involve a commitment on the part of the individual that may color and sway all of his other roles. There are certain achieved statuses that have almost equal power. Class status, which is largely an ascribed status in the United States but which can also be achieved, is both cause and effect of occupation, amount and kind of education, and general standard of living. Some occupational statuses make similar demands upon identity. One example is that of the medical doctor, for aside from placing a person firmly in the upper middle class, the doctor status is highly regarded and treated as a special kind of position. The doctor does not have a "job" but a "vocation," and his fellow doctors and patients alike expect him to maintain a certain dignity of bearing and dispassion in relation to his clientele and the general public. This objectivity toward the patient potentially interferes with other relationships, such as the close ones of kinship, and a doctor is usually deterred from treating members of his own family. The categorization of the entire person as doctor has an isolating effect, introducing a penumbra of distance between doctors and all others. It is no surprise, then, to learn that most doctors socialize with other medical people, just as policemen, another total status, commonly spend their leisure hours with other policemen.

The problem of the doctor's relationship to his family raises an issue central to writings on status and role. This is the simple fact that all of us are holders of multiple statuses and are expected, therefore, to play a number of different roles. In most societies, a single individual will have fewest statuses when very young and very old, and the most in his middle years. The newborn child has the age status of infant; the world relates to him and not he to the world. The child has a sex status, and parents, often unconsciously, handle, speak to, and play with baby girls in a somewhat different way than with their brothers. The newborn comes equipped with a kinship system, for the baby is a son or daughter and will minimally have a mother or a mother surrogate. In most societies, the child will also have a father, aunts and uncles, and so forth, giving him an entire status network. The child acquires other statuses and roles, mostly achieved ones, with his maturation. He or she will become a friend, a student, a scout, or whatever, and the expansion of the status system is concomitant with breaking out of the family shell into a broader social orbit. Full maturity may well bring a wife, or a husband, children, work associates, religious offices, political positions, club memberships, and all the rest, often leaving the middle-aged American to feel that he is smothering in a sea of multiple and frequently conflicting commitments. Finally, retirement, infirmity, and separation from one's children, who are busy raising their own families, causes a radical and usually sudden decline in one's statuses. The result in our own society, which tries hero-ically to prolong life spans and then neglects the old, is the isolation of the elderly.

The adjustment of social statuses to each other to form a working organization of related parts is the way a social system works, but each individual must similarly relate all his statuses to each other in order to allow consistency of behavior and integration of the personality. Children discover the potential for role conflict early in life, when they first learn that the role their friends expect them to play may be at radical variance with the fond hopes of their parents. This becomes aggravated over the years, involving, perhaps, profound internal struggles over one's career aims and obligations to family, over the disparity between one's religious ethics and livelihood, or any of a multitude of other conflicts. The problem of making one's statuses compatible with each other is complicated by the fact that we play the associated roles before live audiences. When a number of roles are enacted before the same audience, efforts must be made to make them mutually compatible. This allows them to remain believable and consistent in terms of the overall self-image the actor is trying to project. An alternative, and common, resolution is for the actor to play his various parts before different audiences.

Every person's social universe can be usefully seen as divided by his statuses. One may have the status of daughter, which prescribes cer-tain behavior toward parents and other relatives, but which may have little to do with one's status as a student. Indeed, the two may interfere seriously with each other, as for example, if the mother is a teacher and the daughter is placed in her class. Each category of other actors with whom we are engaged in a certain status is referred to by anthropologists and sociologists as a "role set." Thus, the role set of the status "daughter" includes the mother, father, and other kin, but the status of "student" involves the girl with teachers and fellow students. Since different role behavior is observed toward teachers on one hand and students on the other, however, each may be seen as role subsets. One of the arts of social life is keeping the role sets apart, called "segregation of the role set," in sociological jargon, a device that has the beneficial effect of separating the audiences as well. In illustration, a friend told me of his young son's belief that his teachers lived in the school; the boy was amazed and somewhat nonplused to find out that the teachers really had homes and families, played games, went to the movies and had nonschool friends. The teachers had apparently been quite successful in segregating their own role sets and thus keeping other aspects of their lives apart from the critical scrutiny of their young audiences.

This process of segregation makes every life a private one and every role set a secret society, something the sociologist Georg Simmel told us seventy years ago. The same requirement that we act in a certain way before one group may dictate that we absolutely do not act that way before other groups. A doctor at an out-of-town convention may properly drink and indulge in uproarious behavior, but he is careful not to do so in front of his patients. Segregation can be accomplished fairly easily in urban, industrial society, for its members are hidden by sheer numbers and may lose themselves in any of the myriad corners of city life. In fact, urbanism may so fractionate one's social life that the person is left with a feeling that bits and pieces of him or herself are strewn about the landscape. A small town may present another problem, one of overvisibility. A child may wish fervently to keep his school performance secret from his parents, but it will be difficult if the teacher lives on the same street. And a storekeeper's business conduct and familial affairs are hard to keep apart when his friends and relatives are also his customers.

The problems of role set segregation are compounded in primitive societies by the nature of the statuses. Statuses and roles in modern society tend to be "functionally specific"; that is, roles are narrowly defined and have relevance to quite particular kinds of transactions. The status has a single, specific meaning; it is single stranded. A clerk in the driver's license bureau has no interest in or relationship with his clientele other than the acceptance of a fee and the stamping of an application. The same clerk may also be a father and will interact with his children in a broad variety of situations. He disciplines them, oversees their studies, goes camping with them, provides for them. This paternal status is multistranded and broadly defined, or "functionally diffuse," meaning that the associated role has a large content, applying to a number of different situations and inferring great depth to the relationship, as well as wide breadth. Simple, primitive societies have all the role visibility of a small town plus the complicating factor that most of their roles are of the diffuse variety. Specific statuses are easy to separate and segregate because they have limited relevance in a limited setting—one may never see the license clerk again. But in a small village in the Amazon, the circumstances of life defy role segregation. Not only are everybody's movements known to everybody else, but each person may interact with the same individuals in a number of ways. A man may be the political leader of his kin group, the group's priest, father and grandfather to many of its members, and a worker in its joint economic endeavors. When shifting from one status to another, special steps must be taken by him to assure segregation of the many aspects of his status. One of these is through ritual and the belief that the person involved in a rite acquires an altered, sacred mode of being. Closely connected is the use of masks and special religious regalia, which similarly transform the person into something different and apart. The supernatural *kachinas*, who whip young boys during initiation rites among the Hopis of Arizona, are men of the community whose identities are concealed by masks. In the same way, a good disguise is necessary to conceal from children at Christmas time that Santa Claus is really one of their uncles. The late Max Gluckman, a British anthropologist, saw the extraordinary requirements of role segregation to underlay a good deal of the elaborate ritual of many primitive societies—a logical conclusion for a professor in an English university, where the dons still wear robes. The alterations of social identity common in sacred situations are means by which life among primitives becomes suffused with religious values. The functional specificity of statuses and roles in modern life is, therefore, a central part of the growing secularization of our times.

Any human personality is, in part, the sum total of its social statuses and of the ways they are adjusted to each other. Our sense of self is largely a product of how we are regarded and treated by others. Since this in turn is heavily influenced by social roles, we are social products. Some anthropologists have compared the human personality to an onion, each of whose rings is a social role. Near the surface of the onion are our specific, more peripheral, less committing roles, whereas those toward the center are more diffuse and total in their command over us. Presumably, as one peels the onion, one gets closer to the person's inner being, the "real" person. Of course, when one peels the last ring of a real onion, one finds that there is nothing left, which agrees with the position of the extreme cultural determinists: "you are what you do." I have taken the position, however, that there is indeed an inner core to the human onion, which is derived from the commonality of the human experience. It is a small, but very unrefractory, human nature that interacts with some of our most basic social statuses. Its archtype is the sex role.

The subject of sex and sex roles is a great reservoir of fears, resentments, defenses, projections of the repressed, displacement of emotions, myth, pure fabrication, and arrant nonsense. It is a topic on which everybody has theories, almost all of which are largely erroneous, because these theories are part of the working equipment of the mind employed by people in relating to one another. The theories, then, are revealing for what they tell us of the social system, rather than what they tell us about men and women; they are socially useful lies. The more respectable, or perhaps just more elegantly phrased, theories of the behavioral scientists are also cultural artifacts and show almost as much inventiveness as those of the layman. As in the question of human nature, there are some who attribute much of what we would call masculine or feminine traits to inexorable genetic programming, and then there are the others who believe that the programming is done by society and that sexual behavioral characteristics are wholly learned. The former theory runs up against the fact that there is enormous variation in sex roles, while the latter cannot explain why, in all this variation, there is still a least-common denominator such that all the females of our species share certain likenesses, as do the males. Anatomy is certainly not destiny, but neither is it trivial.

There is a dearth of information on the behavioral genetics of sex, but we are able to make some inferences about the development of sex-related characteristics through a consideration of the universals of socialization, as discussed in the last chapter. It was argued then that males emerge from the Oedipal period with an orientation toward future heterosexuality, a male identity, and a good deal of insecurity about the strength of their hold on this status. One of the products of the Oedipal crisis, according to Freud, is a deep-seated fear of emasculation, in both the literal and figurative senses, which he labeled "castration anxiety." The Freudian analogue of "penis envy" among females, castration anxiety bespeaks the frailty of the masculine sense of power and an uncertainty of male identity. The masculinity project, a treacherous venture, is fraught with the apprehension that one will lose his autonomy, slip back into passivity, and be swallowed in the ambivalent fantasies that spring from mother love. The male becomes more isolated than the female, for the renunciation of his sexualized claim on the mother carries with it a parallel renunciation of his identification with her. The subsequent identification with the father is never as strong as was the maternal link, and he experiences a more radical differentiation of himself from all others than do his sisters. Men are loners, as compared to women, and women are more secure in their femininity than are men in their masculinity.

Certain very obvious biological facts make for profound differences in the sex roles. Paramount among these is the simple reality that only women can bear and suckle children. This alone does not account for the fact that women's work among primitives is usually carried out somewhere near the group's home base, and that the care of house and fire are ordinarily female chores, but it certainly introduces a strong bias in that direction. Permanent restriction to the home precincts is a continuation of the confinement of late pregnancy and early child care, and there is a logic that the person who first fed the child will continue to provide its nourishment. Whatever the reasons, women stay close to home in their work. In hunting and collecting societies, they commonly gather wild roots and seeds near their camps. In horticultural societies, the women often do most of the garden work while the men go off to hunt and fish or make war. The male specialization in these more athletic activities may also be considered a function of superior masculine strength and greater capacity for large and brief expenditures of energy. Women could undoubtedly be trained for greater feats of strength, but a pregnant woman would nonetheless have a difficult time of it.

Another difference between the sexes is equally obvious: men have to be psychophysiologically aroused for sex, but women do not. This has all sorts of interesting ramifications and nuances. Women can fake desire, for example, but men cannot. Women can also indulge in a frequency of sexual contact that would be impossible for most men to attain or sustain. And preparedness for sex may be problematic for males, though it never is for women. The latter fact may have much to do with the common custom of allowing the male to have the initiative in sexual relations. This is so strong in our own society that aggressive sexual overtures by women are known to frighten men away and have an antiaphrodisiac effect. Another possible social product of the workings of the genitalia is the double standard that censures female promiscuity but encourages it among men. All social systems, except for the one toward which our own seems to be evolving, limit and control sexual expression as a means of political and social control, a point we will argue further in the next chapter. The special strictures and inhibitions placed on female sexuality not only guarantee that children will be born under the socially approved auspices of marriage but also that the relatively unlimited sexuality of women will be harnessed and dampened. Society makes sex a commodity of sorts, forcing men to jump through the hoops of work and paternity to obtain the rewards of a woman. This would not work if there was more supply than demand.

Hearth and home are not the only possibilities for females, for in most societies women carry out some of the central chores of the economy. In Amazonian Indian groups, as an instance, men hunt and fish for the proteins in the diet, but women's work supplies most of the vegetable foods, which usually form the greater part of the food supply. Similarly, women in the agrarian America of the nineteenth century had a substantial role in the farm economy, and many worked farms of their own; and lower-class women have always worked whenever jobs were available. Actually, the popular image that we have of the suburban lady who drives her husband to the commuter station, gets the children off to school, shops, and plays bridge is a transient phenomenon of the early to middle-twentieth century. The type is already disappearing. The women's role in less advanced societies than ours is limited by the technology, but in our own electronic age, most jobs do not require superior strength, and the occupational horizons of women have been greatly expanded. Women are perfectly able, in both body and mind, to do most of the jobs now assigned by men to men in our society. They can fly airliners, pilot ships, program computers, direct banks, manage businesses, edit newspapers, and even serve on police forces. Women are now being moved more closely toward combat roles in the armed forces, though it is doubtful if they will soon be used as infantry, as were the women of the West African Dahomey people. Whether women should be cheered and encouraged by their new military uses is a matter of opinion, for in the shift into occupations that were once exclusively male it should be remembered that many, if not most, male occupations today are either boring, or humiliating, or both.

Americans and Europeans have a penchant for inquiring of all things different, "Which one is best?" When confronted with apples or oranges, white wine or red wine, beer or ale, they immediately assume that a difference in kind means a difference in quality. Similarly, people have been arguing about which sex is most intelligent, most sociable, most artistic, or most anything for centuries without throwing much light on the matter. The sexes *are* different, but this indicates no innate inferiority or superiority of either one. Thus, it is widely believed by men in our culture that they are superior to women, which tells us nothing about women, but a great deal about men. The myth of natural superiority is a way of maintaining the social superiority of men in our own society and in many others. The subject bears close examination.

In all the societies of which we have knowledge, both past and present, there are none in which the female is the dominant sex. In most societies, the men are accorded the dominant role. There are some in which the male and female roles, though different, are accorded the same value. I am well aware that a number of books written by feminists maintain that there was a previous stage of matriarchy in the past of our own and other groups, and it must be stressed that such theorization is based on fanciful and imaginative historical reconstruction. The nonexistence of matriarchies is a fact. Most evidence for ancient matriarchies comes from mythology, especially a type of myth about an archaic time when men were subservient to women. In this genre, the Mundurucú tell of a time when the women ordered the men about, made them cook and live in the dwellings while they took over the men's house, and even had sexual relations with them "whether we wanted to or not, just as we do to them today." Women did not hunt, however, and therein lay their downfall as they could not make ritual offerings of meat to the spirits kept in the men's house. The men took over, and women have had a secondary position ever since. Myths charting the shadowy beginnings of a society are notoriously unreliable as history, and we can well doubt the authenticity of this story, and of the Book of Genesis, for that matter. But the tale is still laden with meanings, albeit covert ones.

There are two things going on in this myth (which has been fully reported in *Women of the Forest*, coauthored by my wife Yolanda and me). Though the myth tells us nothing of the past, it serves as a rationalization, or "social charter" to use the term of Bronislaw Malinowski, of the present order of things. American males often claim hereditary superiority of intelligence over women to justify their dominance. The Mundurucú, on the other hand, attribute the supremacy of the male role to the fact that they and only they do the vital work of hunting. The American notion is self-serving, self-aggrandizing and cockamamie speculation; the Mundurucú charter myth at least has the virtue of offering a social and economic explanation. There is also a psychological component in the Mundurucú myth. Myths are formulated over the generations and without conscious authorship, but they express certain wishes and anxieties of a people in the same way that the dream is a fantasy of the individual. Both are ways of expressing in a socially accepted manner what is repressed in the unconscious mind and are a reliving in symbolic or metaphoric form of past experience. In this sense, the Mundurucú myth states that women are capable of dominance, for they were once dominant, just as every son was once wholly dependent upon the mother. Women are depicted as a threatening force that must be guarded against if men are not to fall back into passivity. And it is significant in this regard that the story epitomizes the secondary position of the mythic men by their sexual passivity. Men have power, but they are fearful of losing it to the women, from whom they first obtained it.

The Mundurucú myth, and others like it, are a form of male defense against weakness, whose giveaway is overprotest. If men were really all that dominant by nature, they would not need so many cultural props, such as male secret societies, virility displays, aggressiveness, and all the behavior bound up in the feminists' favorite terms, "sexism" and "male chauvinism." I would hazard the guess that this overprotest underlies a good deal of the male need for superior status, combining with the division of labor of simple technologies to produce male ascendancy. This division has carried over into modern times and is now disappearing with the advent of a new technology. The prestige of women lags behind modern economic reality, but it will surely catch up in time.

That male dominance is not built into our inheritance is amply indicated by many societies in which women are accorded a status on a par with men. Among the Iroquois, the matrons of a group had the right to nominate and remove chiefs, though they did not serve as chiefs themselves. The women of the Tuareg, a nomadic group of the sub-Saharan region of Africa, do not occupy public office either, but they are respected by their men, politically influential, and occasionally quite wealthy. Both these groups were highly warlike in times past, suggesting that high male bellicosity and high female status can go together and often do. Although it is rare for women to hold public office in primitive societies, it has been quite common in the history of the West. Two of Britain's strongest monarchs were Elizabeth I and Victoria, and the examples of Indhira Gandhi of India and Golda Meir of Israel show clearly that women can govern with a toughness usually associated with men. Moreover, both led successful wars during their terms. The office, we can infer, makes the person and not vice versa.

This variability of female status has been best described by Margaret Mead in her books *Sex and Temperament in Three Primitive Societies* and *Male and Female*. Citing among others the case of a New Guinea people whose men practice dance steps while their women go off to trade in the markets, Mead argues that there is considerable plasticity of sex roles. In some societies women may occupy religious office but in others this would be impossible; in some societies women are independent and self-assertive whereas in others they are forced into a self-effacing modesty. But even where their prestige is low, there are compensating mechanisms. In many groups, women acquire a much higher status in old age, the exact reverse of the United States, and in others women wield influence behind the scene through their husbands and sons. There is often a fine art to these manipulations, and women the world over have discovered how to take initiatives, get things done, and exercise their will without seeming to do so. This has always required a keen sensitivity to social relationships, and it is for this reason that women make such good anthropologists.

Many factors other than the technological division of labor affect female status. A technology that relies less and less on human power allows women to enter economic areas once closed to them, a process that is aided and abetted by demography and economics. One reason why women are entering the job market in such large numbers is that the birthrate is going down. Whereas child bearing once brought honor, a woman today with more than two children is open to denunciation as a litterbug. The industrial economy has reached a dead end and neither employment opportunities nor resources will allow the past population explosion to continue. The female's main product is in oversupply. Free of the burden of the large family, women turn to work for a number of reasons. Some wish to find fulfillment in a career, others are bored at home with little to do, and still others go to work because they need the money. The latter is by far the largest category.

Our standard of living in the West has in some ways drifted downward in the midst of unprecedented consumption. It would seem that we can afford every sort of appliance, adult toy, or gewgaw, but we cannot afford to bring up large families and still satisfy our avidity for things. Moreover, the price of housing militates against large families. Less than 20 percent of the people of the United States can afford their own home, and new apartments in urban regions are commanding exorbitant rents. It would be superfluous to cite the higher costs of food and medical care to document the crushing expenses of large family size, for even small families find extreme difficulty in surviving. One resolution of all these dilemmas is the working wife. There is a television and magazine cliché that portrays the woman struggling to get out of the house and into a job, against the wishes of the male-chauvinist husband whose manhood would be threatened by this. The scenario proves another of Morton Fried's adages, "If enough people believe it, it can't be true." In most cases, the wife goes out to work with the full agreement, even urging, of the husband, who no longer can support the family properly on his own income. The working wife is more the product of industrial capitalism than of the feminist movement, and she is here to stay. But she wants equality of opportunity and salary, and these are inevitable.

The conflicting requirements of work and family have introduced severe strain in the female role and in the kinship roles of wife and mother. The structure and internal functioning of the family have consequently undergone shifts of sufficient magnitude to inspire a host of media Cassandras to predict the early demise of the family. The American family of the future will certainly differ from the family of 1950, but then the latter was a far cry from the family of 1850. The shape of the family and of marriage will change, as it always has, but it will not disappear, for it is a universal and enduring form of human sociation. But this is the subject of the next chapter.

Marriage and Family

Marriage is a truly peculiar institution. Although it is widely regarded as a natural state, or at least one ordained by deity, it is actually one of the more ingenious traps set for us by society. Consider its dubious benefits. A woman (or women in plural unions) agrees to place herself in lifelong thralldom to a man (or men) for whom she will cook and clean, giving herself sexually to him on demand, and bearing and raising his children. His side of the bargain requires that he restrict his sex urges to his wife (or wives), or at least keep his liaisons secret from her, live with her, and support her children under compulsion of custom or law. Both sides experience a drastic reduction in independence and autonomy and both have had a lien placed against their labors. When children arrive, the burdens on each are multiplied, for they have surely given a hostage to fortune. There is nothing natural about any of this, and the entire business defies common sense. For all mankind, however, marriage has been so much a part of life, so routinized, that people rarely thought to question the institution, and it is a sign of an age of doubt that we are doing so now.

Whatever its liabilities, marriage is found in all societies. This does not mean that everybody gets married, or even that most people marry, but only that in every human society there is a socially recognized and valued bond between men and women that we call marriage. I have avoided definitions in this book, for they trap the mind into believing that everything in its purview takes the shape of a neat, hard object, which is not true. Nonetheless, when we speak of a custom so general and yet so culturally variable as marriage, it is well to describe its common features. In the first place, almost all marriages except a nun's symbolic union with God grant the partners rights of sexual access to each other. Moreover, this sexual privilege is generally an exclusive one. One may have intercourse with one's spouse, but with nobody else. I hasten to reassure the reader that cheating and adultery go on in just about every society, and there are some in which fidelity is honored more in the breach than in the observance. And in most societies, the injunction to be faithful rests most heavily on the wife, leaving the husband relatively free to philander. Nonetheless, fidelity is the ideal, and extramarital sex is defined as adultery.

Georg Simmel once wrote that marriage is about sex, but it is more than sex; it transcends it. Similarly, sex within marriage becomes transformed into something more than the mere physical act. Objectively, of course, sex is sex, but a different meaning is placed on it in marriage. Sex in marriage is considered good and proper and within the interests of society because it produces children and continuity. Marriage is also the acceptable means for conferring an identity on children, and the notion of legitimacy, or the recognition of legal fatherhood, is widespread. Sex is a very natural act, but marriage is not, for its very core is not just union but public sanction and recognition of the union. It is a legal and contractual affair, even in societies where there are no written laws and contracts. Finally, one of the more curious features of marriage in most societies is that the participants expect the union to be more or less permanent. Actual experience in many groups suggests that the odds may well be against the marriage surviving for more than a few years, but the fond hopes of people seem undaunted by statistics. Some Tuareg who had been married up to eight times told me that, on each occasion, they expected the union to be lifelong. Americans do much the same thing, and skepticism about the permanency of a union is usually firmly repressed, at least at the time of the wedding.

The structure and conduct of marriage vary from society to society, but the above basic meanings are amazingly widespread. Married anthropologists doing fieldwork commonly find that their status toward each other is understood instantly by the host group, no matter how different and exotic. The people may be surprised and amused by what goes on between the anthropological pair, but they have no question about the fact that this is a deep, diffuse, and proprietary bond similar in kind to their own unions. How do we explain it?

The usual rationalizations for marriage, common to layman and professional alike, are that it provides the setting for the basic division of labor between the sexes, it controls sexual access, and it is the framework within which children are socialized. This is all so commonplace and evident that it may well be distrusted. Those who argue the sex-regulating function assume that the alternative would be a tooth-and-claw competition for women that would result in anarchy. They fail to take into account the fact that it is the very restriction on sexual access to women imposed by marriage that makes for their scarcity. Without marriage, we might well become indolent about sex; at the very least, women might be fighting for men instead of the reverse.

There is no denying that the division of male and female work and activity into complementary chores is also an important component of marriage. One must ask, however, is it the only way that the division of labor can be effected? Why not let brother-sister pairs, or other kin groupings, perform the sexually specialized tasks for each other? Or even more to the point, why not let men do their own cooking and allow the women to do men's chores when they are able? Finally, is the family the only structure within which children can be socialized? This is doubtful on the face of it, because children have been brought up in fatherless families, motherless families, and in collective nurseries and schools. One might make an argument that children brought up under the aegis of marriage are happier and better adjusted, but the family seems just as capable— some say more—of producing neurotics as any other unit.

The family is certainly a useful social unit, but simple utilitarianism makes for bad anthropology. Moreover, usefulness is not sufficiently compelling to make for universality. Let us return instead to some even more fundamental considerations. Sex, as Lévi-Strauss reminds us, is ideally adapted for social control. It is a strong drive, yet it is deferrable, can be directed toward different objects, and can even be sublimated, its energies rerouted into creative activity. Its strength, coupled with its plasticity, makes it a splendid system of reward and punishment when properly controlled. One of the distinctive things about sex is that it always is culturally controlled, and sex is the business of society at large in every known group. Society controls sexuality through the stipulation of norms of sexual morality and regulations governing marriage. Those who conform to these norms, and to a series of others, are rewarded with wives, husbands, or just plain sex. As was said in the last chapter, sex can be used in this way only if it is hard to get, and every society has rules that make it scarce. Many place a premium on premarital chastity, especially for girls, and others impose elaborate taboos on sex during certain periods and under certain conditions. Most human groups condemn rank promiscuity, and all state that marriages are the proper auspices for sex. There are few limits set for sexual indulgence within marriage, and societies encourage the partners to direct their erotic attentions to each other. These closures on sexual contact most often affect women more than men, but it must be repeated that the potential supply of female sexuality far outstrips any possible male demands. Women are thus enjoined to chastity, fidelity, modesty, and reserve, and are expected to deter the improper advances of men. They do not always do so, of course, but they are nonetheless the wild card in the game that society plays with all of us.

Marriage, then, is part of a reward system that we get for work, reproduction, and child rearing, all of which are central to society's continuity. Marriage also promotes the social division of the sexes, a primary axis of social differentiation. We usually think of marriage as a union, but it must also be understood that when a person marries, he changes his relationship to not only his spouse but to all persons of the opposite sex. The very contract that gives a man ultimate closeness to one woman enjoins him to be more aloof and reserved with all others; they become "antiwives." There is thus a disjunction between mankind and womankind that is directly promoted by the unions of individual men and women, and which functions to maintain and perpetuate the division of labor. The division of labor between men and women may be a response to breeding and infantile dependency, but marriage produces an embellishment and formalization of the division.

The anthropologist David M. Schneider has noted of American marriage and family that these ties are based upon a model of diffuse, enduring, unquestioning loyalty and fealty; they embody love. This is an ideal, of course, and our families just as often fester with hates, jealousies, and hurts. But Schneider pointed to something very real. The relation between husband and wife is understood to be close in all societies and the closest of all ties in many. It is a remarkably diffuse relationship, covering a gamut of activities ranging from sex through authority and economics to religion. It is the nearest thing we have to a total relationship save one, the mother-infant bond. Freud saw this parallel clearly and interpreted love as a "refinding" of the maternal figure. I would go beyond this and say that the link to the mother is primal and the anvil of all other social relationships. It continues into marriage as an extension of a total bond and the prototype of all other relations. It is a template of social bonding.

The manifest functions of marriage in the division of labor, child rearing, and sex regulation are undeniably important, but as we have seen there are other processes going on below the surface of appearances. We have found marriage to be a cause as well as the resolution of the shortage of mates and have examined the way in which it introduces and maintains the separation of the sexes, one of our fundamental binary distinctions. Marriage has also been viewed as a basic and total kind of relationship, a projection into adult life of the maternal bond. Capping these latent functions is another, which was alluded to in the last chapter: marriage is a unifier of opposites and a fundamental way of expressing reciprocity.

I have chosen to regard marriage as a model of all social relations because it involves the union of social persons who are considered inherently different. The bond between father and son, no matter how warm, is of a different order, based as it is on the identity of family and sex of the two. Ties that are founded on dissimilarity and complementarity, on the contrary, involve the kind of exchange and reciprocity that underlie the social order, and here I am harking back to the writings of Claude Lévi-Strauss. The first opposition to be resolved in marriage is that between the sexes. There are societies that permit same-sex marriages, but only under special circumstances and only when one of the partners assumes the legal status of the opposite sex. Among the Mohave Indians, male transvestites married other men, but they assumed the female role completely. In West Africa, the daughter of a wealthy and important family without male heirs sometimes assumes a male social status and takes wives who bear sons (with the help of male neighbors) and thus continue the kin group. Similarly, in informal, nonlegal weddings between male homosexuals in this country, one of the pair often wears a bridal gown.

Homosexual marriage in our own society is an interesting case in point. Most Americans have varying moral reactions to the practice of homosexuality, ranging from Biblically spiced denunciations to uneasiness to a completely live-and-let-love attitude. Almost all shades of the spectrum, however, believe that homosexual marriage is illogical—not immoral, but nonsensical. This is usually rationalized by pointing to the fact that no children will issue from the union, an objection that could equally be directed at heterosexual couples who prefer to remain childless. The real problem with homosexual unions, however, is that by bringing together that which is already the same, it is a redundancy and a turning inward. Marriage, on the other hand, is a turning outward from one's own sex and from family too; the prohibition of incest forms the chief means of accomplishing the latter.

If marriage is a positive extension of relations to the other sex and other kin groups, the incest taboo is the negative side of marriage, its counterface. The injunction to marry and the ban on marriage with one's own kin are both universal and parts of the same phenomenon. Two distinctive characteristics of incest fear are the extreme abhorrence it arouses and its seemingly inborn nature. All of us from an early age know that sexual relations with close kin are improper, though nobody may have sat down and explained the matter to us. This spontaneous quality has led some to theorize that the revulsion for incest is genetic and inherited and is an evolutionary development for preventing harmful inbreeding; this is also popular belief among most Europeans and Americans, who believe firmly that a union with one's sister or even cousin will almost automatically beget mentally, physically, or morally damaged offspring. Genes do not work that way, however; they do not punish sin. After all, the beautiful and intelligent Cleopatra was the product of generations of brother-sister marriage.

The problems of mating are rather complex. In the first place, imbalances in the sex ratios of children born to families would prevent equitable distribution of sex partners, were inbreeding the norm. This would be compounded by the fact that the children of a family mature at different times and may thus be unavailable to each other. Mating between siblings would be problematic in a family with, for example, three nubile daughters and one baby son, though the girls would be available to the father. At the very least, systematic inbreeding would be difficult to maintain, and unless the inbreeding were continuous over the generations few deleterious effects would occur or be noted. There is a threat in close unions that the mates might be carrying lethal recessive genes that could become dominant or phenotypical in their offspring, but the discovery of most genetic maladies requires some clinical sophistication and fairly complete family histories. In any event, the explanation of the incest taboo as means of avoiding hereditary damage does not account for the sweeping, categorical, and highly emotional nature of the prohibition.

Another problem with the biological interpretation of the incest taboo is that the ban is variable in scope from one society to another, and even within the same society. Jews may marry first cousins, on either side of the family, but Catholics must seek a dispensation for anybody from a third cousin inward. Every state in this country has laws defining and banning incest, but there are considerable differences among them, though all prohibit sex and marriage between primary relatives, such as siblings and parents and children. At the other extreme, there are many societies that define as incestuous sexual relations with most persons of the opposite sex, leaving a minority in the category from which one can draw a mate. Moreover, in exactly these kinds of societies, there are preferences for marriage between certain types of kin, such as a man with his sister's daughter or a woman with the son of her father's sister. The closest marriages of which we have record are between royal brothers and sisters in the direct ruling line of kings of ancient Egypt, Inca Peru, and Hawaii. Such unions are not known to have produced damaged offspring and were prohibited to commoners. We must turn, then, to other explanations of this universal ban.

Bronislaw Malinowski, whose dogmatic functionalism impelled him to attempt to explain practically everything, theorized that the function of the incest taboo was to maintain the stability and integrity of the family. Sexual relations between members other than the husband and wife would introduce competition, would pit brother against brother and father against son and would destroy the tranquillity and order of this fundamental social unit. This, in turn, would disrupt a series of economic and other functions of the family and would be deleterious to the entire society. There is some merit in this view, though we could add to it that sexuality between first-degree kin would also disrupt the role system of the family, crosscutting and canceling out lines of authority. Malinowski's theory does not, however, explain any taboos beyond the elementary family unit of mother, father, and children, unless by a gratuitously applied extension. It is true as far as it goes, but it does not go very far.

One of the more fanciful theories of the origin and function of the incest taboo was advanced by Sigmund Freud in his book *Totem and Taboo* (1912). Following a common anthropological opinion of his time, Freud speculated that the immediate predecessors of man lived in "hordes," or aggregates consisting of a patriarchal leader, his mates, and their offspring. The patriarch was the absolute ruler of the horde, and one of his privileges was that he maintained a sexual monopoly over his mates, including his daughters. The sons, hating the father and desiring the women themselves, banded together and killed him, enabled perhaps by some small technological advance such as a better stone weapon. They then ate his body to incorporate his powers. The ambivalent side of their feelings for the father then came to the fore, and the sons were afflicted with remorse for their deed. In atonement, they did two things. They symbolized the father by identifying him with an animal, a "totem" in anthropological parlance, from which they subsequently traced their descent. They then imposed a taboo upon eating any animal of that species except at certain ceremonial occasions. In this way, they compensated for the murder and the cannibalism, leaving them next to atone for their guilty wish for the women—their mothers and sisters. This was accomplished by a permanent renunciation of claims on the women and the imposition of a law—presumably the first law in human history—banning sexual relations between people descended from the totem-father; that is, all persons of the same totemic group. From that point on, the men would have to give their women to other groups, which would reciprocate in kind.

Freud saw this fictional episode to be a watershed of human development, for out of it was born man's capacity for renunciation, guilt, and repression, and also the institutions of culture. Outmarriage was the first law, belief in totemic descent the first religion, and the totemic groups man's first formally constituted social units. The parallel with the Oedipal situation is obvious, and for a time Freud believed that the experience of the individual was the reliving of a "racial memory" of the primeval crime, a notion he dropped in his later work. The Oedipal complex is, however, relevant to an understanding of the fact that people do not need conscious instruction on the taboo. Rather, at the time the child renounces the mother, he seems to place all other family members in the taboo category. It could also be said that Americans and Europeans learn the incest taboo negatively, through the repression of open display or discussion of sex in the household. Of Freud's just-so story of human origins, we can doubt that such a sequence of events actually took place and that human culture had so sudden and revolutionary a birth, but he was correct in stating that one sure and necessary step on our way to humanity was the definition and prohibition of incest.

The development of the custom of outmarriage, or "exogamy," is a central element in the Freudian theory, as it is in many others. The late Leslie White wrote that the choice facing early man was to "marry out, or die out," an idea he traced to Edward Tylor and Saint Augustine. In White's reasoning, our protohuman, precultural ancestors may well have mated both within and beyond the limits of their small, wandering bands. Those bands that showed a consistent pattern of inmating became encysted and closed off from the rest of mankind, whereas those that tended to marry out would establish alliances with the groups with which they exchanged spouses. The inmarrying, or "endogamic," groups would become isolated and weak, while the others would grow strong in numbers of allies. In time, the endogamic isolates would be forced out of the best food areas or wiped out in war, leaving the exogamic groups surviving according to a sociological kind of natural selection.

Lévi-Strauss has also promulgated a theory of incest that stresses the need for alliances between groups, but he at once starts from more basic concepts and ends with more rarefied theory. The initial assumption of the French structuralist is that reciprocity underlies all human sociation and is the primary means of reconciling the contradictions posed by social opposites. It at once involves self-denial and altruism and sets up a structure of communication between people. In his scheme, the total gift, an act of complete reciprocity, is the giving of a woman. Let us think again of an imaginary Garden of Eden with a fictive Adam and Eve. Early man found himself in a peculiar dilemma; he neither had instinctive equipment that would govern mating, nor laws to do so. His coupling was random and promiscuous, indifferently with close kin or total stranger. Some individual males must have broken out of this social amorphousness, says Lévi-

Strauss, by entering into compacts with others. Each would renounce rights to a woman of his own group, presumably his sister, and would give her to another man in return for the latter's sister. Each winds up with a woman, as he would have even if he had not made the exchange, but he also has an ally bound to him by a tie whose strength derives from the value of the gift. The union with the woman becomes transformed from mere coupling to a formal agreement between men; it is a marriage. And the relationship between the men is transformed from isolation or hostility into support and cooperation. In this way, mating passes from being a natural act to its status as a cultural artifact. It is in the first instance, says Lévi-Strauss, a relationship between men, and only secondarily between a man and a woman.

Lévi-Strauss pursues the logic of brother-sister exchange with interesting results. By consulting the diagram in Figure 1,* it will be seen that if men A and B, the principals in the original sister exchange, wish to keep their reciprocity going, then the way to do it is to marry off their respective children to each other. B will give his daughter G to A's son and he will be given A's daughter for his own son, F. The same pattern could be followed in future generations, leading to a stable system of alliance and interdependency.

Let us look at the diagram more closely, because though A and B came together as strangers, their children are related as "blood kin," or "consanguines." E marries G, who is his father's sister's daughter, but when one follows the maternal line, she is also his mother's brother's

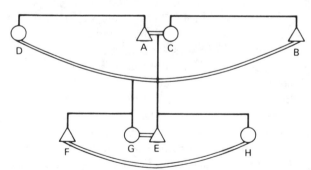

FIGURE 1. Brother-sister exchange and cross-cousin marriage.

*The symbolism of the diagram is quite simple. A triangle stands for a man, a circle for a woman. A short double line between a triangle and a circle indicates that the man and woman are married. A single vertical line extending down from one of the double lines indicates offspring. Finally, brothers and sisters are connected to each other by single horizontal lines.

daughter. Reference to the diagram shows that F and H stand in the same relationship to each other. These two categories of cousins, the respective children of siblings of unlike sex, are called "cross-cousins" in anthropological jargon, and basic brother-sister exchange thus produces cross-cousin marriage, one of the most widespread of all marital preferences. On the contrary, exchange cannot produce parallel-cousin marriage, or the union of the respective children of siblings of like sex (the father's brother's daughter and the mother's sister's daughter). Lévi-Strauss goes on from this paradigm to an exhaustive study in his *Elementary Structures of Kinship* of the varieties of cross-cousin marriage, which is ultimately a theory of the origins and bases of human society.

There are several types of marriage, reflecting the diversity of social institutions in various parts of the world. Marital practices everywhere, however, must take account of the biological phenomenon that sees approximate equality of male and female births globally or in any sizable population. Three fundamental tyes of union are: monogamy, or the marriage of one man to one woman; polygyny, or the union of one man with more than one woman; and polyandry, or the marriage of one woman to more than one man. The latter two plural forms of union are referred to collectively as "polygamy." The term "bigamy" means marriage to two mates, though common English usage extends the definition to be synonymous with polygamy.

Most human societies permit polygamy in one form or another, but in many of them polygamous unions are in the minority. Moreover, monogamy is the rule in the most populous parts of the earth, and the great majority of the world's marriages are, therefore, monogamous. Monogamy is the common and legal practice throughout Europe, most of Asia, Australia, North America, and South America with the exception of some remaining forest Indian tribes. Most traditional African societies permitted polygyny and the practice is consistent with Moslem law, but even here marriages are increasingly monogamous. Monogamy has the clear function of conforming to demography. Moreover, it sets up a simple one-to-one dyadic tie between the partners, usually making for a greater intensity, if not harmony, of the bond as compared to polygamous unions. Monogamy also yields one of the smallest family forms, the nuclear or conjugal family of husband, wife, and children.

We will return to a more detailed view of the monogamous union and the nuclear family later in this chapter, pursuing for now our review of marriage types. Polygyny is by far the more common form of polygamous marriage. It was apparently customary practice in biblical days, and King Solomon was said to have had seven-hundred wives, an ambitious number even at that time. Polygyny is commonly a prerogative of the wealthy and powerful. In many South American Indian tribes, only the chief can have more than one wife, his presumed reward for the burdens of office. The Mundurucú chiefs had this formal privilege also, but it is rarely exercised today. One young chief who had the temerity to do so succeeded only in incurring the anger of the first wife, who tried to drown the younger one. One could say that though the men permit polygyny, they forgot to tell the women. In Africa, polygyny is made possible by wealth but can also be a means of attaining additional wealth. The need for a bride price makes it difficult for a poor man to acquire even one wife, whereas the rich may have many. But once obtained, a wife may add to a man's wealth through agricultural or other labor. Some West African kings in the past were known to have had hundreds of wives, though this would be highly unusual for even a rich commoner. Moslems set four as the limit of wives permitted to any man, a stipulation that was a reform at the time of the Prophet in the seventh century A.D. Mohammed decreed that a husband must treat his wives with justice and equity and must be able to provide for their support. He added that the maximum number that any man could properly keep in this manner was four, a sharp reduction from the huge harems of some Arabs of the period. The same basic logic is now being used by modern-day Islamic reformers to justify a reduction to one wife, for it is maintained that under present conditions of life no man can treat more than one wife justly.

The problem of equity is resolved among West African Moslems by providing separate rooms or huts within the household compound for each wife. The husband eats and sleeps in each wife's quarters in rotation, however much he might favor a younger and prettier spouse. The issue of jealousy always arises when discussing polygyny, for the relationship of cowives is often delicate. Polygyny would, of course, have totally disruptive effects in an American household, but it is an ordinary part of life to those who have grown up in it. Some older African wives urge their husbands to take on an extra wife to help with the housework, or to relieve them of child care while they go to market. Nonetheless, friction can develop. Among the Hausa peoples of Nigeria, cowives are referred to by the word for "opposites," because of the frequency of fights between them. One Hausa told me that he would soon take a second wife but would then wait many years before taking more, as it would be prudent to marry the third and fourth almost at the same time. He explained this as due to imbalances within the household compound. Two wives form a balanced opposition. They may be antagonistic toward each other, but it is a standoff into which the husband does not get dragged. Similarly, four wives usually pair off two against two, leaving the husband again to peacefully receive his male visitors in the front room. But when one has three wives, the antagonisms take a two-against-one form, in which alliances and sides continually shift, pulling the husband into the conflicts and keeping the compound in a general turmoil. Very often, the jealousies do not center on sexual competition over the husband but over real and imagined differences in the treatment of the wives' respective children. It can be added parenthetically that despite the father centeredness of the Hausa and other West African societies, a child's tie with the mother may be stronger in these polygynous societies than in monogamous ones, because the father's attentions are diluted and divided, whereas the mother's are undivided and whetted by antagonisms.

Most people assume that the woman's position is debased by polygyny, but this is a simple extrapolation from our own standards. Married women in France only gained control over their own finances in 1968, but West African women in most of the coastal regions have always had this right. In this area, women are petty traders, selling foods, cigarettes, sunglasses, or whatever off trays balanced on their heads or occupying stalls within the local markets. Some successful ones become small-scale wholesalers in intercommunity commerce, and a very few have become wealthy and notable. They are often organized into tightly controlled guilds, run by market women, and constitute a political force. A woman's earnings are absolutely her own. She may help her husband financially if she wishes, or she may even lend him money at appropriate interest rates, but he has no claim or right to her income. As a consequence, the wife, whether or not she has cowives, is a proud and independent figure within the family. The woman's prestige and value in a polygynous society may be low or high, and each instance is due more to economic factors than to the marital situation itself.

The practice of polyandry leaves most people bemused and unbelieving. "It is against human nature," exclaimed one young African to whom I had just explained polyandry. I pointed out to him that plural marriages were permitted in his own society, but he dismissed this as it was the women who were cospouses and they did not matter that much. The young man's ethnocentrism is understandable, but even American women find polyandry more odd than polygyny. In only a limited number of societies is marriage of a woman to more than one man condoned. It occurred infrequently among the Shoshoni of Nevada, along with occasional polygyny, but the most famous cases come from the Marquesas Islands in Polynesia, Tibet, and certain hill tribes of India. In almost all instances, lack of land or extremely rigorous environmental conditions produce a marginal subsistence level and the need for population control. The logic is simple: a woman can have a hundred husbands, and she still will produce a child only every year or so. Polyandry is not a common response to overpopulation and hard times, however, for most people living at the edge of hunger do not follow the practice. It is simply one solution among many possibilities.

Polyandry among the Tibetan yak breeders of the Himalayas makes good economic sense. A man must build up a herd before he can become economically self-sufficient, and in this harsh area it is a slow process. Men become independent late, but those with older, married brothers are commonly invited to join the unions of those brothers. The older brother remains the head of the household and father to his wife's children, but the younger brother helps in the herding and shares sexual access to the wife. When the younger brother builds up a herd of his own, he usually sets up his own household and withdraws from the polyandrous union; it is thus a means of delaying the age of marriage while taking care of the sexual needs of the younger males. The practice has no necessary relationship to female prestige, for the Marquesan woman has a significantly higher status than the Tibetan female. Like everything else, polyandry can be looked at from two opposed viewpoints. It may be regarded as a woman keeping her own stud stable, or it may be looked upon as two or more men sharing a chattel. Depending on the society, it can be a bit of either, or both.

Fraternal polyandry, as we call the Tibetan variety of the custom, may also be looked upon as a relationship between two kin groups, the wife's and the husband's. From this perspective, the bride is not only contracted to the husband but to his entire kin group. The younger brother's rights in the wife follow from the exchange bond between the groups. This is more clearly seen in the custom of the "levirate," which bears close comparison with fraternal polyandry. The ancient Hebrew levirate is mentioned in the Book of Leviticus, whence its name, and enjoins that when a man dies leaving his wife without issue, it is the duty of a younger brother to marry the widow and to continue the family line. In most societies in which the levirate is followed, the widow is married by a brother of the deceased whether or not she has borne children. In common with the Hebrews, however, it is a younger brother who usually marries the widow, a variety known as the junior levirate. It is thus the kin group as a whole that has residual rights in the wife; not only her person is entailed to the husband's family, but, as the Hebrew custom suggests, also her issue. The basic interest of the kin group is its continuity, and its interest in its brides is in their offspring.

The same principle is involved in another widespread practice, known as the "sororate." Just the reverse of the levirate, the sororate enjoins or urges a widower to marry his deceased wife's sister, usually a younger one. His kin has contracted through marriage with the wife's kin for a woman, and the agreement in the cases of both the levirate and the sororate outlives the people involved in the union. Very much akin to the sororate is the custom of "sororal polygyny," or marriage of a man to two or more sisters. That this is clearly a male right is evident among some of the tribes of the upper Xingú River in Brazil, where a man is given sexual access to his wife's unmarried younger sister. This may result in sororal polygyny or it may be a temporary arrangement until the girl is married to another man.

Marriage in modern industrial society has increasingly become a private affair, and we tend to think of it in this way. In our ideology, whether or not to marry, when to marry, and whom to marry are the individual's choice. Young people, especially young women, are the objects of no small amount of advice and nagging from their elders, but the ultimate decision is supposed to be theirs. Arranged marriages are regarded as barbaric and Old World in our culture and as a definite impediment to the pursuit of happiness. There is no way of determining whether parent-arranged marriages are more or less successful than marriages freely entered into by the partners, for each has a time and a place. Marriages were formerly contracted by families, but our families are so truncated and shorn of function that it would now be meaningless. Moreover, in times past, romance and love were not necessarily understood as a prerequisite to marriage, and the relationship between mates lacked some of the intimacy it has today.

Marriages are no longer arranged in the United States, but they are certainly not random. People marry for love, but they seem more disposed to fall in love with people with whom they have "something in common." What is common is usually race, education, religion, and class status, all of which prestructure marriage through determining the associations, schools, and living places of the parties. Parents may not tell their children exactly whom to marry, but they choose the neighborhood in which their child grows up, they determine his religion, and they dictate the amount and place of his schooling. Thus, if a young man marries a young woman whom he met at a religious fellowship group on a university campus, the respective parents would probably be delighted. They might even observe that it could not have worked out better if they had arranged it.

However limited it may be, the amount of freedom given in mate choice in our society is unusual, but not unique. Most groups consider marriage too important a decision to be left to kids, though several primitive groups grant great latitude to their young. The control of the older generation is most evident in those societies in which substantial wealth is transferred at the time of marriage. Throughout much of Africa, a "bride-price" is paid to the woman's family by the man's kin. Often erroneously interpreted as outright purchase of a woman, the bride-price may be considered as a way of honoring the woman and her kin, as recompense to them for their expenses in bringing her up, and, most importantly, as the means of securing the rights of the husband's group over the wife's issue. The latter purpose is most clearly seen in two aspects of the custom. First, if a divorce occurs before children are born, the husband's kin in many groups can ask for a refund of the bride-price. Second, since bride-price is often payable over a period of years, the child is not fully incorporated into the father's group until payment is complete. If the father's kin default, the child frequently becomes a member of his mother's kin group.

Bride-price is part of a pattern of exchange relationships that may go on between in-laws for the lifetime of the couple. These exchanges have considerable economic significance, which will be discussed in the appropriate section. In simpler societies they may be the chief means for the circulation of wealth. In more complex societies, bride-price becomes increasingly rare. In pre- and early industrial Europe, the principal marital exchange was the dowry, a bestowal of wealth on the bride or the couple by her family. Dowries, unlike bride wealth, have nothing to do with gaining rights over children or recompensing the groom's family for bringing him up. They seem to operate mainly in stratified societies to guarantee a husband of proper class and occupation for one's daughter. The amount of dowry is in part a function of what her family can afford, but it also varies with the social worth of the prospective groom. Dowry is a fast disappearing custom, as is the arrangement of marriages of which it was a part.

Marriages are contracted in a variety of ways, but almost all produce a cohabiting couple that will form the nucleus of a family. The absolutely basic, elemental family form consists of a woman and her children. In almost all human societies, the mother's right over her children is considered prior and natural, a function of the fact that she bore the child. That is, her natural role as mother is sufficient to establish her social role as mother. On the other hand, except in a few East African groups, a man does not become a legal father by the biological fact of siring a child. The only way in which he can become a legal father is by marrying a woman, who bears a child; the mother's right is considered natural, the father's is cultural.

A bit of expansion and illustration are in order. Among the Kuikuru Indians of Brazil, a child addresses as "father" all the men who had intercourse with his mother at the time of his conception. Such fatherhood is not a diffuse and lasting tie, however, and the person who carries out the main role of father is the mother's husband. We go considerably beyond this in our own society. A man is treated as the legal father of all children born to his wife. If the wife has an illicit relationship that results in a child, the husband may divorce her, and he may even disown the child, but he would have to go before the courts and plead for relief. If the husband, however, wishes to recognize the child as his own, he may do so, whatever might be the natural father's disposition in the matter. Actually, natural fathers have responsibilities, but few rights, in the United States. If a man is found by a court to be the biological father of an illegitimate child, he may be compelled to pay medical costs and a child-support stipend. This differs from child support payments after a divorce, for the divorced man remains the father and has certain rights over the children. The natural father acquires no rights at all. He is paying damages, much as if he had injured the woman with an automobile. By the same logic, the mother may decide to yield the baby for adoption, and there is little that the biological father can do to intervene.

Marriage, and with it legitimacy, bestow on each child a full and rounded kinship status, a network of relatives that has extensions outward on both the father's and mother's sides. Illegitimacy means that the child has a truncated kinship status, as in the case of a young Mundurucú child who had no clan name because his father was unknown. His status was referred to by the word for excrement, but he was well treated, though somewhat forlorn. Marriage guarantees a man support and kin connections, for it is also a way of linking the men firmly to the reproductive process and to younger generations. Lacking marriage, a man may relate to the young through special ties to his sister's children, but the rules of incest prevent him from taking part in her reproductive activities. One of the more extreme cases of devaluation of the nuclear family and the husband role comes to us from the Nayar, a caste of former mercenary warriors in India. Young Nayar women go through a ritual marriage with a man, who may well have no further part in her life. The woman then has a series of lovers; some unions are stable and long lasting, but the frequent absence of the men for military campaigns results in considerable turnover. For their part, the men do not have close relations with the children they sire and find their nearest ties to their sisters' households and children.

Americans look upon the nuclear family of husband, wife, and children as an absolute good, ordained by God or nature or both. All departures from this divinely given institution are seen as pathological. In this ideological climate, the news that a significant percentage—though a clear minority—of black urban families were headed by women came as a shock to official America, which promptly decided that this was the root of the poverty of black Americans. This was a convenient conclusion, for it relieved white America of any responsibility for the situation, which, in any event, could be handily dismissed as hopeless. Once again our social physicians had concluded that fevers cause malaria and that measles derive from a rash; cause and effect had been reversed, and a period of "benign neglect" of the American black had begun.

Anthropologists have long known that mother-centeredness is a striking characteristic in many black families. In the United States, this takes the common form of a particularly strong mother-daughter bond, expressed in joint living arrangements. The younger woman may have a succession of lovers or may have been divorced or abandoned. Left to her own support, she sets up a common household with her mother, who takes care of the children while she goes out to work. The household may include other daughters, and perhaps sons, and men may be in transient residence. The core of the family, however, is the mother and her daughters; we call a female-weighted group of this kind a "matrifocal" family. Matrifocality is in part a creation of our aid-to-dependent-children programs, which provide subsidies only if the household is without a male breadwinner. Men are either driven out of the house in order that their children may be supported, or their presence as regular household members is concealed. In either case, the tendencies to matrifocality are aggravated.

Matrifocality is even more pronounced among West Indians of African descent. There are sections of the island of Jamaica where 75 percent of all unions are consensual. Women are the permanent occupants of the houses, whereas the men come and go. Some of the common-law unions are quite stable, however, and last until the death of one of the mates. I knew an old man in the Brazilian Amazon who had been living with his common-law spouse for forty years and had raised a number of children to maturity. Each year, the priest on his annual rounds would try to marry them, offering the ceremony absolutely gratis. The old couple refused regularly on the grounds that one should not tamper with anything that works.

Matrifocality has been treated by some as a peculiarly Afro-American phenomenon, but it is much more widespread. American Indian reservations often contain a high number of female-led households, though the mother-daughter tie usually does not pose a division of labor between child rearing and job, as it does in many black families. A study done a number of years ago in East London among lower-class English showed a similar importance of female links. Most of the subjects in the study were legally married, but the center of gravity of family life was the woman. Newly wed daughters would try to live as near their mothers as possible, relying on their support, help, and companionship. The Cockney "mum" is a classic mother figure, ranking with the Jewish and Italian mothers so celebrated by novelists.

Almost every ethnic group lays claim to having the world's champion mothers, noted for their cooking, smothering affection, eternal nagging, and capacity for inducing guilt in their offspring. In this sense, most families are matricentric, for mothers are generally the center of familial affect or emotion, whether for better or for worse. This should not, however, be confused with matrifocality, which refers to a certain kind of structure and the placing of authority as well as affect in female hands.

Strong women do not necessarily breed weak men, but the strength of the female role in matrifocal families is a function of weakness and vulnerability of male status. Some scholars believe that black matrifocality was a result of the African heritage and a cultural residue from the close links between mother and children in polygynous households. Others see it as a product of slavery and the systematic efforts of slave owners to inhibit the growth of black families. These factors may have been operative, but they do not explain the modern American Indian or the East Londoner. Actually, male roles were central to the economy of the post–Civil War rural black family, and matrifocality is more strongly imbedded in the cities of the north than in the southern countryside. Poverty contributes to the pattern, but more critical is a kind of poverty in which male employment is marginal, sporadic, and unstable. The man can provide for his family at times, but there may be long periods in which he would be no more than a drain on its limited resources. In the West Indies, men are forced into semimigrant seasonal plantation work and, like Nayar warriors, are continually breaking away from domestic units. Women, on the other hand, may work as domestic servants or laundresses, jobs that do not pay much but have the virtue of being steady and close to home.

Matrifocality usually implies something beyond the centrality of a woman in the household, for it is an intergenerational matter. The female head of the household is often not simply a mother but a grandmother as well, and her role can verge on the matriarchal. Matrifocality skews the division of labor whereby husbands earn and wives cook and have children; it is characterized by a situation in which younger women have babies, which their mothers tend while they go out to work. It is thus a practical and rational adaptation to poverty and male status-deprivation. Marriage and family are still considered the ideal institutions, but the people often complain that they cannot afford it. Looked at in another way, the turnover in common-law marriages bespeaks marital instability, raising parallels between matrifocality and high divorce rates, to which we will return later in this chapter. Finally, the matrifocal family enjoys a certain stability that is disappearing in the modern conjugal family. The latter is based on the always problematic and vagrant bond between a man and a woman, but the former is fixed in the most enduring of all human ties, that between mother and daughter.

The principal difference between the Nayar family or the matrifocal type and the kind of family typical of middle-class America is the central role played within it by related adults other than the husband-wife duo.

We will look more closely at the standard American family soon, but we can note for now that one of its chief features is the degree to which it forms a kinship isolate; the family has relatives, of course, but they do not play important roles toward each other. The matrifocal family is notable for keeping together a group of blood kin; in its classic form it is a three-generation group of women related through women. In simple, primitive societies the conjugal family is commonly lodged within an even larger matrix of kinsmen, many of whom play roles that we normally associate with first-degree relatives.

The Mundurucú Indians provide a fine illustration of the ways in which larger kin groups take over functions that are the responsibility or right of the nuclear family in our own culture. Each Mundurucú village consists of a number of dwelling houses and a men's house. Most Mundurucú, except for the very old, are married, but spouses do not sleep together. Rather, the men spend their leisure time in the men's house, eat their main meals there, and sleep in it at night. The residences are the province of the females of the village and of boys under the age of puberty. Women usually remain in the residences of their mothers after marriage, their husbands moving into the village men's house, and the core of each dwelling is a group of sisters and their married daughters. For those whose thinking is addled by the American euphemism of "sleeping together" for sexual intercourse, I hasten to add that the men make frequent nocturnal visits to the hammocks of their wives or have trysts with them in the daytime outside the village. Husbands also visit the wife's house during the day to play with the children or to take a snack or a drink of water.

There is a strict division of labor between the sexes which assigns child care, cooking, garden work, and fetching water and firewood to the women, leaving the men to hunt, fish, and do the heavy work of clearing forest for the gardens. Most of these chores involve cooperation among members of the same sex. Men do much of their hunting collectively, and the women of the village all help each other in harvesting and in the tedious work of preparing cassava. Gardens are considered to belong to the people of a household and their yield is enjoyed by the entire group. Moreover, garden foods are usually distributed among all the village women who help in its harvesting and preparation. Game is similarly widely shared. A monkey or bird may well be consumed by the hunter's wife and children only, but a wild pig or tapir will be quartered and pieces distributed throughout the village. It is then cooked by the women of each household, and a share is eaten by the men at a communal meal in the men's house.

Thus far, we have seen that husbands and wives neither sleep together nor form separate domestic groups. There is no independent conjugal family economy. The division of labor is carried out by men and women as separate groups, within the context of household and village. The women of a house also run an informal day-care center and children are passed from one woman or girl to the other all day long. Divorce is easy among the Mundurucú. All a man has to do is bring his kill of game to another household rather than to that of his wife. The community is thereby informed that the marriage is ended. He may move to another village, but he often stays just where he is, in the men's house. If he has a kinswoman in the village, he will bring his game to her house and will go there for small meals and a drink of water. His ex-wife's life will likewise continue along the same lines as before. She will work with the other women and will receive meat through sharing; in fact, she may well eat of her former husband's kill whenever he is lucky. Both will experience some inconveniences. He will need a woman to patch his clothes and make his hammock, and she will lack for the trade goods that her husband used to buy for her from his rubber-collecting proceeds. And they will both have to find other sex partners, which is never much of a problem in a Mundurucú village.

We may well ask, as I did, why do these people get married? For the answer, I can only refer the reader back to the earlier part of this chapter and my contention that one could never explain marriage on simple utilitarian grounds. It is sui generis and as central to human society as the incest taboo, with which it is one. The same stricture is true of marriage in Western society. In some ways, the form of the European family has been quite stable over the past two-thousand years. The family has been monogamous, divorce has been difficult to impossible, illegitimacy has been severely stigmatized, and the nuclear family has been the primary kinship unit. The traditional European family, and the American family until recent years, have always been the center of a large network of kinfolk extending out through both the father's and mother's lines. One starts off in life with the "family of orientation" and forms his or her own "family of procreation" at maturity, extending one's skein of kinsmen beyond those of one's mother and father to those of one's spouse and ultimately to the families of procreation of one's grown children.

These links of blood and marriage—of consanguinity and affinity, respectively—set up a vast chain, which would see each of us with uncountable thousands of relatives were it not for those social mechanisms that make us forget all about some kin but maintain ties with others. The means by which we define kin are also the means by which we exclude other, potential kin from our orbits. Thus, not even the largest and most ramified kin groups include all of one's blood and in-law links, but those of the past were larger than today's. In rural America, farming districts were often seats for large aggregates of relatives, whose numbers were kept down only by land shortages and westward or urban migration.

Traditionally, relatives bore responsibility for each other. If a child was left orphaned, he or she was reared by an aunt and uncle; if a family became impoverished, they were fed and even housed by kinfolk; the expenses of illness and death were often born by kin; and the elderly were unquestioningly cared for by their children or by nieces and nephews. In contrast, the chain of kinship today is shorter and thinner.

The big family has not disappeared entirely from the American landscape. The great migration to the United States of the late nineteenth and early twentieth centuries brought entire kin groups and whole villages to this country. First one immigrant would arrive, who would save his wages and send them back to the old country for the passage of others. They, in turn, would repeat the process until scores of relatives were brought in. The migrants tended to settle near their kin, their fellow villagers, and their countrymen; the upper Midwest drew Scandinavians and whole sections of American cities became ethnic neighborhoods, where European language and custom persisted. As in the process of coming here, the immigrants helped each other in their new land. The knowledge and influence of relatives were used to get jobs or to mediate with officialdom, and kinfolk helped each other in much the same way as the rural Americans of an earlier period did. The Jewish "cousins clubs" or "family circles" were typical phenomena of the postimmigration period. The membership of these groups, some tracing their ancestry back to a long-dead couple in a Russian or Polish village, often figured in the hundreds. They were important in arranging marriages, educating the more promising young people, and in providing economic assistance.

Most of these associations are moribund today, but large kin networks are still found among the blue-collar descendants of the immigrants. The American working class has greater stability of residence and occupation than the middle class, and their neighborhoods remain remarkably intact. In Hamtramck, Michigan, the Bridgeport district of Chicago, and Bayonne, New Jersey, there are many adults who were born in the community, as were their parents and perhaps grandparents. They were baptized in the same church where their funeral services will be held, and the men may well have worked in the same factory as their fathers. Their spouses are generally drawn from the town or its vicinity, thereby compounding, extending, and intensifying the overlap of kinship and neighborhood. Over the three or four generations since the original immigration, the family network will have grown to make each neighborhood a kinship center, and their numbers will have spilled over into adjoining communities. These people still rely on each other for job information, small loans, political support, and friendship. Every Sunday dinner sees parts of the family network reunified, as does every church service. And one often finds an elderly grandfather or grandmother living in the household and taking a full and active part in its life.

Large families are also a characteristic of the rich. The poor stay together because they are weak, whereas the wealthy keep their kin ties alive because they are profitable. This is clearly seen in our euphemistic expression "an old family." Now, unless the hoi polloi were born from test tubes or by parthenogenesis, every family is as old as every other one. Old, in popular usage, means that the family has been wealthy and notable for several generations and that there is manifest material advantage in tracing one's origins to it, for it confers upper-class status. Obviously, when descent is traced back even a hundred years to the goose that laid the golden egg, a large number of people will find common kinship. These ties may be well worth keeping. They put bank presidents in contact with industrialists and senators in touch with governors. They know and understand each other; they have a common "blood" bond; they wash each other's hands.

The greatest constriction of kinship networks has occurred among America's middle class. There have been a number of contributing factors to this. The middle class consists of strivers and climbers; these people have not yet made it big, but they have hopes of doing so. Many of them are newly up from the working class and expect further status improvement by either themselves or their children. The mobility of the newly arrived may or may not be helped by kin. If one's cousin is a lawyer or a doctor, he can obviously be of assistance, if only to get one into his country club. On the other hand, if your cousin still speaks with a heavy accent and has manners considered gross according to middle-class American standards, he can only be a drag on your social ascent. People part company from such relatives with great ease. "We didn't have much in common anymore," will be the excuse of the successful, whereas his lower-class cousin will complain that his relative has taken on airs.

One gets rid of kinfolk on the way upward, and also on the way outward. Part of the mobility of the middle class is a relatively high rate of turnover of place of residence. With affluence, one moves from the Bronx to Scarsdale, a few miles as the crow flies, but a long distance the way people move. The middle-class youngsters also go off to college, where they may marry people from other parts of the country, and at the end of which they will usually apply for jobs most anywhere. If a man becomes part of the huge army of middle-level corporation executives, he may well live in one place for no more than a few years at a time. Nationwide firms have now made frequent transfers so much a part of policy that they routinely buy the houses of transferees and resell them to their replacements. Life for many middle-class Americans is a bit like being in the Army—one is always on the move. And as in the Army, people lose track of old friends, and old relatives, and bits and pieces of themselves.

The middle class does not completely shed its kin but rather attenuates ties with them. A special event such as a wedding or a funeral ("It's been too long—let's get together soon under happier circumstances. I'll call you.") brings kinfolk together, and small family reunions are held at Thanksgiving. Christmas brings greeting cards and often a dittoed newsletter on family events during the past year. But the members of the middle class do not usually go to kinsmen for help. A father or a sister may be called on for material assistance, but not a cousin or an aunt; the codependency group shrinks back to the nuclear family. Similarly, when looking for a job, a person will rely on friends and business associates more often than on a relative, if only because one ordinarily makes many friends in his line of work. If a professor is looking for a college post, he will not seek support from his brother, except in the unlikely event that the brother is a dean. Even then he might not be able to help, for the dean would go against the universalistic rule in giving a job to his brother. The professor will instead contact his peers from graduate-school days, his old professors, and friends in his discipline. The same general situation prevails in much of middle-class employment. If a person loses his job and experiences a long period of unemployment, a brother will usually neither have the resources nor be expected to support the man's family. He turns instead to savings and unemployment insurance, just as health insurance and not family is what sustains people when they are ill.

The expanded social-service functions of every level of government have relieved the family of many burdens but have also taken away part of its reason for existence. The family ceded its educational role to the schools during the last century, and some modern parents even blame the poor behavior of their children on the educational system. Families also had productive functions in the agrarian economy of the past, for the labor of every member was needed on the farm. The family farm, like most other family enterprises, is now disappearing, and kinsmen rarely band together in their work. The work efforts of the middle class, especially, are done in separation from family and home. Given the complex nature of their occupations, the children of the middle class often have no understanding of what their parents do for a living, and to the degree that the principal waking activity of the parents is impenetrable to the child, so also is the parent. A farm boy can see his father at work, and a child in a mining town knows of his father's occupation from an early age. But a father who disappears on the 8:02 every morning and does not get home until 7:00 poses an enigma that deepens if he is also a computer programmer or an ad-agency account executive.

The economic unity of the family in the past was predicated on direct, though delayed, reciprocity. A couple raised children who were expected to provide for them when they grew old. Social Security and the growth of private retirement plans, however, have relieved the nuclear family of financial responsibility for the old, and in the process have shorn the family of the very presence of the grandparental generation. Communities of people of a certain age bracket made their appearance in the United States at the end of World War II, when veterans bought houses in large suburban tracts, producing neighborhoods where few were older than thirty-five. Retirement funds have since that time given us the old-age, or "golden-years," villages that started off in the Southwest and Florida and are now found throughout the country. These are the places where middle-class Americans go to die. The less-prosperous wind up with their children, if they are lucky, but are frequently abandoned in the cities by their suburban young; they then eke out life on Social Security. When they can no longer take care of themselves, both the well-off and the indigent end their days in nursing homes, sustained by Medicare and Medicaid, but still alone.

The structure of the Social Security system has had one interesting effect on marriage and the family. Benefits for an eligible husband and wife are substantially less than they would be for two single people, and many perfectly decorous oldsters resolve their loneliness by entering common-law relationships. There is no evidence that their sons and daughters are sufficiently shocked to offer to make up the loss of stipend if they were to marry. Beyond this, the separation of the old from the rest of society has truncated family life and lopped off some important roles. The grandparent-grandchild relationship in most societies is warm, permissive, and almost conspiratorial, in tacit recognition of the fact that they have a common enemy—the young-to-middle-aged parental generation. The children see the parental generation as disciplinarians, threats to autonomy, and frustraters of pleasure. As for the grandparents, the child-rearing experience has left them with as much ambivalence as the children, and they often bear a sense of betrayal and abandonment toward their offspring. But the alliance of the alternate generations against the proximate one cannot be effective if the grandparents live in Florida. Other benevolent older relatives, such as a favorite uncle, are still available, but the children may not see them very often either. Friends may informally play out the role of the nonauthoritarian and egalitarian elder with each other's children, but there is an inherent impermanence in this position. The family, then, gets forced back and turned in upon itself.

The status and role system of the nuclear, or conjugal, family was never neatly and tidily arranged, the rights and responsibilities never allocated without overlap. The sociological notion that the mother is the emotional center, or "expressive leader," of the family, while the father is the practical director, or "instrumental leader," is a cliché at best and wrong in most cases. Mothers are indeed the centers of love (and ambivalence) in most families, but there are many in which the reverse is true. Authority in the middle-class American family ideally lies with the husband, but it would be a fair guess that the balance of real decision-making power is in the hands of the wife. Major decisions, such as the choice of an apartment or a house, a change of job and location, or the education of the children, are commonly joint affairs, though most wives have an effective veto. But in the usual day-to-day, month-in-and-month-out decisions, the wife's wishes are often paramount—and it should be kept in mind that most important choices are predetermined by a long series of previous little decisions. The woman makes all the decisions about the running of the house and she has the responsibility for directing the activities of the children. Very few youngsters were ever fooled by the admonition, "Wait till your father gets home." This passing of the buck left them with little doubt that it was the mother who was punishing them and simply added the further grievance that she had sold them out.

Although the situation shifts with the working wife, men are ideally supposed to worry about the workaday world, while women tend the home. Part of the business of home and family is the task of maintaining proper contact with relatives. Since the wife usually sends out the greeting cards, buys the wedding presents, and invites people for dinner, she effectively controls the domain of kinship on both her husband's and her own sides of the family. One of the commonest in-law complaints is that they are given short shrift by the daughter-in-law. This is nicely expressed in the adage that when a daughter marries, you gain a son; but when a son marries, you lose a son.

Women have large areas of discretion in the modern family, and few seem to be ready to give up their traditional prerogatives when they go out to work. Most simply increase their instrumental roles. I believe that fathers have also moved toward the emotional, or expressive, center of the family in recent years, compounding the crosscutting of roles. These multiple and conflicting aspects of the parent role are in part a result of the attrition of more extended kin ties and the need for the parents to fill the vacant statuses. Mothers want to be confidants and friends with their daughters, and the father will attempt the "pal" role with his son. The girl soon learns that if she confides too much, she will evoke the disciplinarian mother. If the son plays ball with his father, he will acquire a coach. I think that this was one of the sources of the famous "generation gap" of the 1960s. Actually, children and parents never did communicate well, and in our culture role-set segregation can be so complete that a teen-ager may be mortified to be seen by his friends in the company of his parents. A couple of generations back, children organized their own ball teams, went on kids-only hikes, and formed clubs without adult advisers. There was comparatively little parental intrusion in their affairs, and the youngsters were equally separated from the activities of their parents. The gap arose at exactly the time when parents decided to take part in the pastimes of their offspring, and followed upon Little League, dance lessons, orthodontist, and other devices for bedeviling children. The elders organized the time of their children, scheduled their activities, and worried them with instruction that the parents considered middle class and uplifting. Children had become extensions of the parents' egos and integral to their quest for immortality in an unbelieving age. When the children grew old enough, they rebelled and asserted a demand for separation and privacy that was once theirs by default. It is not over yet.

There is in the modern conjugal family a great contradiction between the decrease in its utilitarian functions and the intensification of its emotional climate; both are root sources of the rising divorce rate in this country. The increased involvement of women in the work force has eroded some of the traditional division of labor of the family and contributed to the kinds of role conflict and blurring we have been discussing. Moreover, the woman can now more easily contemplate financial independence; one no longer has to be wealthy to afford a divorce. In the event that the divorced woman is unable to support her children, even with the ex-husband's contribution, there is always public assistance. And with the lower birthrate, the welfare of children is not as big a factor in holding unhappy marriages together as it was in the past. While all this was going on, the family became emotionally isolated and encysted. Parents cling to children for security and the hoped-for realization of their own failed dreams, and the children struggle to free themselves from this emotional pressure cooker; but they have been ill trained for autonomy and they often fail. The marriage compact itself has become a matter of great expectations—and crushing disappointments. Lacking some of the older rationales of marriage, the union is forged of love and continued by love. It is a fragile base, and half our marriages end in divorce. Our emotions become more intense as they focus on fewer people, and it is this very depth of feeling and its ambivalent expression that so commonly make family life intolerable for its members.

This dilemma has led some to predict the death of the family. A high divorce rate tells us something about the structure of the family but little about its supposed demise. Actually, there are scores of societies that have far higher divorce rates than our own. My Tuareg informants were amazed to find that I had been married only once and that our union was (at the time) ten years old. Five or six marriages and divorces were common among them, and they usually had to comb their memories for examples of people who had lifelong marriages. Divorce, after all, means a turnover of husbands within the family, and white middle-class unions are simply acquiring some of the structural features of the matrifocal family—and for similar reasons.

Interestingly, most divorced persons remarry after a few months or a few years and, taking a leaf from the musical comedy *Candide*, it can be said that these repeaters are the true enthusiasts of the institution. To marry once is conformity; to marry three times is zealotry. Another symptom of the death of the family is said to be the growing number of consensual unions. If one looks at these arrangements closely, however, it is found that they often end in marriage. The period of premarital cohabitation, is then, a kind of trial marriage, and those liaisons that break up are merely instances of unsuccessful courtship. What impels young, childless couples, both of whom work, to give up their ill-defined common-law unions for the legal toils of marriage? I believe that the very fact of the relationship being ill-defined leaves the social statuses of the people involved correspondingly ill-defined and ambiguous. There is in all of us a drive toward fixity, boundedness, and definition, an impulse toward order that is the eternal enemy of freedom and the handmaiden of society.

Marriage is, finally, the antidote of a fractionated world. With the progressive bureaucratization and compartmentalization of life, human relations are becoming more narrow and specific, increasingly devoid of emotional content, engaging less and less of our total identities. Moderns, many of them refugees from the family, complain that it is a shallow and plastic world we live in and express a craving for deep and "meaningful" ties with others. "One should love everybody" is the cry of the emotionally dispossessed, a plaint that means that one should also love nobody. It is the essence of narcissism. There is an aching nostalgia in these yearnings, a pining for a time when social life was whole and our inner lives undivided. But there are few possibilities for whole and enduring bonds in life other than those of marriage and filiation. The family is not dying; I doubt whether it is even ailing much more than it always was. Families are simply experiencing a greater turnover in their memberships, and they are dissolving in time, as they always did and must. The breakup of individual families is not the breakup of *the* family, for, as a particularly astute undergraduate once wrote in an examination, "The family is the only social unit whose main function is to destroy itself."

V

The Net of Kinship

People are born and die, conjugal families form and are dissolved, but lines of kinship transcend person and family, providing continuity within the chaos of life. The ramifications of kinship in both time and space spread a network of loyalties and common identities that weld together neighbors or are the stuff of alliance between areas. They also seal a bond among the generations, uniting each person with his forebears and defying the carnage of history. In our own individuated and socially riven civilization, kinship remains the principal source of our closest ties; but in the simpler groupings of the past and among the remaining primitive peoples, kinship did more than provide the individual with love and support, for it formed the very structure of entire societies.

To understand the importance of the net of kinship in simple societies, we must recall our definition of society as an organized and internally differentiated aggregate of people. Out of this systematization come our specialized statuses, the formation of groups and classes of people, and the division of labor. In a way of life such as ours, there are a number of criteria for internally dividing the society and allocating certain rights and duties to the divisions. There is, as we noted, an extremely complex division of labor, which divides the population into an almost unlimited number of occupational groups and statuses. Differences of wealth and power split us further into social classes, converting the natural fact that any one human being is by birth much like the others into the social fact that there are qualitatively different kinds of people. Other criteria for dividing people include race, religion, ethnic background, education, avocation and many more. The result is a society of such remarkable complexity that one may well wonder how it keeps going. Most probably, having become convoluted beyond the capacity of its members to understand it, it has an inertia and life of its own. Our civilization could die, and we would not know it. Maybe it has.

By definition of the word, "simple" or "primitive" societies are those that have few internal divisions, statuses, and subgroups, and correspondingly fewer criteria for differentiation. As we observed in the third chapter, many groups are internally ordered by age, sex, and kinship only—three ascribed statuses that are universal whatever the level of technology. The first two are of limited use as structural principles, for most groups and communities must have in them people of both sexes and all ages. One of the few exceptions to the latter rule, aside from our retirement communities, is found among the Nyakyusa of central Africa, where young men and their brides form new villages in the company of their age-mates. In East Africa and parts of tropical South America, many societies are divided into age-sets of young men who have been initiated at the same time. These sets pass through the socially recognized stages of maturation, or age-grades, as groups, displacing the next oldest set, which in turn passes to an older grade. Age-set and -grade systems have important political and economic functions and are central in the determination of male roles, but they are quite limited in the variety of divisions they can yield.

For all the varieties of sexual expression, there are only two sexes, and no matter how one cuts up the age continuum (most primitive societies, for example, do not have a category of "teen-ager") the possibilities are limited. Kinship, on the other hand, may yield a rich diversity of groupings and statuses, and it has the advantage of versatility and malleability when applied as a criterion of differentiation. This is critical, for every social system needs flexibility, the capacity to transform itself as circumstance changes, just as much as it needs stability.

Most Europeans and Americans think of kinship as a biological affair, or at least a direct expression of biological ties. This is part ideology and part sloppy thinking, but it must be granted that kinship speaks in the language of biology. It concerns the biological fact of mating and procreation. The web of kinship is extended by the mating and procreation of one's parents and their parents, one's children and their children, and on and on until it would seem that one has millions of relatives of whom track has been lost forever. The trouble with this reasoning is that we do not just mate—we marry. And we do not just have offspring—we have children who are legally recognized as ours. The element of culture thus intruded, we should recall the stricture of the previous chapter that kinship systems not only embody rules for defining who is one's kin but also norms for keeping people out of this category. No kinship system anywhere includes within an individual's orbit of relatives all the people to whom he is genetically connected. Even in tribes where everybody is considered a kinsman of everybody else in the group, the kinship net will not include the issue of past outmarriages or adulterous affairs that begot children. As for our own society, it is manifest that each individual's world of socially recognized kin is but a tiny fraction of all the people to whom he is genetically connected. And this in a society that speaks of "blood relatives" and says, "Blood is thicker than water."

The rules of kinship, or the standards by which we recognize a person as kin and assign him a status relative to our own, are exclusionary, for no person would be able to cope with or even remember all the people to whom he is biologically related. These exclusionary rules are sometimes slanted in certain ways, favoring in one case the father's line and in another the mother's. There are many societies, as we will see, that allot to one's maternal kin expectations entirely different from those allotted to the paternal side. The mother's and father's brothers are both called "uncle" in English and are of equal genetic closeness, but in many societies the two categories of uncle are called by separate kin terms and treated very differently. Moreover, there is a very wide spectrum of kinship groupings in human societies, exhibiting a range of diversity of form and functioning that would be inexplicable from the rigid framework of biological connections. This plasticity of kinship, which makes it so useful in structuring societies, is realized by ignoring biology or standing it on its head. A person is a kinsman because we have bestowed that meaning upon him. A sister is simply another woman, not too different from all the others, just as her brother is one more man among millions, but they cannot mate because a certain meaning has been imposed on their relationship. And there are no natural meanings, only cultural ones. We can recognize certain people as kin while sloughing off others; we can attach a particular value to one category of relatives as opposed to others; we can warp and twist kinship around to produce a variety of configurations. These gambits become intelligible only in relation to other social institutions, and not to biology.

The social nature of kinship is most evident in genealogy keeping.

That genealogies are useful social fictions has been understood ever since the first person faked his ancestry to gain prestige. Genealogy tracing among Americans has been common among social climbers and those struggling to hold on to their status. It usually takes the ancestor hunters back to colonial days and to England; it has been truly said that no ocean liner ever built could hold all the people who are said to have come over on the Mayflower. Others seek to shore up their sense of identity—to find out who they *really* are—through discovering their ancestry. Lest we consider genealogies a fragile framework for the notion of the self, it should be remembered that identities, too, are social fictions.

Genealogies are partially fictional maps of the past used to justify present realities. As an example, the Arab Bedouins keep genealogies that go back to the time of the Prophet. Their genealogists can rattle off the names of great-grandparents and their brothers and all their issue with ease, but they become a bit fuzzy about names on the fifth or sixth generation. This seems rather odd until we understand that groups of men tracing their descent back to an ancestor of five or six generations in the past constitute basic political units. The variable memories of the genealogists allow relationships to be fudged at this level for the purpose of making and breaking alliances. Thus, when two groups decide on peaceful cooperation and mutual defense, they will commonly rationalize it by saying that they are related. Kinship in this case is the product and language of solidarity and not vice versa. The Arab genealogies are also remarkable for their omission of reference to the names of most women. This drops out the entire maternal side of the family, except in cases in which preferred inmarriages merge the ancestry of the mother and father.

The Mundurucú Indians, along with many tribes of tropical South America, make the genealogist's task impossible by a total suppression of genealogies. It is forbidden for a man or woman to speak the name of the dead, especially a dead relative, and the result is that one has a difficult time determining which people were second and more distant cousins to each other. Despite such vagueness, the Mundurucú belief that they are all related to one another is not negated by the lack of genealogy but rather supported by it, for there is no way to refute the claim.

Americans do not have name taboos, but they do have bad cases of genealogical amnesia. Most remember the names of their four grandparents, but far fewer will know the names of all eight of their great-grandparents. And how many know the maiden names of all four great-grandmothers? Who knows who were his great-grandparents' siblings? Or even the brothers and sisters of his grandparents? This strikes many Americans as much useless ado about people long dead, but knowledge of the links is what allows us to establish relationships with the living. The children of your parents' siblings are your first cousins; the grandchildren of your grandparents' siblings are your second cousins; and the great-grandchildren of your great-grandparents' siblings are your third cousins. As a matter of fact, in most American families we do not know our exact relationship with people beyond the first-cousin position. Second, third, and more distant cousins are referred to diffusely as "distant relatives" or are totally and completely forgotten. It was not always thus. The English language has a rich nomenclature of cousinhood, giving distance of removal and generation relative to one's own. But people no longer refer to another as a "second cousin, once removed," and so forth; they do not know the proper terminology, and they do not even know the relatives. Just as among the Bedouins, our genealogies reflect current social reality. Kinship is a cultural construct.

American and European kinship has been described thus far as based on the primacy of the nuclear family, which in recent decades has lost some of its functions at the same time that more extensive kin ties beyond the conjugal family have weakened. Paradoxically, then, the conjugal family has become at once more fragile and more central. We have also observed that each nuclear family is a knot in the web of kinship, a coming together of people in a small cluster that is related through marriage and parentage to similar clusters. Looking outward from our conjugal families, we trace through links of intervening kinfolk to ever more remote relatives until the domain of kinship ends. Our English terms "relative" and "kinsman" include both consanguineal (or blood) relatives and affines, or in-laws. The latter may be a little less related to us in our minds but they still fall within the orbit of kin, although we usually do not reckon too many of an in-law's consanguineal kin as part of our own network.

This skein of kinfolk, toward whom we feel a diminishing sense of solidarity as the ties become more distant, is called a "kindred" by anthropologists. The kindred is not a fixed group with a membership and delineated limits, for every individual's net of kin is different. Two siblings will share a kindred of parents, grandparents, uncles, aunts, and cousins, but when they mature and form their own families of procreation, each will acquire different affines and beget a different line of descent. The kindred is not a stable group, but rather a network radiating out from each individual. The network spreads out equally through both the mother's and father's line; that is, it is "bilateral." Bilaterality indicates an equal weighting of the maternal and paternal lines for the purpose of determining the formal rights and responsibilities of kinsmen to each other. It does not necessarily imply equality of feeling toward each side of the family, which can vary from one family to another and from individual to individual. To give an example from American law, if a man dies without a will and has only two surviving nephews, one the son of a sister and the other a brother's son, the two will divide his estate evenly. This contrasts sharply with "unilateral" or "unilineal" societies, which allot quite different duties and privileges to kin on either side.

The degree of closeness we feel for our maternal as opposed to our paternal kin is often a simple function of proximity. Absence does not make the heart grow fonder at all. Nearness of residence makes for nearness of emotion, and there is some evidence that our own residence choices after marriage are more often close to the bride's parental home than to the groom's. Despite our formal and legal bilaterality, it is women, as we said, who control the realm of kinship. It would come as no surprise to learn that they keep in more frequent contact with a larger number of their own relatives than they do with the relatives of their husband. Moreover, the strong, however ambivalent, bond between the mother and daughter often solidifies further in our society with the birth of children.

Residence and physical closeness are major factors in determining the strength of kinship bonds and the definition of the roles. This was first stressed by the pioneer anthropologist Robert H. Lowie and further developed by his student Julian H. Steward. Lowie wrote at one point that there is no opposition or gulf between ties of neighborhood and ties of kinship, for kinship is often simply a symbolic language for stating territorial relations. In the same vein, Mischa Titiev noted that the incest taboo is often applied to one's coresidents, whatever the degree and mode of relationship. Kith and kin, then, are often one and the same. The principal reasons for this overlap lie in the rules and preferences that determine where people reside after marriage, and in a complementary tendency to treat as kinfolk those among whom we live.

Proximity is one of the forges of kinship, for the bonds of deep loyalty and solidarity of the nuclear family ultimately derive from the physical closeness and dependence of mother and child, father and child, and brother and sister, and not from some mystical relation of blood. In much the same way, the more extended ties of kinship are closely related to the arrangements of people in space. Children most commonly, but not always, grow up in the parental household, and their first shift of residence usually occurs when they get married and form a new family unit. They may reside in this postmarital home for a period of time only or for the rest of their lives, but in either case the choice is a critical one for the entire society as it determines who lives with whom, and, therefore, who cooperates with whom, who worships with whom, and who whiles away his leisure time with whom.

Few societies leave such a critical decision to individual fancy. All have preferences of varying compulsion on where people should go after marriage. Let us start off with simple premises. The rules of incest generally prohibit marriage with a person of one's own household, and one of the partners at least will have to move after marriage. The question is: move where? The first possibility is for the new couple to form their own independent household, as in modern America and Europe. We call this choice "neolocality." Neolocality works in our own society because kinship no longer functions in mutual defense or in economic production. Moreover, the overall structure of the society lies in the political and economic realms and not in the family. In simpler societies, the newly-weds cannot go off all by themselves and set up a home in the wilds, for they would be the prey of enemies and would lack the help of others. They must live with their fellowmen, but they cannot live randomly among them, for this would result in a chance and formless composition of local groups. The decision, which is fraught with political and economic considerations, will turn on prior links and ties between people, that is, on their statuses relative to each other. It is possible to reside after marriage with one's age-mates, a practice that we noted for the African Nyakyusa. Even the Nyakyusa, however, located their villages near those of their elders, and generations remain integrated with each other. One other possibility of residence choice in a very simple society is post-marital residence among people of the same sex, but this would be a contradiction in terms. Actually, the Mundurucú men's house poses one of the most complete separations of the sexes of which we have record, but the men are still only about one hundred feet away from their women and children. This leaves kinship as the remaining ascribed status that could be used as the criterion of residence, and its potential for variation makes it ideally suited to the purpose.

In most primitive societies, newlyweds live among kin, for there they can find loyalty, support, trust, and cooperation. They will also find jealousy, ambivalence, and suspicion among their relatives, but at times of need the positive side of the relationship is supposed to emerge, and it usually does. Having determined that one lives with the kin of either the bride or the groom, the next question is: which? There are a limited number of possibilities, which we will briefly list, returning to each later for more complete discussion. The first possibility is to live with the family of the husband, an option known as "patrilocality." A second is to live with the family of the wife, which we call "matrilocality." In some societies, the couple live with relatives, but the choice of side is optional, a situation termed "bilocality." Neolocality, patrilocality, matrilocality, and bilocality together account for the residence preferences of most of the world's societies, but there are three interesting and rare variations on these themes. "Avunculocality" is residence with the brother of the groom's mother; "duolocality" refers to a situation in which each mate remains in his or her natal residence; and "ambilocality" finds the spouses shifting back and forth at periodic intervals between the kinfolk of each.

Some anthropologists further clutter up the nomenclature with the terms "virilocal" and "uxorilocal," which mean, respectively, living at the husband's or the wife's abode, without reference to whether relatives live there also or which relatives. It is a valid distinction, but not a particularly useful one.

In the discussion which follows, it should be stressed that residence rules range from mild preferences in some societies to absolute injunctions in others. In the former cases, it is possible that not even half the marriages will conform to the residence rule, and even where it is strongest there are usually exceptions. The result of this laxity—a flexibility characteristic of most cultural norms—is that the domestic units that develop from cumulative residence choices are generally not monolithic in composition. The rule of residence will produce a strain in the direction of keeping together certain types of kinsmen, and thus will be an important factor in structuring local groups. But these groups will usually have a somewhat eclectic and varied membership, allowing the society to cope with the vagaries of circumstance and fortune.

Our own hankering for neolocality is halfway between preference and hard rule. It is not enjoined in either civil or religious laws, but it is an ardently held value. Indeed, the worst thing that can happen to a young couple is to be forced into residence with the parents of one or the other. Neolocality makes sense in an industrial society. It is congruent with the demands made upon American families for geographic and class mobility and fits into a kinship system characterized by the truncation of its functions and the shortening of its links. Neolocality is one condition of the isolation of the nuclear family in a society that individuates its labor force and redirects the loyalties and associations of its members from kin to friend. The American family is not, however, totally on its own. We commonly live in the same areas or neighborhoods as kin, if only due to the chances of employment and knowledge of available housing. Relatives thus may remain in proximity to each other, and the actual degree of dispersal of kin after marriage is partly a function of social class and occupation.

Most primitive societies do not practice neolocality, for all the reasons we gave for its predominance in our own. Two of the most notable exceptions are the Eskimo and the Western Shoshoni of Nevada, both of whom lead lives of rigor and austerity in extremely forbidding environments. The vicissitudes of life in their harsh climes kept residential units small among both the Shoshoni and Eskimo, for they lived by hunting, fishing, and gathering and the food resources of a district might be enough for only a few families. Newlywed couples could live with the family of one or the other mate, a bilocal arrangement, but if local resources were insufficient for them and their children, they would be

forced to go elsewhere and become neolocal. Mutual defense and cooperation were not vital considerations, for warfare was rare among them, and
most of their food-getting activities did not involve extensive cooperation.
When mutual help became necessary, due to a whale hunt among the
Eskimo or an antelope drive among the Shoshoni, people from adjoining
areas were invited to participate. These occasions, however, were not frequent enough to build up large and consolidated aggregates of population.

Patrilocality is very widespread among societies throughout the
world. It brings the bride to the groom's household, to live with the
groom's father and brothers and perhaps with his paternal grandfather
and some of his father's brothers as well. The result is a congregation of
men related in the male line, to which we will return later. Most anthropologists attribute the patrilocal residence preference to economic factors.
According to this reasoning, there will be a tendency toward patrilocality
when certain of the key subsistence activities are carried out by cooperating groups of males. These pursuits may include collective hunting of
game animals, group fishing using drugs, seines, or weirs, nomadic herding
of large domesticated animals, and plow agriculture by men. As a matter
of fact, almost all societies based on pastoralism are patrilocal, as are
most of those featuring plow agriculture. Hunting groups tend toward
either bilocality or patrilocality. In some hunting societies the patrilocally
formed segments occupy defined territories and are exogamic, getting their
wives from other, similar bands. In all these societies, the joint contribution of the men is so important that it is functional to the best operation of
the economy to keep together a group of men who have been raised in
the territory they will exploit and have been trained to mutual loyalty
and cooperation through their common kinship. Other factors are operative, but those of economy set up a strain toward patrilocality.

Matrilocal societies may be regarded as those in which the female
economic contribution is sufficiently critical to make it worthwhile to
keep together cooperating groups of women and their daughters. There
are not as many matrilocal groups in the world as patrilocal ones because
the far-ranging activities of men in hunting and war require a kind of
cooperation that is rarely necessary in the female sector of the economy.
There are, however, some matrilocal hunting and collecting societies that
are probably disposed in that direction because of the importance of wild
vegetable and berry gathering by the women. Most matrilocal societies
are based on simple hoe horticulture, in which female labor is paramount.
This was true among many of the Indian tribes of the eastern United
States, such as the Iroquois and the peoples of the southeast, and across
a swath of central Africa. On the other hand, among the matrilocal Zuñi,
a pueblo-dwelling group of Arizona, the men farm while the women grind
corn; the tedium of the latter work and the long hours consumed by it

make it congenial, if not utilitarian, to consolidate female relatives as workmates. Lest an easy determinism be inferred, it should be said that, though most matrilocal societies are based on hoe horticulture, most societies with this kind of economy are not matrilocal. Matrilocality produces delicate living arrangements that make for its comparative rarity. It forces men into coresidence with their in-laws and thus threatens the prestige and autonomy of the groom by surrounding him with people with whom he shares all the built-in antagonisms of the affinal relationship. Patrilocality does the same to women, of course, but women are seldom central political figures and their hostilities are therefore less threatening to the political order. This is a theme we will revisit.

Bilocality is one of the more common modes of postmarital residence. It is found in cases in which there are no compelling reasons to keep together either related men or related women, and it functions well in an economic setting in which flexibility is a virtue. Bilocality is part of generally loose-jointed social systems; it both expresses and promotes flexibility and variation. People join relatives, but whether they join the parents of the husband or of the wife depends on situational factors. The newlyweds may opt for either patrilocality or matrilocality depending on the availability of agricultural land, or they may be motivated to join certain kin because of good hunting in their locale or the prestige of the group's chief. Whereas the so-called "unilocal" (patrilocal and matrilocal) modes of residence yield groups of men related through men or groups of women related through women, bilocal communities tend to be eclectic in composition and their members can usually find kin in the group who are related in either line, or sometimes both at once.

The three minor modes of residence are more intriguing. Avunculocality is best known from the descriptions of the culture of the Trobriand Islands in Melanesia by Bronislaw Malinowski, to which we made reference in Chapter 2. According to Trobriand custom, when a boy reaches about twelve years of age, he leaves his natal home and joins the household of his mother's brother. He matures there and when he marries, he will bring his wife to the uncle's house. In time his own sons will leave for the houses of their mother's brothers and his daughters will go off in marriage too. Their places will be taken by his sister's sons and their wives. The result of avunculocality, then, is a household whose continuing core is a group of men related through women.

Ambilocality is not to be confused with the opportunistic shifts of residence that characterize bilocality, for it implies a regular and cyclical change of location. Its prototype is found among the Dobu Islanders of Melanesia, among whom there is inordinate and numbing dread of witchcraft, especially at the hands of one's in-laws. Understandably, neither spouse relishes life among the menacing affines, and the problem is partially resolved by periodic moves from the household of one set of kin to that of the other side.

Duolocality is equally rare. Its best expressions are found among the Ashanti of Ghana and the people of Torry Island, a speck of land in the Irish Sea. In Ashanti, when a man and woman marry, they each stay in their own households and continue their responsibilities there. Such unions are usually endogamic to the town to make communication between the mates easy. The Torry Islanders, described by Robin Fox, do much the same thing. Each mate stays in his or her natal residence for periods of up to several years before finally joining each other. This time allows them to continue to care for their old people and permits the man to become economically independent. It is a sort of "half marriage" and a way of beating the Irish pattern of interminable courtships and middle-aged weddings.

All of the residence rules except neolocality result in households consisting of several nuclear families, groups that are termed "extended" or "joint" families in our lexicon. Extended families consist of a number of nuclear families, or a group of closely related ones, sharing a domicile and engaged in common endeavors. The degree to which the nuclear family is autonomous within this milieu varies. Among the Trumai Indians of the Xingú River, Brazil, each wife has her own hearth, and husbands and wives jointly work conjugal family gardens. But the couples live in extended-family households brought together by a bilocal residence rule, and family space within the house is marked only by the fact that its members hang their hammocks close to one another. The Mundurucú, a few hundred miles away, submerge the nuclear family to a greater degree, for the husbands do not sleep in the joint-family household, there is only one cooking fire for all its women, there is a common larder, and gardens are made and used by the extended family as a unit. In some societies, the extended family is not always found under the same roof, and its component nuclear families may be lodged in different dwellings of the same compound or in adjoining houses. In such cases, the conjugal unit usually has greater independence and distinctiveness.

The conjugal family is eclipsed to different degrees by the extended family, leading some anthropologists to argue that the latter is the primary kinship unit in primitive society and might well be prior to the nuclear family in evolutionary emergence. The issue is largely a moot question; there are no real answers, but it is instructive to engage in the debate. It is unquestionable that the functions that Americans normally associate with the conjugal family are often superceded and taken over by more extended units in primitive societies. There is a catch here, however, for we are using the American family as a measuring rod, falling into the trap of treating it as a natural unit. Actually, the functions of our nuclear family may also be looked on as grossly exaggerated and over-burdened with emotional freight. Instead of looking at the nuclear family as atrophied in its joint-family context, we may regard it as normal in human society that no unit consisting merely of a man and a woman and dependent young can be autonomous, self-sufficient, and capable of answering most of the needs of social life. Ours are not. Why should we expect it of primitives?

One problem with the argument is that we measure the relative importance of extended vs. nuclear families by the simple, manifest functions of division of labor, child rearing, and allocation of sex. When we find that the first two are often carried out by extended families and the last one is arranged by them, the conjugal unit seems very diminished indeed. When we look on marriage and the nuclear family, instead, as constituting vital links in exchange relations, as the positive expression of the incest taboo, as means of linking men to the cycle of regeneration, as a fixing and regulation of the statuses of the marrying pair and their children, as a device for creating an artificial scarcity of women and thus capturing sex in the service of society, and as means of maintaining the social division of the sexes, then we can see that the institutions fulfill these invisible purposes everywhere. The extended family can take over most of the manifest uses that we associate with the nuclear family without lessening the central role of the latter in all social systems. At the same time, it must be acknowledged that in most societies the nuclear family is firmly imbedded in larger kinship matrices that mold and alter the shape of the conjugal union, but can never eliminate it. Both sides of the debate are right—and wrong.

Returning to our earlier summation of the extended-family forms resulting from the different modes of residence, it will be recalled that patrilocality produces a group consisting of a male elder, or two or more brothers of a senior generation, their sons and the sons' wives, the sons of the latter generation, their wives, and their children—if longevity of the elders allows for a four-generation family (see Figure 2). In addition to the men of the extended family and their wives, the group will include unmarried daughters. In virtually all cases, the incest taboo prevents the men from marrying a woman born to the household, for she would not only be a coresident but she would also be related to them as a daughter, a niece, or a sister. The rule of patrilocality, then, makes it necessary to send all women of the extended family out in marriage and to bring wives in from the outside in exchange. The continuing residential core consists of men who are related through men. Thus, a father's brother will be a member of one's patrilocal extended family, but a mother's brother will not. The maternal uncle will have stayed home, sending his sister off in marriage. Also, men who are father's brother's sons to each

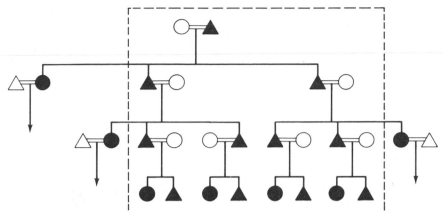

FIGURE 2. Dotted line encloses members of a patrilocally formed extended family. Blackened symbols indicate members of the patrilineage, when descent rule is applied. Arrows point toward offspring who will belong to their fathers' lineages.

other will belong to the same extended-family household, but all the kin related through female links—the father's sister's children, the sister's children, and those of the mother's siblings—will live elsewhere because of patrilocality.

Matrilocal extended families are at first glance the mirror image of patrilocally constituted ones. The senior generation consists of a group of sisters and their husbands, their daughters and the inmarrying husbands of the daughters, and so on down to the younger generation of unmarried children, as diagrammed in Figure 3. The continuing core of the extended

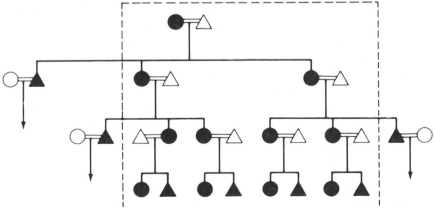

FIGURE 3. Dotted line encloses members of a matrilocally formed extended family. Blackened symbols indicate members of the matrilineage, when descent rule is applied. Arrows point toward offspring who will belong to their mothers' lineages.

family consists of women, related to each other as sisters, daughters, and so forth, through linking female relatives. That is, a woman remains in the natal home with her mother and sisters, and her children will also form part of the household. To the contrary, the woman's brother will depart for the household of his bride, where his children will be born and brought up. The household is based on a line of women, related through women.

The units we have described thus far are loose aggregates of kin of a certain kind brought together through a mode of postmarital residence. As a group, such an aggregate may well acquire certain assets. It will have a house, or a cluster of houses, and may even own the land on which the houses are built. The extended family may also acquire other resources of an economic nature. Kin groups often have rights to tracts of tillable land or will hold a section of river for fishing. In time, the group may also acquire religious and political prerogatives, which are held by it in collectivity, further increasing the common stake. To the extent that a kinship group holds rights and assets in common, it acts much as a corporation does in our own society. That is, it can be viewed as a fictive individual, a single entity, which has a common property and outlives its members. The quality of "corporateness" infers that the members of a kin group possess collectively held valuables. Therefore, it becomes increasingly necessary for the group to set rules stating who has rights to these corporately held properties and who does not. The extended family thus passes from being an ad hoc group assembled by a residence preference to being a formally defined, continuing group with rules of membership and exclusion.

The principal mechanism for effecting the formalization of the unilocal extended family lies latent within its structure. This is the fact that, whether in reality or in ideal, the extended family can be looked on as a group of people descended from a common ancestor. The reader can conjure up such a common descent group in his own mind. Starting from a founding man or woman and their mates, locating their children patrilocally or matrilocally, respectively, and following the same residence rule for a few generations, we find ourselves with almost exactly the same kinds of units that we have described for patrilocal and matrilocal extended families. The chief method of transforming an extended family aggregate into a formally constituted and bounded corporate group, then, is to include within it all those people who trace descent from a common founding ancestor through a line of intermediate ancestors of the same sex, as shown in Figures 2 and 3. This at once sets the limits on membership and applies a label to the unit that will survive its members. We call such a kin group a "lineage."

Just as there are two modes of unilocal residence, so there are also two principal types of lineage, which we label as "patrilineal" and "matrilineal." The word patrilineal, sometimes referred to as "agnatic," means simply "father's line" and matrilineal "mother's line." Patrilineality refers to the practice of inheriting kin-group membership, or some other asset, through one's father, who inherited it from his father, and on back in time. According to the logic of the usage, a person may inherit from his father's brother, but not from his mother's brother. Patrilineality does not mean inheritance by men only, for daughters may inherit patrilineally, but rather inheritance through a line of men. By this reasoning, a patrilineal lineage—we will avoid the redundancy by saying "patrilineage"—consists of a group of people who trace common descent from a founding ancestor through a line of linking men. The same logic defines matrilineality as the inheritance of kin-group membership or other valuables through a line of linking females. Men as well as women can inherit matrilineally, and they can inherit from men also. Thus, by a rule of matrilineality, a man can inherit from his mother's brother, for he is related through a linking female and will belong to the man's matrilineal descent group. By simple extension, a "matrilineage" is a group of people tracing common ancestry through a line of linking women.

A closer examination of each type of unilineal descent system will show that in their operation they are not at all simple mirror images of each other, though certain salient characteristics aer common to both. Both patrilineages and matrilineages are exogamic units. It is forbidden to take a mate from inside the lineage; the women of the group must marry men of other lineages, and the men must seek their wives outside. This is consistent with the basic principle of marriage as alliance and exchange, and it is through their affinal ties and the links set up through the inmarrying spouses that lineages relate to each other to form a larger society. The rule of exogamy also defines the boundaries and membership of the group, distinguishing a "we" category of those too close to marry from a "they" class from which wives or husbands come. Lineages are stable, continuing groups of at least three generations depth, giving them persistence over time. Moreover, their members derive an important set of statuses from them as well as a good portion of their overall social identity.

There are fundamental differences between patrilineages and matrilineages that stem from the fact that one traces links through men and the other through women. That men hold the balance of authority but women are the agents of procreation makes for a skewing that becomes reflected in structures. Patrilineal groups are generally patrilocal as well, and the local group often corresponds to the lineage, or a unit of the lineage. Women are brought into the group from other lineages, which often means other communities. They generally keep their membership in the natal lineage, but long distances may make the bond increasingly tenuous as the years go by. In the patrilineages, or "gens," of ancient Rome the estrangement of the wife from her own lineage was complete and she became a member of the husband's gens. The female position was low, the wife's status servile, and women rebuilt their prestige by consolidating their positions in the marital households and influencing their sons. Much the same situation prevailed in old China, and the cowering, bullied bride aged into the influential old wife, the terror of her daughters-in-law.

The congruence of descent and locale in patrilineal societies is conducive to a budding process, called "segmentation," whereby lineages subdivide. Let us take as an example an imaginary patrilineage of people descended from X, who, according to the genealogies, founded the group some generations ago (see Figure 4). The rule of patrilocal residence coupled with population increase has caused the lineage to wax in numbers, resulting, in time, in pressures on neighborhood resources. At this point, two brothers may decide to set up a new residence a few miles away, where there is perhaps more farmland or better hunting. The two men, who are sons of Y, keep their tie to the home lineage, but consistent with the pattern identify their new group by the name of their own immediate ancestor. It thus becomes sublineage Y of lineage X. In time, Y can grow and send off buds itself, and a new minor lineage Z may spring from intermediate range lineage Y, which in turn is a part of major lineage X (see Figure 4). Each one of the component lineages will be organized on exactly the same principles as the others. The only difference will be in numbers of people included, which in turn will be a function of how many generations one goes back to find the founding ancestor. A member of lineage Z may trace back only four generations to its founder, but he may continue backward in time to the seventh generation to locate ancestor Y. And to find X, he may have to go back ten generations or more, depending on the calculations of the genealogists. Since X may have spawned sublineages A and B as well as Y, and since each of these, in turn, may have sent out offshoots C, D, and so forth, it is clear that the

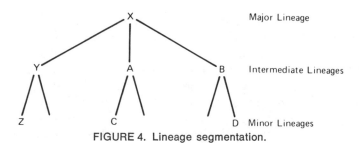

FIGURE 4. Lineage segmentation.

further one goes back to trace ancestry, the more inclusive the unit, and the greater the number of people included.

Patrilineal descent, with long genealogies, can provide a social and political framework for entire districts. Major lineages among the Nuer of southern Sudan include thousands of people. The Nuer conceive of villages as small lineages, which are viewed as parts of large-scale lineages that integrate the entire area in which the component communities are located. Nuerland is not that tidy in reality, for there is a great deal of population shifting and each community has a large number of persons who are not lineage members, or even Nuer. The anthropologist E. E. Evans-Pritchard noted this in his writings on the Nuer and stressed that the system of patrilineages gave a conceptual order to Nuerland, making its people and landscape intelligible as parts of a stable system. It has been suggested by Marshall Sahlins that Nuer social structure was ideally suited to a society expanding in territory and numbers, for the segmentation process was adapted to colonizing. Moreover, the nesting of smaller lineages within larger ones and the reliance on genealogies for reckoning closeness provided a mechanism for the mobilization of populations for war or feud. If attacked by another tribe, the Nuer as a whole would mass against the enemy. And if a Nuer minor lineage was threatened by another Nuer lineage, it could count on the help of closely related lineages. A fight between two men could escalate into a fight between their minor lineages. If the two were parts of the same intermediate-level lineage, then no other units would become involved, but if they were of different intermediate segments, all of the component segments of each could become opposed. This massing effect, through a process known as "segmentary opposition," allowed the Nuer to become effective warriors, for thousands of people could band together and then split up again into small units without disturbing the social system.

Patrilineages are based on the link between father and son, for descent is transmitted and authority maintained along this axis. In matrilineal societies the line of descent goes through women, but authority still passes through men. The status of women in matrilineal, and especially matrilocal, societies is generally higher than in patrilineal, patrilocal ones for two reasons. First, women are recognized as the legal as well as the biological sources of social continuity; they cannot be treated as simple vessels in which fetuses grow, as is the ideology in many patrilineal groups. Second, matrilocality embeds a woman among her kinfolk. In any difficulties that she may have with her husband, she finds support in her coresident sisters and in her brothers. Among the patrilocal Yanomamo of Venezuela and Brazil, the people understand clearly that a woman's position in life worsens as the distance between her natal and married homes increases. In matrilocal societies, on the other hand, the woman remains in place at marriage and the solidarity of sex is further strengthened by the loyalties of kinship. Women may exercise considerable prestige and influence in such groups, but the formal public offices are almost always occupied by men. For this reason, men continue to play larger roles in their natal matrilineages than women usually do in their home patrilineages. Thus, in matrilineal societies, the line of descent goes through women, but authority is held by men.

Men do not usually have a large role in their wives' matrilineages, for they are outsiders to it. Rather, they maintain close ties and have rights and responsibilities in the lineages of their mothers and sisters, where they have authority as senior members. The principal link, then, in a matrilineal group is between brother and sister. This has profound implications for postmarital residence, for their obligations require that the men remain relatively close to home after marriage. Many matrilineal societies are, accordingly, patrilocal; one can hypothesize that the descent system first evolved in conjunction with matrilocality but that the need for continued solidarity of groups of brothers impelled a shift to the patrilocal preference. Another common residence choice in matrilineal societies is avunculocality, for it keeps together the mother's brother and his principal heir, the sister's son; their home is the seat of the lineage and it receives the sons of its absent sisters. The matrilocal residence rule in matrilineal groups also reflects the continuing part men play in their home lineages, for it is usually coupled with local endogamy, or inmarriage. In the Puebloan towns of the Zuñi and Hopi in the southwest United States, matrilocality is the rule, but men marry women of their own community. Matrilocality may take a man only a hundred feet away from home, where he has recourse to the support of his fellow matrilineage members.

The central role of the brother-sister bond poses a number of problems for matrilineal societies. The need for close and continuing contact between the two dampens the segmentary process we noted for many patrilineal societies. If a lineage woman and her husband were to move out to a new location, her children would lack their mother's brother, the main authority figure as they grow up. And if a lineage man and his wife move out, he will lose track of his sister's children, and his wife will lack the support and counsel of her brother. The resultant tendency toward local endogamy makes for rather inflexible social systems. Communities tend to be tightknit and crosscut by bonds of household and descent. The price of this close integration, however, may be a relatively immobile population, in which conflict festers but is contained because the parties cannot bud off easily and must maintain an uneasy peace.

The husband's position in a matrilineal and matrilocal society is equivocal, just as the wife's is in patrilineal groups. But unlike the woman's, the male role usually requires a greater public show of autonomy and independence; societies seem to be able to get away more easily with deprivation of the female status than of the male's. The husband brought into his wife's household is in a delicate position. In-law conflict is a very real thing in all societies and not just a subject for stale jokes. Any mate's affines and consanguines will have somewhat differing expectations of him or her, and the families on either side of the union will tend to support their own in a marital disagreement. Moreover, discord between the related families can produce disharmony in the marriage, as each spouse sides with his or her own relatives. Surrounded by these potentially threatening people, husbands are hard put to keep a grip on their public prestige and self-esteem. There are ways of accomplishing this, however, one of which was mentioned in Chapter 1; this is the avoidance of the mother-in-law and the observance of rigidly proper and formal relations with the father-in-law. Another device for tempering the male situation is found among the matrilocal Mundurucú, who are in the unusual position of being also patrilineal. Here, the men are only loosely incorporated into the households of their wives, for they dwell in men's houses. These strategies only ameliorate the condition, however, and marriage in matrilineal and matrilocal societies rests on a bed of shifting alliances and antagonisms. It is for this reason that the average divorce rates are significantly higher in such groups than in patrilineal ones.

Marriage is brittle in matrilineal groups because the husband has potentially conflicting loyalties. This same problem arises with respect to inheritance. Malinowski long ago noted that Trobriand men experienced conflict between the matrilineal rule requiring inheritance by their sisters' sons and the bonds of affection that grow between them and their own children. Men were generous toward their offspring, bestowing presents upon them during their life that their sisters' sons expected to inherit upon their death. One might hypothesize that the descent system was changing toward patrilineality, but this tension between the two lines appears to be a standard feature of matrilineality and an integral part of its structure. This balancing off of interests and antagonisms and the presence of barely contained internal strain form the hallmark of the matrilineal system and the foundation of its close, but chancy, integration. But it is also this general rigidity that makes matrilineality relatively rare.

The lineage has been interpreted as an outgrowth of a unilocal mode of residence, with corporate closure around a group-held estate. There are other kinds of descent groups of a more inclusive nature that differ from lineages in their mode of operation as well. The "clan" is the best known of these, for we even use the term in English to loosely designate the bilateral kindred. Thus, newspapers refer to the "Kennedy clan," which includes those kin of the late president bearing the Kennedy surname, but also numbers of in-laws. For it to be a clan, and one based on patrilineal descent, only relatives named Kennedy could be members; the husbands and children of the sisters of the family would not belong. All that would be needed to make this hypothetical lineage of Kennedys into a true clan is the stipulation that everybody named Kennedy, whether or not they can trace kinship to one another, is a member, and then to prohibit marriage between any of these Kennedys because they are too closely akin. A clan, then, is an exogamic, unilineal descent group in which the members believe, but cannot genealogically demonstrate, that they are all descended from a common ancestor.

Lineages are held together and their unity rationalized by genealogies. These are often of dubious authenticity, but the people nonetheless believe that they can trace back through them to their founding ancestors, and they use them also to calculate the mode and distance of relationship between themselves and their lineage mates. This is not the rationale of the clan. Clansmen may be able to trace part of their descent through such genealogies, for lineages are often component parts of clans, but after they reach the apical ancestor in their reckoning, the genealogies end. From there on up to the founding ancestor of the clan, there is only the belief that they are somehow linked. Lineage ancestors are conceived of as ordinary mortals; they may have been remarkable for their power and virtue and may be the center of ancestor worship, but they were still people. Clan founders, however, are usually thought to have lived in a mythical time in the most remote past of the people. If given human shape, they are believed to have possessed supernatural qualities, but quite commonly they are not considered to have been human at all.

The most frequent means of designating a clan founder is by identification of him and the group with a plant or animal species. Thus, the people of a wallaby clan in native Australia believe they are descended from a mythical wallaby, giving them a sense of oneness with the living wallabies of their environment as well as with each other. Mundurucú clans are all named after animals or plants, and the people believe that both they and the current species were descended from the same ancestor. The anomaly of descent from an animal is partly resolved in Mundurucú thought by the parallel belief that in mythical times animals had not taken their present forms. Much of Mundurucú mythology tells of how the animal-humans of the mythical age acquired their present forms, for characteristic of all mythical times, including the Garden of Eden, the great schism between nature and culture had not yet occurred.

The labeling of a group and its ancestor with a plant or animal name is called "totemism" by anthropologists. Earlier scholars were impressed by the distinctiveness and prevalence of totemic clanship and thought it to be an archaic social form, indeed the first human social institution. Subsequent generations of anthropologists showed that totemism was not a single, unitary body of practice, but that its supposed elements, such as animals' names, exogamy, and a taboo on eating the totemic object, could be found in isolation from each other or in differing combinations. This was a blow to theories like Freud's that built a world view out of the "complex," but it left unanswered the question. "Why use names of natural species at all?" Lévi-Strauss writes that there have been two approaches to the problem. One says that totems are good to eat—that is, they are considered ancestral because they are useful and central to the diet—and the other claims that totems are "good to think." Lévi-Strauss disposes of the first argument by showing that some totems are not used economically by the people and that many useful plants and animals fall outside the purview of totemism. He opts instead for the explanation that natural speciation of flora and fauna provides a model for the "social speciation" of totemic groups. Speciation divides the natural world, and these divisions are used to express the differences within the social world. Totemism, in this view, is a classificatory system and a taxonomy of social units; it is good to think.

There are many groups, it has been noted, in which there are lineages within clans, but many clan-based societies have no lineages. The two types of descent group are not necessary to each other and actually function in different ways. Reckoning of distance between kin and fissioning on the basis of the degree of closeness is central to lineage operation, but not to clanship. The essence of the clan is that the kinship of all its members is only imputed and cannot be demonstrated, as in a lineage. The Mundurucú, for example, have no lineages and suppress genealogies, but have patrilineal clans. Relationships within these groups is a matter of faith and consensus, and kinship is accorded evenly and amorphously throughout the clan. Most people have no idea exactly how they are related to fellow clansmen, but neither do they make the invidious distinctions of closeness between them that are at the root of segmentation. The spirit of brotherhood and solidarity is sometimes accorded to other clans, which together form a fraternity of clans called a "phratry," but these aggregates reflect an extension of a bond rather than a division. Clanship, per se, does not lend itself to fissioning, but to a kind of generalized brotherhood. One knows his immediate kin and perhaps more remote ones by their exact relationship, but all other clan mates are simply kin, toward whom one owes loyalty and mutual support.

Unilineal descent ascribes membership in kin groups and assigns important rights and duties to the individual members, but this does not mean that the other side of the family is neglected or ignored. In matrilineal descent groups, the father enjoys a closeness to his children that is unalloyed by any disciplinary powers exercised through the lineage. In patrilineal societies, the mother's brother, who is of the mother's patrilineage, usually has a generous and kindly role toward the nephew. He can be confided in, he is a source of aid, and he mitigates the sternness of the senior generation. A. R. Radcliffe-Brown saw the role as a counterbalance to the authority of the father and other members of the patrilineage. In this sense, the mother's brother's role is modeled on the nurturing warmth of the mother. The complementary line to a person's lineage—a bond of "complementary filiation" in Meyer Fortes's terms—may also carry out important functions on his behalf, such as making sacrifices for him or ceremonial sponsorship at initiation. Indeed, these ties, arising in the first instance out of marriage, promote the integration of the several descent groups into a working whole.

Two types of kinship system illustrate the continuing importance of both sides of the family. In one type, persons trace descent to an apical ancestor, but they can do so through either the mother's or father's line. These units have been called by various writers "ramages," "nonunilineal descent groups," "ambilineal descent groups," and "cognatic descent groups." For no good reason, I prefer the term nonunilineal descent group. Nonunilineal descent groups differ from kindreds in that they stem from ancestral figures, and they also have fixed memberships and boundaries. In the Pacific Islands, a center of this practice, each such group has an estate, consisting of agricultural land and residences, and the choice of the group of either the father or the mother is largely dictated by availability of land and the decision to reside there. As a rule, it is an either/or proposition, and one does-not exercise rights in more than one kin group. Among the Amhara of Ethiopia, however, people are able to claim rights in a number of nonunilineal descent groups, amassing use of considerable tracts of land. Not everybody can do so, for the kin group must accept the new member, and only the wealthy and powerful have sufficient social muscle to make their claim stick. The other type of descent referred to is termed "double descent." In societies having double descent, every person belongs to two descent groups, one a patrilineage or patriclan and the other a matrilineage or matriclan, memberships in which are inherited through the father and mother, respectively. In Africa, where the institution is principally found, the patrilineal group commonly has control over land or other resources and the matrilineal one is the repository of religious participation and knowledge. The overall yield of double descent is a remarkably intricate set of interlocking, overlapping, and crosscutting memberships and bonds.

The structure and operation of descent groups is vitally connected with rules of marriage. This is nowhere more evident than in societies that are split, in essence, into two exogamous unilineal descent groups, called "moieties" by anthropologists. In a moiety system, a person is ascribed membership in the group of either the father or the mother. It is forbidden to marry or have sexual relations with any comember of the moiety, and one must choose a mate from the opposite one. This division into inter-marrying halves is found among the Mundurucú, where one becomes a member of either the Red moiety or the White through patrilineal descent. Figure 5 diagrams the pattern of marriage in the group. If Ego's father is a member of the Red moiety, then he and his siblings will also be Reds. The father's brother and sister will be Red too, but the children of the father's sister will bear the moiety designation of their father, who must be a White; the father's brother's children will inherit his Red membership. On the mother's side, the mother and her siblings will be White, for the mother married a Red man, and the offspring of her brother will be Whites like their father. On the other hand, the mother's sister must marry a Red man, whose children will also be Red. A glance at Figure 5 will show that Ego's father's brother's daughter and mother's sister's daughter will be members of his Red moiety, and thus taboo to him. The daughters of the mother's brother and the father's sister, on the other hand, will be of the opposite moiety and therefore marriageable. In short, cross-cousins belong to the opposite moiety and are suitable mates, but parallel cousins belong to one's own moiety and fall under the incest pro-hibition. Now, if we turn back to Figure 1 (p. 64), it will be seen that this marriage pattern corresponds exactly with brother-sister exchange. It is a simple, direct exchange of spouses between two groups, and no more than two groups. Due to the limited scope of the marriage network, Lévi-Strauss refers to such a system as one of "restricted exchange."

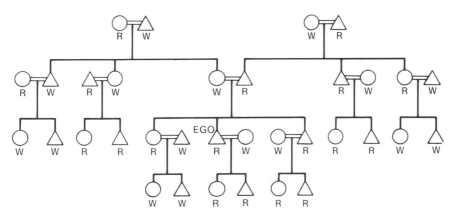

FIGURE 5. Patrilineal moiety relationships among the Mundurucú Indians (R = Red; W = White). Intermoiety marriage is equivalent to cross-cousin marriage in diagram, yielding a system of restricted exchange.

Cross-cousin marriage and an accompanying ban on parallel-cousin marriage is the single most prevalent marital rule; preferred parallel-cousin marriage is found principally among Arabs and societies influenced by Arab culture through Islam. The moiety system, or restricted exchange, prescribes marriage with a cross-cousin of some degree, for everyone in the opposite moiety in Ego's generation falls in that category. One can marry either cross-cousin, making it bilateral cross-cousin marriage; in cases of direct brother-sister exchange, as in Figure 1, the same person stands as both kinds of cross-cousin to Ego at the same time. In many societies, but particularly widespread in native Australia and southeast Asia, there is a preference for marrying one or the other kind of cross-cousins, but not both. Some groups prescribe marriage with a man's father's sister's daughter, but prohibit it with the mother's brother's daughter, whereas a much larger number prefer mother's brother's daughter unions and ban mating with the father's sister's daughter. Lévi-Strauss built a massive study of kinship on the contrast of the two, in all their nuances and subtypes, but a review of his work would go beyond our present scope and into the muddied complexities of Australian kinship. I will spare the reader and restrict the presentation to his model of "generalized exchange," in order to contrast it with the restricted-exchange regime associated with bilateral cross-cousin marriage.

Figure 6 diagrams mother's brother's daughter marriage over a three-generation span. At the senior generation, on top, a man of patrilineage A marries a woman of B, whose brother marries a woman of C. We can close the marriage circle by having the man of C wed the sister of the A-man. On the next generation down, an A-man again marries a B-woman and a B-man a C-woman, a pattern that is repeated again on the junior genera-

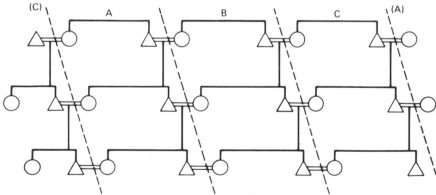

FIGURE 6. Mother's brother's daughter marriage and generalized exchange. The dotted lines separate patrilineal descent lines A, B, and C.

tion. The marital link is not based on simple, direct exchange as in a moiety system, for B always gives women to A without getting any back from that patrilineage. B does, however, get its women from C, which, in turn, marries A-women. Every group ends up with wives, and the debt of one group is paid by another. The main differences between this system of generalized exchange and that of restricted exchange is that whereas the latter is between two groups, the former must involve at least three and usually allies many more than that. It is a system that casts a wider net, integrating a large number of kin groups, and as Lévi-Strauss says, it involves a kind of trust. The exchanges are indirect, and each group gives away its women in the firm expectation that they will get some back from someone else. And they do, as long as the system works.

In any two-party interaction system, Georg Simmel tells us, there is direct reciprocity between the two, and they usually stand in a balanced, egalitarian relationship. In three-party systems, however, reciprocity is always indirect in the sense that you give something to another and get it back from a third party. Moreover, due to the inequalities inherent in the possibility of two-against-one combinations, there are frequent inequalities among the three parties—hierarchy is introduced. Thus far, our little sociology of numbers sounds like Hausa polygyny, described in Chapter 4, but closer examination reveals a striking parallel of three-party systems with generalized exchange. Not only is there indirect reciprocity, but the lineages of the system in many societies conceive themselves to be unequal to each other in the sense that the givers of wives are, ritually and in their conduct, superior to the receivers. This hierarchy is a relative one. In our diagram in Figure 6, C is superior to B, which is superior to A, which is superior to C, closing the circle. Every group is superior to one and inferior to another, an expression of their indebtedness for their wives and mothers. Under certain circumstances, such systems can change into an absolute order of rank and class, something that moiety systems cannot do.

The mutual statuses defined by kinship go beyond marriage, reciprocity, and hierarchy into elaborate protocols between affinal relatives. It has been noted that the in-law relationship involves two kin groups with common, but conflicting, interests in the same married couple. The tie is loaded with real or potential hostility that is handled in various ways. One of these is the previously mentioned custom of avoidance, whereby one party does not speak to another and may even be required to avoid being in the same locality. The anthropologist Elliott Skinner tells us that a West African of the Mossi people cannot enter his wife's home village, so strong is the avoidance. Thus, when a woman goes to visit her mother and overstays her time, the pursuing husband must sit outside the village under a tree and send for her; the wife's kin sometimes leave him under the tree for two days. A milder expression of the same sentiment requires a Saharan Tuareg to put symbolic distance between himself and his parents-in-law. He does this by raising the veil that covers the lower part of the face to a point leaving just a slit for the eyes.

Avoidance stems from the principle of respect for the older generation, but it is an exaggerated respect that makes for rigidly formal behavior or total aversion. Carried to an extreme, respect turns into noninteraction, consistent with the tendency of all things social to turn into their opposites when pushed far enough. The same thing happens with egalitarianism and camaraderie of age-mates. Men and women who are in the same exogamic group behave with the reserve appropriate to people who are taboo to each other; but in the same society it may be perfectly proper to make joking sexual references to a kin person in a marriageable category or for both male and female cousins to engage in riotous or bawdy behavior toward each other. Institutionalized joking between marital prospects or toward the siblings of the eligibles is a common feature of simpler societies and is found in almost all groups having bilateral cross-cousin marriage and moieties. Intermoiety joking reduces some of the tensions between possible affines through laughter, but it is also camaraderie stood on its head.

Avoidance and joking relations are not simply curious customs of the primitives, for we do some of the same things ourselves. How many newlywed couples have not worried over what to call their in-laws? If you call your mother-in-law Mrs. Jones, it will sound too formal, and if you call her mother, you had better not do so within earshot of your own mother. And although we do not have joking relations with kinsmen, it is a standard part of our behavioral repertoire in delicate situations in which role conflict is possible. Laughter and humor seem superficially to be the essence of good fellowship, but they are, equally, effective ways of keeping people, and even the whole world, at arm's length.

The terms we apply to kinsmen—mother, brother, aunt, and so forth—describe and classify the world of relatives, placing in the same-named status those toward whom we play similar roles. It is a form of categorization which, like all classification, both lumps and splits, listing one group of kinfolk under one term and distinguishing them from others. We like to think of our own kin terms as natural and reflective of biological ties between people, but nothing so completely refutes the genetic model of kinship as the terminologies used in different societies. Other societies not only have different words for kinsmen, but they also have entirely different systems of classifying them. These systems of nomenclature are of interest to us because they fall into a limited number of types, each of which appears independently in otherwise unrelated societies and may have worldwide distributions. This regularity of recurrence suggests a corresponding similarity of conditions for the appearance of each type system. Therefore, it is ideal grist for the scientific process.

The variety and significance of kinship terminological systems was first recognized by the pioneer anthropologist Lewis Henry Morgan in his classic *Systems of Consanguinity and Affinity of the Human Family (1871)*. Morgan believed that each type of terminology evolved from a custom of marriage or family form at some time in the remote past and remained fixed since that time. He was on the right track, for nomenclature does reflect marriage, descent, and other social practices, but he was wrong in his assumption that once established, the systems would remain unchanged. Thus, the Hawaiian usage whereby all kin on the parental generation are called mother and father was seen by him to be a survival of a stage at the dawn of human social evolution in which there was group marriage, and individual parents therefore indistinguishable. There is no evidence that such a stage ever existed, of course, and we have historical evidence of other type kin systems actually in the process of changing into the Hawaiian kind. Kinship terminologies label social statuses and thus reflect the social structures of which they are a part; they tend to change more slowly than other aspects of society and may thus tell us about conditions in the immediate past, but they are not at all so unyielding as to tell us of archaic periods in the life of man.

There are six basic types of kinship terminological systems, called by anthropologists after the tribe or people in which they were first found or are best exemplified. These are Eskimo, Sudanese, Hawaiian, Iroquois, Crow, and Omaha. We will review each of these, making reference in all of them to Figure 7, which gives a genealogical grid from the perspective of a male Ego, the person who will be conceived as using the kin terms. Each of the positions is numbered, for our own English kin terms do not describe the classifications of other societies and would only distort the facts and confuse us through imposition of our own meanings.

We start off with Eskimo terms because they are the same as those used in most of Europe and the Americas. Eskimo terminology is sometimes called "lineal" terminology because the terms used in Ego's direct line of descent are not applied to his collateral relatives, or those we call uncle, aunt, nephew, niece, and cousin in English. Thus, positions 1 and 2 are called mother and father, respectively; 7 and 8 are sister and brother, and 19 and 20 are daughter and son. These terms are applied to no other relatives. Among collateral relatives, those outside the direct line of descent through Ego, the children of Ego's brother and sister (17, 18, 21, and 22) are called niece and nephew and are distinguished only by sex. Similarly, the siblings of one's mother and father (3, 4, 5, and 6) are called uncle and aunt, without reference to which side of the family they

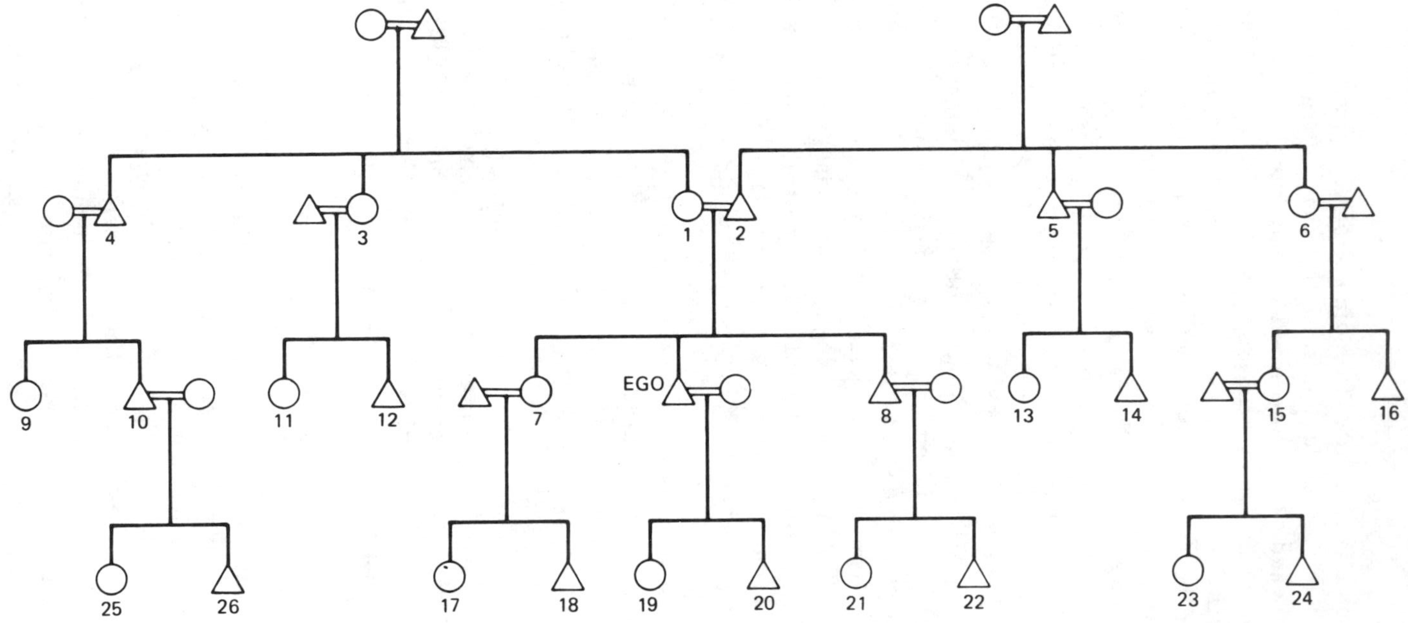

FIGURE 7. Diagram of genealogical positions relative to Ego, to be consulted in connection with discussion of kinship terminology.

are found on. All children of the aunts and uncles (9, 10, 11, 12, 13, 14, 15, and 16) are referred to as cousins, without distinction even of their sex. Romance languages, which have gender, do mark the difference, as in French *cousin* and *cousine* and in Spanish *primo* and *prima* for the male and female cousins, respectively. The indifference with which a number of relatives occupying a range of genealogical positions are thrown into the cousin pigeonhole suggests that cousin roles are ill defined, which is correct. Moreover, the consistent omission in Eskimo terminology of any distinction between the mother's side of the family and the father's shows its thoroughgoing bilaterality. Finally, the restriction of primary-kin terms to the conjugal family expresses the primacy of this unit and the comparative weakness of other ties.

Sudanese terminology may be simply described as one in which every numbered position on our chart has a different kin term. Maternal and paternal aunts and uncles are distinguished, and there are exactly descriptive terms for the cousins, and for the nieces and nephews too. These systems are found in a wide belt across the Sudan zone of Africa; thus the label. Earlier European kinship terms also veered toward the Sudanese model, and the balance of anthropological opinion is that the systems are associated with societies in which kinship is important and pervasive, but which have no unilineal descent groups. The detailed calculations of Sudanese terminology fit well with the equally detailed and ramified relations within European kindreds of the past. As extended ties of kinship atrophied with the industrialization and urbanization of Europe, most of the continent drifted toward the Eskimo type.

Hawaiian terms distinguish relatives only by generation and sex, and for this reason are sometimes referred to as "generational systems." Numbers 2, 4, and 5 on our diagram in Figure 7 are all called by one term, and 1, 3, and 6 by another. Similarly, 8, 10, 12, 14, and 16 are lumped under one rubric, which we would translate as brother, and 7, 9, 11, 13, and 15 are included under another. On the generation below Ego's, all the young are called by the same terms one would apply to his own children. As the category "Hawaiian" suggests, the Pacific Islands are a center for this kind of nomenclature, just as they are also known for the wide distribution in the region of nonunilineal descent groups. The broadly inclusive and highly generalized, almost amorphous, nature of the Hawaiian system is ideally adapted to the latter type of descent, which leaves an individual's group membership undetermined until maturity. Not knowing exactly how any one person will stand toward another in terms of group affiliation, they categorize them in a nonspecific way, a kind of vagueness appropriate to their undetermined kinship status.

Iroquois kinship terminological systems are found throughout the Americas, in Africa, and in other parts of the world. Their salient characteristic is that they divide the mother's line from the father's and that they merge the mother and her sister and the father and his brother. For this reason, they are also called "bifurcate merging" systems (and Sudanese is "bifurcate collateral," because it splits up all the parents' siblings from each other). In Iroquois systems, therefore, 2 and 5 are called by the same term but distinguished from 4, and 1 and 3 are merged, but 6 has a separate term. The other terms follow logically. All the children of somebody called father (2 and 5) are termed brother and sister (7, 8, 13, and 14), and all the children of a "mother" (1 and 3) are also called brother and sister (7, 8, 11, and 12). All the other cousins (9, 10, 15, and 16) are lumped together, distinguished only by sex. Continuing down the family tree, the brother's children (21 and 22) are called by the same term as Ego applies to his own (19 and 20), and the sister's children (17 and 18) are given separate terms, which we would translate as niece and nephew.

The first reaction of English speakers to this is that addressing both the mother and her sister by the same term does violence to biology, something that does not seem to bother us in our own cousin terms. But kinship is not about biology. It is about social relations and social groups, and the Iroquois system is splendidly in keeping with this purpose. Study of the diagram will show that, whether the system is matrilineal or patrilineal, Ego's own line of descent is distinguished in such a way that kin can be divided into two categories: Ego's own descent group and all the others. If the society has matrilineal clans or lineages, the mother's sister will be called mother, and her children, who are one's clan mates, are brother and sister. If the system is patrilineal, the father and his brother are merged, and the latter's children are called by sibling terms. In short, the parallel cousins (11, 12, 13, and 14) are termed brother and sister in keeping with common descent and the fact that they are not marriageable. On the other hand, the father's sister's children and the mother's brother's children, the cross-cousins (9, 10, 15, and 16), are all called by another pair of terms. It will be noted that not only are they often preferred spouses, but they can never, under either matrilineality or patrilineality, belong to Ego's descent group. The Iroquois system, then, is usually found in societies having unilineal descent groups, or cross-cousin marriage, or both.

The above four systems of kinship terminology are the most common ones. Much less frequent in occurrence are the so-called Crow and Omaha systems, which resemble Iroquois with certain key differences. All the other kin systems we have reviewed have observed the separation of the generations (though the English cousin term does not), but Crow and Omaha override them in an interesting way. In Crow systems, numbers 2, 5, 16, and 24 are all called by the same term, and 6, 15, and 23 by another. From our point of view it would seem that Ego may be calling an age-mate or a child father or aunt, but if we examine the diagram, we will see that they have something else in common. First, it is necessary to understand that the Crow Indians, and nearly every other group with their type terminology, are matrilineal; Ego belongs to the descent group of his mother, her brother, the mother's sister, and the mother's sister's children. On the other side of the family, the father (2), his brother (5), the father's sister (6), her son (16), her daughter (15), and the daughter's children (23 and 24) all belong to the father's matrilineal kin group. These are also the people we noted as having been lumped together despite generation level. The terms, then, mean "members of my father's matrilineal descent group" and bespeak the common identities of clan and lineage fellows. The exact mirror image opposite applies to the patrilineal Omaha. In groups of this type, numbers 1, 3, 9, and 25 are given a single term, and 4, 10, and 26 another. These are all members of the mother's patrilineal descent group. Crow and Omaha are associated with matrilineality and patrilineality, respectively, and we may infer that the overriding of the generations indicates a strong descent principle.

Anthropologists have devoted an inordinate amount of attention to kinship terms because the results are so frequently neat and tidy, unlike the messier aspects of social life. The terms, and more importantly the groups and statuses with which they deal, are also basic to the lives of primitive peoples and have deep importance even in our own society. In modern America, however, family stands apart from other things, just as religion and politics do. For a wage earner, family is what he returns to at night and weekends; it entails a range of emotions, attitudes, and activities that are somewhat distinct from those of the workaday world. We compartmentalize job, church, and politics in the same way. In simpler societies, however, life is cut out of a whole piece of cloth, and institutions that we consider separate interpenetrate and are imbedded in one another. For this reason, the study of kinship has a certain priority, for its principles define groups whose major functions are economic, political, and religious. We turn to these subjects in the following chapters.

VI

Ecology and Economy

The career of our species has been largely wrought out of our struggle to control and exploit the environment, an assault on nature that has accelerated sharply in recent decades. The resultant threat of exhaustion of Earth's resources has stimulated a new sensitivity to the finitude of our planet. We no longer think of our fuels, ores, and vegetation as limitless in their abundance. The sense of shortage and scarcity has even extended itself to water and air, which used to be thought of as free commodities. But we now buy potable and swimmable water with sewage-disposal plants and clean air with smoke scrubbers on factory stacks and smog suppressors on our cars. Everything has its price in our civilization.

Popular understanding of ecology, as we call the science of environmental relations, has gone beyond simple appreciation of the limited nature of natural resources to a quite sophisticated grasp of the inter-relatedness of plants, animals, and their natural settings. Ecological scientists had known of this for a long time, of course, but the lesson was first brought home forcibly and dramatically to the general public with the publication in 1962 of Rachel Carson's book *Silent Spring*. Carson

114

showed that the insecticide DDT, considered a boon to man because of its effectiveness in eliminating crop-destroying and malaria-bearing insects, actually had a profound and unanticipated effect on the entire chain of life. Insects were killed, but the birds that fed on them died off from lack of food, and from the DDT, thus allowing insects to again multiply, requiring even greater dosages of DDT, and so on in an endless spiral. The DDT was also picked up by grazing cattle and passed to humans through the milk; it washed into the rivers and destroyed or contaminated the fish; and it flowed out to the estuaries of the sea, where it devastated shellfish and entered the marine food chain. We had upset the balance of nature once again and we did so—as is usually the case—in the interest of human well-being and profits.

We have emphasized throughout this book the paradox whereby we sapient, planning creatures are unable to forecast the full results of our actions before we take them. In fact, we cannot even understand what happens after our actions were taken. This is nowhere more true than in the domain of ecology. Nobody was able to predict the ultimate and far-ranging effect of DDT on the delicate adjustments of the natural environment, and the farmers and chemical industry alike derided Carson's work and vilified her personally until the truth of her assertions became indisputable. This has been the story of all of human technology, for good or for ill. The pioneers of automobile manufacture did not anticipate that they would revolutionize the American landscape, spreading homes and industries throughout once-rural areas and leaving the cities hollow shells. And for that matter, few people today realize that, if energy and other shortages end the age of the automobile, the cities may become the only viable places to live in. Not all of our innovations produce such immediate results, and agriculture, for example, was born out of a slow process of trial-and-error experimentation. The primitive innovators had no idea that they were laying the basis for the development of civilization. Whether this was a propitious event or man's fall from grace is debatable, but the creative acts were small, their purposes limited, their ultimate consequences vast. Who tampers with nature reaches into the wellsprings of human society.

Along with flora, fauna, and the features of the natural terrain, man and his activities are integral parts of most ecosystems. The human impact upon the environment is manifest, but not so evident is the environment's influence in molding culture. The study of the latter process has preoccupied anthropology almost from its founding. Much of the earlier writing on the subject revealed naivety and a poor knowledge of history that persists today. There is, for example, a prevalent popular belief that the supremacy of societies of the temperate zone is due to the rigors and variations of climate, which make for sturdy, active folk. Correspondingly, the backwardness of most of the tropical world is supposedly a result of the hot, sultry weather, which presumably affects all the residents of those zones in the same way that a heat wave does New Yorkers or Chicagoans. This sounds plausible until one realizes that most workers in the tropics expend far more energy in their jobs than the average American or European workers, whose physical efforts are magnified hundred- or thousandfold by the machines they operate. Moreover, the premise that there is a neat and simple relationship between environment and culture makes light of the fact that wholly different cultures can occupy the same area sequentially, and that the environmentally unfavorable regions of one age can be the storehouses of the civilizations of another. There is indeed a deep relationship between man and his setting, but it is a bond that is as complex and elusive as it is delicate.

The modern study of ecology in anthropology began with the attempts of several writers to explain the similarities of culture that characterized certain geographic areas. One obvious explanation was that neighboring groups would share many elements of culture through "diffusion," or the spread of customs, knowledge, arts, and so forth from society to society. Another reason given for the cultural distinctiveness of areas was the similarity of subsistence pursuits of the resident peoples. Thus, the tribes of the Great Plains area of the United States exhibited many common features, which were in part an outcome of their frequent communication with each other, but also a result of their common economy of buffalo hunting from horses. In the same way, the reliance of the peoples of the north Pacific Coast on salmon and sea-mammal fishing produced a specific way of life, just as did acorn collecting among the societies of California.

Subsistence areas and "culture areas" overlapped in the work of the pioneer anthropologist Clark Wissler of the American Museum of Natural History, as they did in the later writings of Alfred L. Kroeber, who founded anthropological instruction at the University of California. But our most important body of theory on the subject comes from the writings of one of Kroeber's students, Julian H. Steward. Theories generally emerge from the practical problem of interpreting data. Thus, Wissler's notion of the culture area arose from the need to sort out and arrange museum collections, and Steward's ideas on "cultural ecology" came out of his research among the Nevada Shoshoni. The essence of cultural ecological theory is that there is a dynamic and creative relationship between culture and the environment, involving technology, resources, and labor. Phrased simply, it states that certain kinds of social groups and institutions emerge from the application of a body of technology to specific resources through human labor. There is a fit and accommodation—a functional relationship—between the ways a society must seek its livelihood and the social context within which this occurs. Put somewhat differently, when a resource is exploited with available tools and knowledge, a specific organization and cycling of work is usually called for. These modes of grouping, patterns of cooperation, and forms of leadership that are functional to getting the job done have a carry-over into all other aspects of the social system, and in this sense the ecological adjustments of a society are integral to its structuring. This is not a form of environmental determinism, for Steward considered technology to be historically derived and the critical parts of the environment to be resources, which are known through culture and are accessible through technology. It is a very cultural theory.

An example or two will illustrate Steward's use of cultural ecology. The central and eastern Nevada areas occupied by the Western Shoshoni Indians are mostly high semidesert. The topography is dominated by parallel mountain ridges of up to eleven-thousand feet, running in a north-south direction, with valley floors between the ranges of four to five thousand feet elevation. The climate is arid, and rainfall is inadequate for agriculture; summers are hot and dry, and winters are cold with some accumulations of snow, especially at the higher elevations. It is tough country even today; it was forbidding for the native peoples.

The Shoshoni lived at the very edge of survival. The main resources of the environment were thinly distributed game and wild seeds and roots. The principal animals hunted were deer, antelopes, rabbits, occasional mountain sheep, and assorted rodents. Wild vegetables included bunchgrass seed, the yamp root, and several varieties of mountain-growing berries. The technology was truly primitive. The Shoshoni used the bow and arrow as their principal weapon, and they had a meager material inventory of basketry containers and utensils and sharpened digging sticks. Shoshoni protection against the climate was slight and consisted of crude skin moccasins and breechclout, and rabbit-fur robes in the winter. The people were completely nomadic; the principal type dwelling, summer or winter, was a windscreen of sagebrush. Yet, in all this austerity, they managed to survive.

The annual round of the Shoshoni started with the breakup of winter camp each spring and the splitting off of small foraging groups of two to four families or so. Rabbits and occasional deer were hunted, and the women searched for early growing roots. Larger groups were not feasible, as the countryside was too poor to support many people in any one place. Summer would see the small nomadic clusters wandering still, harvesting the ripening grass seeds, though the melting of the snow in the mountains would enable them to ascend into the Alpine zones in search of berries, mountain sheep, and deer. Fall was a critical point in the annual subsistence cycle, for the yield of that period would have to support them throughout the long winter. Life was made possible in the region by the fact that a winter staple, the pine nut, reached maturity in September and was sufficiently abundant to make available labor the only limit to accumulation. Each fall, the Shoshoni went to the mountainsides where the piñon tree grows and gathered large quantities of the nuts, which they stored in underground caches at the bases of the hills. The people gathering pine nuts at a mountain would then form winter-camp groups nearby, numbering up to ten or fifteen families. This was the most sedentary period of the year, and the stored nuts and occasional game sustained them until the spring.

Shoshoni natural resources and the tools they used to exploit them lent themselves to individualized economic efforts. Women were responsible for the gathering of grass seeds, berries, and roots, all of which chores involved the labor of only one person, with perhaps another for company; the pine-nut harvest was carried out by nuclear family units. Most of the male hunting was done by solitary tracking and stalking for, except for antelopes, none of the animals moved in herds. The only occasions for large-scale collective hunting were infrequent antelope and rabbit drives. Antelopes are too fleet to be taken by a single hunter, and the Shoshoni would drive a herd down a valley floor to a defile where they had set up a crude corral of sagebrush. Frightened into the trap, the antelopes were dispatched with club or bow and arrow. A number of people would take part in the drive, which was under the direction of an "antelope shaman" who magically charmed the beasts in advance. Women and children would help set up the noise and clamor that would stampede the herd, and other hunters were responsible for ensuring that the animals entered the corral and stayed there. The hunts took place every couple of years in shifting locales, for a good drive could decimate a local antelope population for a decade. Rabbit drives were movable feasts for the same reason. When a valley floor grew rich in rabbits, men from a wide area would converge on it, at the invitation of a rabbit-hunt leader, and stretch grass nets across the valley. The beaters drove the animals into the nets, where they were clubbed to death by waiting men.

The Shoshoni lacked stable, multi-family local groups and forms of political integration beyond the simple leadership of the oldest male of a foraging group. There were no villages, no territory-holding bands, and no chiefs. The reasons for this are found within their system of environmental exploitation. First, the thin distribution of wild foods called for an equally thin distribution of people. Second, most economic activities called for individual work only. Those ventures involving people from several neighborhoods were infrequent and held in shifting locations, with corresponding variations in personnel taking part. Finally, the one time of the year when a large number of people joined in common residence was winter, but the same people did not winter together year after year. The reason for this is quite simple. The pine nuts in any single grove failed to yield about once in every three years. When this happened, the component families of last year's winter village would scatter in all directions to more favorable stands of trees. Winter-village sites constantly shifted, and different groups of people would reside together each year. Under these circumstances, patterns of leadership remained situational and ad hoc, and social groups were small, undefined, and shifting in composition. The crude Shoshoni technology and the sparse resources of aboriginal Nevada made for an individualized pattern of work that was reflected in an amorphous and individuated social system. Indeed, work group, political unit, and kin are one and the same among the Shoshoni, and in much of the primitive world.

Cultural ecological theory is also illustrated by the process of lineage formation. It will be recalled from the last chapter that when an extended family based on a unilocal rule of residence acquires an estate, a set of corporately held assets, it may close around these possessions to become a lineage. In reviewing the literature on South American Indians, one is struck by the almost complete absence of either patrilineages or matrilineages in the entire vast area of the Amazonian rain forest. The reason for this hiatus, I would venture, is that there are no shortages of agricultural lands, hunting territories, or fishing rights in most of the area and, therefore, no closed estates to build a lineage corporation upon. The lack of proprietary rights in land by either individuals or groups is inherent in the system of horticulture. Gardens among Amazonian Indians are made by clearing an area of forest at the end of the rainy season, letting the felled vegetation dry for several months and firing it just before the next rainy season commences. The garden is planted after the first rains with a variety of vegetables, including maize, squash, beans, yams, and manioc (or cassava), the principal crop. The tropical soils are poor in minerals, and in the following year, or the second planting of the garden, the manioc takes almost 50 percent longer to mature, and the depletion of the soil prohibits replanting of maize. By the third year, the garden is allowed to revert to jungle and may lie fallow for decades until it acquires a new forest cover. Land is abundant near most Indian villages, and a garden site only has value after labor has been expended upon it. Land that goes back to forest loses this temporary value and is freely available to anybody else who wants to work it. There is no ownership. The anthropologist Mervyn Meggitt reports a similar situation in the highlands of New Guinea, where there is a direct correlation between land scarcity and strength of lineage.

The directness of interchange and mutual influence between ecological setting and social system, and the prominent role of technology in the process, suggest that ecology is an important factor in social change and evolution. Steward recognized this early; however, in 1938 he wrote that the influence of environmental factors would lessen as the overall social system grew more complex. Superior technology would override environmental constraints and, although social groupings would still be forged by labor, labor would be less contingent on nature. One could well argue that as man gains progressive control over the environment, social evolution is effected by transcending the limits of nature. The nub of the relationship between man and nature, then, is not so much passive accommodation and adjustment as struggle.

The importance of the ecological factor in the growth of culture finds its aptest example in the development of the earliest civilizations. In the year 1853, Karl Marx wrote that the history of India followed a separate path from that of Europe because of the wide practice of irrigation in the former land. This theme was elaborated by the noted historian Karl Wittfogel into a theory of the evolution of Chinese civilization and of a kind of regime he referred to as "Oriental despotism." Wittfogel, in turn, had a profound influence on the thinking of Steward, who applied these ideas to a general theory of the rise of territorially defined polities governed by ruling classes—the state. Steward noted that the earliest states arose in rather unpromising areas, such as the flood-prone Yellow River valley, the arid valley of the Nile, the equally dry area of the Tigris and Euphrates rivers of Iraq and Syria, the parched lands of the Peruvian coast, and the high and rain-short Valley of Mexico. The distinctive feature of each was that agriculture would have been either risky or impossible without irrigation.

Irrigation agriculture lent itself to state formation for a number of reasons. It is a most effective method of farming, for irrigation waters bring fertilizing silt as well as moisture, and two crops a year can often be taken from the same land. It thus provided the abundance needed to support specialized artisans and a ruling class. The very building of irrigation dams and canals promoted central control and authority, for somebody had to plan these complex engineering works, amass a labor force, and supervise their construction. After the waterworks were finished, a continued authority was needed to allocate the precious water and to maintain the canals. These requirements were met at first by priests attached to temples, which became the nuclei of city-states. In time, these grew into regional states and empires ruled over by secular dynasties, held together and expanded by force of arms. Irrigation agriculture is an intensely communal venture that, like most collective effort, can lead to despotic control, but this despotism ushered in the very beginnings of the modern world. The trinity of technology, environment, and work—irrigation agriculture, aridity, and mass collective labor, respectively—underlay man's great leap into civilization, and into exploitation by his fellowman.

The cultural ecological method, as enunciated by Steward, was not premised on a rigid or monolithic economic determinism. Rather, he saw it as a strategy for social analysis, a way into understanding a body of cultural data, a series of first questions that one asks before all others. The theory recognized that the destinies of cultures were shaped by many other things than the environmental and the technological, but it quite rightly stressed the urgency and importance of these factors, people do have to eat. There are other problems, other questions, other theories, and cultural ecology does not preempt the discipline, but it remains among the more fruitful of our endeavors.

Anthropological interest in economics stems quite logically from its concern with subsistence and environment; however, there is surprisingly little overlap between the two professions. This is due in part to the fact that to understand modern economics one must have a background in advanced mathematics, but it is also a result of the kinds of people anthropologists study. Economics is concerned with the allocation of scarce means to different ends, which refers simply to the choices that people make in spending their money. These choices, according to most economics textbooks, are arrived at and expressed through prices, those ideal points on a graph where supply and demand meet. The economist makes a number of assumptions about the people doing the economizing, but the most important is that there is an "economic" or "rational" man, whose actions will be motivated by a calculation of maximum benefit and whose acquisitiveness is unlimited.

Good economists recognize that economic man is a useful myth in their profession, but they know that there is more to human motivation than this. Nonetheless, European and American businessmen (most of whom would make woeful economists) carrying on enterprises in certain parts of Africa are amazed when a worker whom they have trained for six months quits peremptorily a few months later and goes back to his home village. The worker is condemned as lazy, improvident, and unintelligent, but in reality he may have done a perfectly logical thing. It could well be that he left his farming community to earn cash for a specific purpose—a motorbike or a bride-price—and once this purpose was served, the sensible thing is to take the money and go home. Rational man, however, is supposed to work indefinitely, because his wants are indefinite. This may describe Europeans and Americans, but it is not at all a part of human nature.

The rationality of economic choice is profoundly conditioned by culture. Purchases are made because the price is right, but they are also made because the individual is under some social compulsion to choose one item rather than another. One of these biases is taste. Lobster sells now for princely sums, but a century ago Maine fishermen were throwing them away as inedible nuisances. We also have a penchant for grain-fed beef, though there would be a savings in slaughtering the animals at a younger age as veal. And there are a host of purchases that we make because their acquisition brings prestige. Does a Mercedes-Benz automobile work three times as well as a car costing one-third its price? Why does a house in one neighborhood cost 25 percent more than the identical dwelling in another part of town? Economic choice is not a matter of cold, calculating rationality, but a blend of bargain hunting, culturally induced and cultivated tastes, and prestige seeking.

By the very nature of his inquiry, the anthropologist is just as interested in the irrational elements in economic choice as the rational ones. He is intrigued by canny calculation, of course, but he finds fashion, fad, imitation, and prestige to be equally deserving of attention. Classical economics is also totally based on the presence of a least-common denominator of value, in terms of which all values can be quantified. This means money, but in most of the primitive societies we study, there is no such thing as money or its equivalent. No matter how elegant, then, modern economic theory is of limited use to the anthropologist.

Anthropological economics deals with the values, institutions, roles, and groupings that are parts of systems of production and distribution of goods and services, an area that has been referred to as "substantive economics," as opposed to the "formal economics" of price and money theory. Every economic system contains an area of production of goods and services, a network of distribution, and patterns of consumption. Holding the entire economy together and integrating labor and resources is a system of exchange, whereby materials are brought into the process of production and eventually end by satisfying consumer needs. The economic historian Karl Polanyi distinguished three types of exchange system, called market, redistribution, and reciprocity, which characterize different economies, and which are reviewed below.

The simplest mode of exchange, and the earliest in human history, is reciprocity. This entails the giving of something to another person in expectation of receiving either the same kind of item or some other good in return. Reciprocal transactions are economic exchanges, but they are also personalized; they take place between people who have a bond, and they serve to strengthen these ties. In this sense, gift giving is the perfect example of reciprocity, for a gift may have economic value and significance, but it also is symbolic of the relationship between the donor and donee. Christmas is America's great occasion for giving, involving billions of dollars worth of goods and exchanges among a host of different social statuses. There are gifts within the family, those made to fellow workers, presents to employees, and so forth, and the experienced gift giver knows that there is a subtle politics in all this generosity.

One of the first rules of Christmas is that equal statuses beget equal presents, unequal statuses entail presents of unequal value. Two brothers or cousins of close age are expected to spend approximately the same amount on their gifts for each other. They do this by familial hints on what the other wants or from the experience of past Christmases. Each may play it safe and give the other a necktie. This may make as much economic sense as taking in each other's washing, but the purpose of the gift is to reaffirm the bond. The parity of the presents reflects parity of status, and if one cousin departs from form and gives the other a fifty-dollar present while getting the same old ten-dollar necktie in return, he has upset the parity. Is the recipient happy with his expensive gift? Hardly. He probably feels that he has been upstaged and made to look cheap. The gift will be looked on as an act of self-aggrandizement and covert aggression.

Absence of parity in gift giving is usually found between people already in a relationship of inequality. Parents give their children expensive toys and receive small tokens in return. When the time finally arrives when the children's gifts are more valuable than those they receive, then a fundamental change has taken place; the parents have become semidependent. Hierarchies outside the realm of kinship have the same imperatives. An employer will be expected to give an employee a more expensive gift than he receives. There is a quid pro quo here, for the employer is not only symbolizing his superior status but is also gaining the loyalty of the employee. Gifts obligate as, for example, when a seller of a commodity gives expensive gifts to a purchasing agent. If the gift is expensive enough, it is considered to be so compromising as to constitute corruption, for ultimate repayment is expected. The donee is beholden to the donor, a principle we have already examined in marital exchanges.

Reciprocity goes far beyond gift giving in all societies. American parents give freely to their children, who may not directly reciprocate by supporting them later but will pay back indirectly when raising their own children. Reciprocity underlies the family, but it is also found in almost all aspects of life in the simple performance of favors. "You scratch my back, and I'll scratch yours," goes a favorite American saying, which can be applied to economic transactions, political tradeoffs and the mutual accommodations of friendship. Important though reciprocity may be, it does not bind our economy together by any means, for all of this is taking place within the framework of a vast system of markets and public finance.

There are, however, many primitive societies in which reciprocity is the only mode of exchange, in which there is no buying or selling, no taxing authority, no money. Nobody goes without food among the Mundurucú Indians, for most foods are shared. An unfortunate group whose garden failed will be supported by the entire community. Kills of large game animals are distributed throughout the village. This is a form of risk sharing, for a man might be unlucky in hunting for weeks, yet eat meat almost every night. If a man wants an arrow or some other object belonging to another man, he will usually be given it, with the tacit understanding that a similar claim can be made in return. Gift giving among the Mundurucú, and in most primitive societies, follows lines of kinship. A Mundurucú can make a heavier claim on a fellow clan member than on somebody from the opposite moiety, but reciprocity is also expected between neighbors regardless of kinship ties.

One of the principal occasions for gift exchanges in simple societies is upon marriage, which is a form of reciprocity itself. A union may involve the affinally related families in a cycle of feasts and gift giving that can continue for years. Abraham Rosman and Paula Rubel have shown that the structure of gift-giving relations is congruent with the structure of marital exchange and services to publicly stress the affinal tie and reinforce the marital alliance. The overlapping of economic exchange and kinship in primitive societies is but one more expression of the multifunctional nature of their kin groups. Moreover, the requirements of exchange are made simple by the fact that almost all adults are food producers, and that the division of labor is minimal. The reciprocal-exchange economy is not burdened with allocating products and rewards to specialized producers and functions to promote the diffuse bonds of kinship.

Societies in which the principal mode of exchange is reciprocity tend to be egalitarian, but redistributive societies are always hierarchical. This follows from the nature of redistribution, which refers to a kind of exchange in which goods flow in from the producers to some central authority or person and are then reallocated, for certain purposes, throughout the society. The very existence of such centralization bespeaks stratification. One of the better examples of a redistributive economy is the ancient Inca empire of Peru. This massive state, which at its maximum size stretched from Ecuador to Bolivia and from the crest of the Andes to the sea, was founded on irrigation agriculture. This provided the material base for an extensive division of labor and a far-flung distribution system. The cities were the locales of the rulers, a large priesthood, units of the standing army, scribes and other public servants, and a host of artisans. City populations ranged to over fifty thousand people, most of whom were not producers of food but were fed by the excess production of the rich farming economy. The economy was as centralized as was the polity, and the empire was crisscrossed by roads connecting the cities and all parts of the countryside. Private property in land was absent. All wealth belonged in

theory to the king, who was also considered a Sun-deity. This centralization of control was consistent with irrigation-based states in most of the
world. Property institutions were also weak in ancient Egypt and Mesopotamia. The monolithic nature of the economy precluded the emergence of
relatively free economic agents, who could enter into independent buying
and selling in markets. Though small markets existed, the main form of
exchange in the Inca empire was by redistribution. This was effected by a
formula that allowed the producers of food to keep one-third of their
yield, taking the other two-thirds to be divided between the state and the
temples. The surplus production beyond the subsistence needs of the food
producers was used to support the specialized craftsmen, priests, soldiers,
and officials of the cities, and a portion was also placed in storage against
the possibility of famine.

Like reciprocity, redistribution may exist side by side with other
types of exchange. In many parts of Melanesia, excess food production is
funneled into the hands of chiefs, or "big men," who in turn give the
food away through the feasts and gift giving expected of a man of rank.
Through much of the world, high status requires great generosity; the
tribute and gifts showered on a leader are commonly given away by him.
He bestows wealth selectively and politically, however, and the surplus
production actually becomes invested in power and prestige. A big man
will feast people of another village and increase the status of his own, for
the gift entails a tacit debt that must be repaid with its equivalent in wealth
or honor. Unlike the Inca state, however, the principal mode of exchange
in most of the Melanesian societies is reciprocal, with redistribution serv-
ing only one aspect of the political order.

The market system of exchange is characteristic of the capitalist
economies of Europe and the New World. Producers send their goods to a
marketplace, where purchasers bid for them. The market may be a series
of stalls in a public place, like the markets of Africa and the Caribbean,
it may be a store, or it may be the trading floor of a stock market or a
commodity exchange. The market is any place where sellers gather and
receive the bids of buyers for their product, agreeing on a price. It can be
and increasingly is located in the memory banks of a computer.

Market economies were prevalent in much of Asia for centuries, and
they have been equally a part of the African landscape since before
colonization. Markets also existed in pre-Spanish Middle America, in the
Aztec and Maya domains. These were all areas of considerable social complexity, in which the state and social stratification were the main political
forms. The markets served to unite the different economic contributions
of areas producing a variety of foods and raw materials and to bring together the specialized contributions of artisans. Vegetables were traded
for fish, metal tools for woven cloth, meat for pottery, and grain for

animals. Some areas operated within a money economy, but many of the markets of the primitive world did business by barter. The atmosphere of the market and the mechanisms by which prices are agreed upon are best seen in street bazaars in which buyers and sellers haggle with each other, the one demanding a price too high, and the other offering too little. The adjustments and compromises that finally produce agreement are often done amid much shouting and gesticulation, but it is essentially the same process by which the price of a share of ITT common stock is set.

Markets, redistribution, and reciprocity are not mutually exclusive categories and all may exist side by side in the same economy. In fact, the only economies that are purely of one type are those of very simple societies that operate exclusively by reciprocity. The decision as to how to categorize an exchange system, then, is a matter of the role of the mode of exchange in integrating the whole economy. The economy of the United States is of the market variety, because buying and selling is what makes it all hang together. Reciprocity goes on at the family level and among friends and associates, but it consolidates only small sectors of the social system. Redistribution is also an important but subsidiary part of the American economy and includes almost all of public finance. The government draws off a significant portion of the wealth of the nation each year in the form of taxes and then redistributes it to ends judged important to the public and national interest. These ends include the armed forces, part of the cost of the postal service, educational support, health facilities and research, parks, and all the other multitudinous enterprises and concerns of the federal government. Local-level governments provide schools, sanitation, police service, fire protection, and many more things that we have come to expect and which most people believe are free. A park seems free if there is no admission charge and a school if there is no tuition, but tax money pays for every bit of the cost. In a pure market economy, the users of the parks and public schools would pay entry fees and tuition, but in a redistributive economy the costs are borne by the taxpayer, whether he sends children to school or not and whether he ever enters the park or not. Redistribution, then, is not only a method of allocating goods and services, but it may also be used to level wealth differences, making available to sectors of the population things that they could not otherwise afford. Moreover, redistribution provides for many items deemed to be in the general public interest, whether a person uses them or not. A citizen may never have occasion to call the police, but he benefits from public security. A person may have no children, but he derives certain rewards from living in a community of educated and effective people.

The redistributive sector of our economy, sometimes called "welfare economics," is a social and political instrument as well as an exchange system. It is a departure from the model of the pure market economy, classical capitalism, but there are no such economies anywhere in the world, nor have there ever been. A good deal of the private and corporate wealth in this country derived directly or indirectly from government subsidy, or redistribution. Industries were built behind tariff walls paid for ultimately by the consumer, and American railroad fortunes were the direct result of government land grants. In more recent years, the government has subsidized agricultural businesses and failing aircraft companies, underwritten cost overruns by defense contractors, and provided investment incentives through tax reductions to corporations. The cost to the taxpayer of these giveaways dwarfs the outlays made for public welfare, or relief, a truly ironic note in light of the outrage expressed by many taxpayers toward the dependent poor. There has been as much truth as sarcasm in the comment that the American economy is communism for the rich and capitalism for the poor.

It may have occurred to the reader that the Soviet Union presents a case of pure redistribution, but this is not at all clear. An economy of "from each according to his ability, to each according to his need" would indeed be redistributive, but Soviet workers are paid according to how much they do and what they do; their real position is not too unlike other industrial workers. They use these wages to buy in stores, much like their fellows in capitalistic societies, with the difference that the stores are usually state run, the prices set by administrative decision rather than the interplay of the market place—a practice reminiscent of monopolistic price fixing in capitalist economies. Productive units are all state owned, but they buy materials from other units, sometimes bidding against competitors for scarce supplies, and they even advertise. There is also a busy black market. The economy, then, is based mainly on redistribution, due to the central role of government control, but there is a strong market element; and reciprocity, of course, still obtains on the family level.

Trade and the transport of goods from place to place is characteristic of market economies and redistributive ones as well, but it also goes on in some of the most simple. One form of barter, called "silent trade," formerly took place between Polar Eskimos in Canada and their Athabascan neighbors to the south. The groups were usually hostile to each other and assiduously avoided physical contact, leading them to conduct their trade by leaving proffered goods at a traditional trading spot, withdrawing, and returning later to see what had been given in return. If they were satisfied with the trade, they took the goods and departed, but if they felt too little was offered, they left the goods until more was added. The same kind of silent trade took place centuries ago between people of the upper Niger River basin of West Africa and the outside world; the main commodity of the Niger group was gold, and the silent trade protected their secret sources of the metal.

Trade was widespread among North American Indians, and objects have been found in Puebloan ruins in Arizona that could only have come from the Pacific Coast; archeological remains in the area also suggest connections with Mexico. After the horse had been introduced into North America by the Spanish in the seventeenth century, equestrianism soon diffused from the Southwest to the northern plains of Canada. Horses rapidly became the objects and carriers of an extensive trade whose origins lay back in foot-going times. The Nez Percé Indians were major raisers of mounts, and each summer troops of Indians from other tribes went to northern Idaho to trade for horses. So extensive was the commerce that when Lewis and Clark visited the Shoshoni of Idaho in 1803, they found a mule with Spanish markings. Not all of the horses were obtained through peaceful trade, however, and the intensification of warfare on the plains was due as much to horse raiding as to competition for the buffalo herds.

Trade and transport were extensive in the great civilizations of South America, but they were found also among the more primitive peoples of the Amazonian forest. In the upper Xingú River area of Brazil dwell a number of tribes, each occupying a single village and most speaking separate languages. There is considerable cultural similarity within the area, and visiting, intermarriage, joint ceremonies, and trade have welded the people of the different villages into what is, in effect, a single social system. The trade is based on a peculiar division of labor among the tribes. The Mehinaku and Waura, speakers of Arawakan-family languages, are the only makers of pottery, the Cariban-speaking Kalopalo make gourd vessels, the Tupian-speaking Kamayura make bows, and the Trumai, whose language is unrelated to the others, formerly made salt, which they extracted from the ashes of a waterlily of the region. Trading takes place during visits and at intertribal ceremonies or is often itself the purpose of a trip to another village. Bargaining is loud and spirited, and a rough set of equivalencies between goods is observed. The trade seems matter-of-fact and pragmatic at first glance, but it should be noted that the materials for each of the specialized products are found throughout the area, and the skills for their manufacture are easily learned. One may well suspect that, though it would seem that the purpose of the trade is to exchange the results of specialized production, the purpose of the specialization may well be to sustain the trade. Trade, in the upper Xingú, has its economic aspect, but it also functions to solidify relations among the tribes, unifying them in a common network of marriage and mutual defense.

The social functions of trade are spectacularly evident in one of anthropology's more famous cases of ritual exchange, the "kula ring." Off the eastern tip of New Guinea are a number of islands and island groups, including the Trobriands, the Amphletts, and Dobu, between which a thriving trade goes on. The things traded fall into two groups;

there are everyday utilitarian items such as foods and objects of technology, and there is a separate category of valuables consisting of armbands and necklaces. The latter "kula" objects are highly prized, though
neither the scarcity of the raw materials nor the labor that goes into making them explains the esteem in which they are held. They are truly ritual
objects, whose intrinsic worth lies less in their making than in their
history. New armbands and necklaces have far less value than old ones,
and the fame of any one of them derives from the frequency with which
it was traded and the luster of the traders.

One does not hoard kula objects, for to do so would cause them to
lose value and would cause the possessor to forfeit prestige. Rather, they
must be traded, and to this end the islanders embark on lengthy sea voy-
ages to other islands. The trips and the trade follow a traditional pattern.
The armbands pass from island to island in a counterclockwise direction,
and the necklaces go clockwise. Armbands can only be obtained with
necklaces and vice versa. Neither food nor money is considered an equivalent value, because neither has the ritual attributes of the kula items. The
islanders are normally hostile to each other but, in common with practice
elsewhere, traders are considered immune to attack. To guarantee their
safety abroad and to facilitate the trade, each man involved in the kula
ring has trading partners on the adjacent islands who receive him and
offer hospitality and protection. The kula trade is deeply involved in the
prestige hierarchy, for only important men take part in the commerce, and
of these only the most powerful come into possession of the more famed
kula valuables. The objects and their owners contribute to each other's
fame and prestige, a process that is reinforced by the fact that "big men"
have equally "big" trading partners.

The kula ring serves to solidify the hierarchy of rank and to unite
the upper strata of the different islands. But at the same time that all this
is happening, ordinary utilitarian goods are also being traded on these
expeditions. This exchange has a decided economic function, because
many of the commodities are unavailable on certain of the islands and
must come through trade. The mundane trade is not conducted with the
solemnity of the kula exchange, nor are the objects themselves regarded
in the same light. It would be easy to take this fact and say that the kula
simply provides a cover and veneer for the important trade in useful commodities, but one could also ask why do they need such a rigmarole to
conduct pragmatic trading? Lots of other groups with little love lost between them engage in trade without a ceremonial system to support it
and we must ask what the kula does that makes it necessary. The answer
is a political one; the kula serves to keep the ordinary folk out of all commerce and thus functions to promote and protect an emergent class structure.

Anthropologists like to argue over whether a practice or institution is "at heart" ceremonial, or economic, or political, or almost anything except fun (anthropologists are very serious people). These are idle arguments, for it is clear that the kula ring is all of these things at once, including fun. Most practices are indeed multifunctional, just as any single function can be fulfilled by a number of diverse practices. There is no such thing as a purely "economic" or "political" institution, for, as we have noted, these compartments exist more in our minds than in empirical reality. A religious group that controls billions of dollars worth of assets and the loyalties of a substantial segment of a citizenry and its political representatives obviously has more going for it than trinitarian doctrine. And a government that has an annual budget of several hundred billion dollars per year, as does that of the United States, must surely be the country's most potent economic force, as it is. This plurality of function and meaning of cultural usages, the mutual imbeddedness of the aspects of culture in each other, is more pronounced in primitive cultures than in our own, but it is still very much with us. Thus, the economist Thorsten Veblen spoke of the prestige economy of the United States and the pattern of "conspicuous consumption" of its upper classes, referring to a mode of spending and displaying wealth that labels a person as rich and powerful. The so-called profit motive, then, is not some abstract and innate force, unique and sui generis, as it is imagined by those who see human nature at work in coupon clipping, but a very complex phenomenon that is rooted in human fears and a culturally induced desire for esteem and power.

The craving for wealth as a vehicle toward prestige is nicely illustrated by a custom of feast and gift giving called the "potlatch," found among the Indians of the northwest coast of North America. The tribes of the area, which number the Kwakiutl, the Bella Coola, the Tlingit, the Haida, and many smaller groups, had a system of rank stratification that is unique, for they were the only hunting and gathering peoples of which we have knowledge who had a systematic social hierarchy. And although most hunters and gatherers are nomadic or seminomadic, the Northwest Coast groups lived in permanent wooden longhouses in sizable villages. All of this was made possible by an unusually bountiful nature, which lavished them with sea mammals, shoals of migratory salmon, and rich hunting grounds.

There were three ranked social categories among the people of the British Columbia and Alaska littoral: nobles, commoners, and war captives. Each noble held a number of titles of rank, which were inherited by him or acquired at some point in his career. The titles had to be revalidated each time they were transmitted, however, for just as the title conferred honor on its bearer, so also did the bearer bring honor, or shame, to the title. Titles were validated, or "made good," by elaborate feasts hosted by the titleholder and to which were invited residents of other villages and the noble's rivals, such as his in-laws. The feasts reached elaborate proportions in which Gargantuan amounts of food were eaten or given away and in which wealth was lavishly bestowed on the guests. Casks of whale oil were thrown on the fires, canoes burned, and an occasional longhouse consumed by fire in extreme expressions of generosity and displays of wealth somewhat reminiscent of the party scene in F. Scott Fitzgerald's *The Great Gatsby*. When the time came for the guests to validate their own titles, they had to repay the hospitality with an equivalent or better feast. The process has built-in escalators, and the Canadian government tried to stop potlatching in the early twentieth-century, because it felt that the Indians were impoverishing themselves.

The feasting of the nobles was financed by the gifts of the commoners, whose stake in the matter was the renown and honor that their title bearers could bring the entire community. This, as we have noted, was a redistributive mechanism, which had the additional functions of encouraging excess production and then converting this surplus to political purposes, as well as distributing the wealth from group to group throughout the population. Potlatching was at one and the same time a political and an economic practice, and it was the primary focus of attention and source of excitement of the people of the area. Once again, we see that asymmetry in gift giving produces asymmetry in social rank; the giver takes his return in prestige, and generosity may indeed be a selfish act.

Egalitarianism is closely linked to economies based on reciprocal exchange; rank and class stratification fit with redistributive and market economies. Market economies lead to the growth of inequality through the appearance of landowners, middlemen, and entrepreneurs, and the profits taken by them, and redistribution involves a central authority who, or which, has the right to receive and allocate wealth. There is thus an evolutionary gradient that takes us from the relatively undifferentiated societies to those crosscut by distinctions of rank and differences of economic role. Economic factors are important markers and promoters of social evolution, for the development of complex societies has been completely contingent upon the simultaneous emergence of an economic base that will support nonproducers of food. In the city-states of ancient Mesopotamia, these specialized groups were only a very small fraction of the total population, whereas in the United States only 5 percent of the population is directly involved in farming. This virtual explosion in the division of labor has been one of the products of the harnessing of nonhuman energy and a burgeoning technology.

There are a number of other striking differences between primitive economies and those of modern times. Money, for example, is rarely found among primitive peoples because exchange is not sufficiently developed or depersonalized to require a portable least-common denominator of value. Wampum among the Indians of the northeast United States and cowrie shells in Africa had many of the attributes of money, but they were used for only a limited range of transactions. On the island of Yap, in the Pacific, huge stone disks were a "money" of sorts, but they could barely be moved and thus lacked the quality of portability; besides, they were used only in ritual exchanges and other values could not be reduced to them. Money need not take the shape of scrip or coin, though this is its modern form, for small, easily divisible and quantifiable commodities can serve the same purpose. Immediately after the end of World War II, with the currencies of Europe in ruins, much of the economy was conducted through the black market. This illegal exchange was largely fueled by the hoarded wealth of Europe and United States military supplies, either purchased or stolen by American personnel. The goods of the black market included jeeps, whole or disassembled, tires, nylon stockings, liquor, gasoline, Leica cameras, and above all American cigarettes. So constant and intense was the demand for cigarettes, and so neatly did they meet the criteria of money, that they soon became a standard unit of value. Prostitutes charged in cigarettes, a decent Leica could be bought for about thirty cartons (at PX prices of one dollar a carton), and all except the largest purchases were translatable into the ubiquitous cigarette. To smoke one was to burn money, a very curious feeling.

Another contrast between primitive societies and most modern ones is the relative unimportance of private property in the former. Lewis Henry Morgan, in his book *Ancient Society* (1877), wrote that private property arose with the development of plow agriculture; prior to that, through hunting and collecting to the simple horticultural periods, the goods of life were said to have been held in common. Morgan's thesis did not lack for critics, and anthropology dismissed the idea of primitive communism along with some of his more fanciful notions on clanship, marriage, and the family. It was pointed out that private property in weapons, utensils, and other artifacts was almost universal. This posed no problem to the Morgan theory, which chiefly concerned communal holding of productive resources and the main instruments of production. But the critics hit here as well and the late Frank Speck, joined by Father John Cooper and others, claimed that private ownership, by individuals or nuclear families, of hunting territories existed among the Indians of Canada. There was no doubt that Canadian Indians held such lands in 1900 and for many decades earlier, but subsequent research by Diamond Jenness, Julian Steward, and Eleanor Leacock showed these to be fur-trapping territories and, therefore, postcontact. A hunter was permitted to kill game on another's territory if he had chased it there, but he was also expected to leave behind the animal's pelt to be sold by the holder of the territory to a white trader. It was, however, totally prohibited to trap in another's district. All of the earlier documents pointed to communal holding of hunting lands before the arrival of the Hudson's Bay Company, and we may conclude that private territories were one of the many far-reaching results of European influence.

Hunting territories are nowheres owned by individuals, and fishing sites and wild-seed gathering areas are also under communal regimes everywhere. Moreover, private property in agricultural land is, as Morgan said, rare among horticulturalists but common in plow agriculture with animal husbandry. A hoe gardener may have usufruct, or use, rights to land he is working, but title is almost invariably held by a larger community. The resource-holding group may be a lineage, clan, village, nomadic band, or a tribe, but it is rarely an individual, or even a group of individuals in a contractual, nonkin relation to one another. It was the absence of any idea of land as a private commodity, held in perpetuity regardless of its use, and alienable at the owner's will, that made the American Indian so easy a prey to the Europeans. Indian grants of lands to the settlers, so common in early colonial history, were not made with the expectation that European-type ownership would prevail. The Indians were merely granting permission to use the land in the same way that they were using it themselves. Access to land was not a personal legal right among them but a human birthright, and its total, unconditional seizure by the whites was, to the Indians, a crime against nature as well as against mankind.

Differing economic values, concepts, and practices were integral elements in the conflict between the American Indians and white colonists, demonstrating once again that the economic and political orders are inseparable. Economics deals with decision making, and so also does politics; politics deals with power, and so also does economics. Political power is used to gain economic ends, and wealth is used to buy political control. Whether the economic is prior to the political is a moot question, but that they are totally enmeshed with each other in every society is a fact. It is to the political aspect of society that we now turn, keeping in mind that there are no walls separating the topic from the subject matter of the chapter now ended.

VII

Order and Authority

Man's intelligence and self-interest combine to make him a most unruly animal, and we may well ask, with our favorite sociologist Georg Simmel, — "How is society possible?" How are the disparate urges, goals, and motivations of people accommodated to the need for public safety and order, and to the requirement that the work of life be done? How is it that seemingly independent individuals yield a part of their autonomy and submit to the will of others? We have been answering these questions throughout this book, for order and control are conditions of social existence. Humans are socialized to life in a particular society, organized along certain lines, and having a distinctive culture. Its ways are impressed upon the personality in a deep and lasting manner. We are not totally puppets and creations of our cultures, but our "enculturation" assures a strong correspondence to people's expectations of each other and serves further to render the seemingly most bizarre practices natural and matter-of-fact. Childhood socialization is our first experience of the profound dependency that all humans have on their fellows. Combined with the capacity for love that is first communicated through the ministrations of the mother, we are held together by bonds at once so deep and extensive that we are indeed social creatures by nurturance, if not by nature. Despite this, our intelligence sets the limits of our existence and our identities and counterposes the self to others; we are all in the final analysis very much alone and vulnerable. Love and dependency are at once our strength and our weakness, for they may produce conflict and social inequality, as well as solidarity and oneness.

The prevalence of the lust for power has led to some speculation that our species has an instinct for it. Like most notions of inheritance of behavior patterns, the belief that humans have a specific tendency toward power or toward the acquisition of wealth, which is somehow built into the chromosomes, does little more than explain a set of data by an attribute of the data. It is rather like saying that fire burns because it has a heat principle. The virtue of this kind of logic is that we can stop thinking of a problem in the belief that we have solved it. No behavioral geneticist has isolated any factors underlying social hierarchy, and the inference that such exist is wholly derivative from the generality of prestige and rank in societies and from observations of certain species of animals. There is a pecking order among barnyard fowl that places each bird in a dominant or subordinate relation to the others. Dominance orders have also been noted among primates, but it has been observed among baboon troops that the presence or absence of dominance hierarchies is contingent upon ecological circumstances. In this respect, we can note of humans too that not all societies are stratified and that egalitarianism and hierarchy are also in good part functions of economic conditions. The earliest human condition was one of equality; hierarchy is an embellishment of time.

Systematic, formal hierarchies, such as those found in European class structure or Indian caste, and rigidly authoritarian regimes of the kind characteristic of ancient despotisms or modern dictatorships are not at all standard features of the cultural landscape, and we must infer that they do not spring from human nature, but from the forces of history. The psychological preconditions for systems of human inequality are, instead, much more general and simple than power hunger and lie in the universal human desire for the esteem and respect of one's fellows, as well as in the urge to live. The drive of all organisms to survive is indisputable, and linked to this will to live is the libidinal or life force of the psychic apparatus. This, in turn, is at the root of the primary narcissism of our species and of our capacity to attach some of this self-love to others. Human survival drives lead man to avoid dangers and to physically repel or destroy a threatening creature or object. This places a value on forcefulness and further motivates people to try to secure their safety through gaining predictability and control over their environment, both human and nonhuman. One is always dependent upon others but is properly fearful of completely resting his security on the whim and caprice of even those closest to him. One sure way of guaranteeing some degree of safety is by gaining the esteem and affection of others, rather than their hostility, a position that is made even stronger by the ability of the individual to physically resist threats. Another survival technique is to control the external world through the technological dominance of nature and through influence over the behavior of one's fellowman. To the extent that others are dependent upon and respondent to an individual, that person has made his situation in life more predictable and less threatening; he manipulates the social environment rather than being manipulated by it. Fear and anxiety thus produce a strain toward a search for autonomy and prestige, an impulse that often conflicts with the even greater need for cooperation in society. The search for prestige and respect is well-nigh universal, but it must be cautioned that it does not explain elaborate social hierarchies. These, we will see, arise in the course of social evolution out of a number of cultural factors. Hierarchies may utilize the quest for power and esteem as individual motivations and rewards, and they may encourage its intensity, but they are not caused by it.

The principle of "Occam's Razor" states that the best explanation is the most "economical" one, that is, the one that involves the fewest unproven assumptions. Prestige seeking, which under the proper social conditions can become magnified into power hunger, needs no specific genetic explanation beyond the animal will to survive and the human expression of this will in the love of self and others. It is a combination of these factors that make most humans crave the good opinion of their fellows, for public esteem reinforces both self-love and personal security. This may lead to conflict and competition for favored social position, but it also is a powerful agent in social control. The control of behavior is built into the interaction process, which sees a continuous shifting and adjustment of each person's conduct according to what each thinks the response of the other will be. It is like a continuing chess or checker game in which every move is an outcome of past moves and a prediction of what the opponent's responding move will be. In this interaction game, a number of elements must be taken into account, including the cultural norms governing the situation and the social statuses of the actors, and the individuals involved must play a complicated hand that sees them pursuing their own pleasures and benefits while observing social conventions and securing the approval of others. Social life is a bit like walking on eggs, every encounter a possible threat. And in this dangerous play, an individual's course of action is modified and constrained by the expectations of others, expectations that ultimately are nothing more or less than the standards and values of the culture. We receive approval and respect for playing the game properly, ridicule and loss of prestige for playing it wrong. Conformity and behavioral control, then, are immanent in all our relations with other people.

There is a prevalent belief in our society that social control, or the maintenance of public order, is wholly contingent upon the formal laws governing conduct and the legal sanctions taken against deviants. We have seen, however, that the process is more subtle and general than that, for it is imbedded in social life. Social control is also obtained by informal, noncodified means in our own society, and these are remarkably efficacious in keeping the majority of the population in line. As an example, New York City has an ordinance prohibiting spitting on the sidewalks, but the only people ever prosecuted under it are suspect types that the police have decided to harass. Nonetheless, few people spit on the sidewalk, for to do so would visibly disgust onlookers. There is also a biblical commandment against "coveting" one's neighbor's wife (or husband, I suppose), but it is doubtful whether this is the reason why adultery is not even more rife than it is. Rather, one can suspect that the chief inhibitor would be the neighbor whose wife one is coveting.

Open disapproval or ridicule of a person's actions by verbal or expressive means by associates and bystanders is one of the main deterrents of deviance, for it arouses that most acute of all afflictions of the ego— shame. The sense of guilt connected with the incorporation of social standards into the "superego," or conscience, part of the personality forces conformity to values through the activity of one part of the mind censuring the other. Guilt can inflict self-torment as retribution for our lapses, but shame may entail even greater damage to the ego and total loss of self-esteem. The person who has been shamed is stripped of his personal worth, robbed of the carefully cultivated self-image that he presents to the world, and made to feel a fool or a knave. He has been depersonalized and all of his other social statuses have been compromised. Shame operates best in communities in which there is face-to-face interaction between all members and in which the miscreant can neither hide his deeds nor escape their consequences; it is thus the means par excellence of social control in small towns and primitive societies.

Shame is contingent upon the fame of the offender and the degree to which he finds difficulty in segregating his role sets. One author tells of the Arab Bedouin who passed flatus in public, a very gross breach of etiquette, and who was derided for years throughout a vast area inhabited by many tribes as "the man who farted." Shame is most effective when coupled with good communications, thus adding up to gossip. Gossip takes news of one's error from the immediate observers to the entire community, often becoming embellished and more lurid in the retelling. The diffusion of the story leaves the person with no place to hide and confronted with the difficult task of rebuilding his reputation. Gossip also sketches out the limits of a community, for it is passed on only to people who have knowledge of the victim. It produces an inverted sense of belonging, for you gossip only about people you care for.

There are many other ways of enforcing social standards without resort to formal agencies of justice. One of the most widespread of these is through the use of witchcraft, or of accusations against alleged witches. Among the Navaho, there is fear of arousing the envy of persons possessing the supernatural power to do harm, which serves to inhibit aggressiveness and competitiveness. Among the Mundurucú, the shaman, or medicine man, has the power to heal and do good, but he also has the power to harm, either through changing into the form of a jaguar and attacking a specific victim, or by spreading evil objects that cause illness. While sickness stays at a low, normal level of incidence, the Mundurucú do nothing to find the culprit, but when it reaches epidemic proportions and people die, a witch hunt starts. A powerful shaman from another community is then called in to identify the sorcerer through his supernatural powers. The accused are often deviants from Mundurucú values. In one village a chief and his son were both killed as sorcerers, though it should be noted that he had habitually exceeded his authority as chief. In another community, a man who worked very hard at rubber collecting, acquiring substantial amounts of trade goods, was accused of sorcery though he had never been a practicing shaman. The people were well aware that they were executing as sorcerers men who had departed from the egalitarian ethic, but they had a ready answer. "Sorcerers are people who are angry with everybody," they explained.

The Mundurucú got rid of their male deviants in this way and, in the process, further promoted social control by projecting their own repressed hostilities onto the person of the victim. Control of women was exercised in two ways: women gossiped about each other, and the men retaliated against female deviants by gang rape. Tales were told about men by men, but the most intense form of gossip was by women, and against women, a common enough phenomenon that has been erroneously attributed to female "cattiness" or to lack of solidarity among women. Gossip, to the contrary, works well among women exactly because they form such close-knit groups. In one case of a suicide—a dreadful event to the Mundurucú—a woman ingested poison because "her sisters were talking about her." Simmel once noted that women are harsh judges of each other because they are an oppressed group, and the lapse of one exposes the entire sex to the sanctions of the men. Mundurucú gossip therefore served to enforce female roles and values before the men intervened. If a woman's transgressions against the female role—usually for aggressive promiscuity or spying on the men's ritual musical instruments—could not be dampened by gossip, she would be gang raped by all the males of the community except her immediate relatives, who, disgraced, would not protect her. True to Simmel's insight, when these events occurred, however infrequently, all the women of the victim's village felt that they, too, had been violated.

The only alternative for the loner who had been accused of sorcery or the woman whose sexual behavior had become notorious was to flee from Mundurucú villages and settle among the Brazilians. In doing so, they and their families became effectively isolated from their fellowmen, from people who spoke the same language, from prospective marital partners, from economic help, and from almost everything that endowed their lives with meaning. Today, refugees from the moral order are at least able to escape to some safety, whereas in times past, the lone family would have been an easy prey to enemy war parties. Ostracism, whether voluntary or imposed, is one of the worst penalties society can exact, for it inflicts a social death while the person is still alive. Social ostracism in small-town America has sent many people to seek refuge in the anonymity of the city, but in primitive societies there are no alternatives to life in tight little communities.

Social control and the maintenance or restoration of order may, paradoxically, be achieved through seeming disorder. One of the more common ways of gaining redress for a wrong, without intervention of government, is through the feud. The feud follows the principle of taking an eye for an eye and a tooth for a tooth, though what is usually involved is a life for a life. Feuds differ from war in that they are generally between people of the same society, between whom all-out conflict would be unthinkable. The essence of the feud is that when one member of a group is injured or killed, his relatives band together to avenge him. Moreover, they hold both the culprit and his kinsmen responsible, and anyone of them can suffer retaliation. Among Arab Bedouins, when a man is killed, all of his kin within five degrees (that is, out to second cousins) of patrilineal kinship must band together to seek revenge. If they can dispatch the killer, then so much the better, but if they cannot find him, any man within five degrees of relationship to him will suffice for revenge. Ideally, the feud is settled when a life is paid for with another, but feuds sometimes keep going for years, until depletion or a third party intervenes.

Arab feuds redress imbalances, but in most cases an attempt is made to avoid further bloodshed. Usually, a deputation is sent from the killer's to the victim's group offering "blood money" as compensation for the life, and no further fighting ensues. The basic principle that members of a kin group are equivalent to each other is also expressed in one form of settlement that sends a woman from the transgressor's group to the victim's group, where she stays in marriage until she has borne them a son as a replacement. The involvement of kinsmen in revenge would appear to escalate violence, but it also may dampen it. People are constantly afraid that some rash act by a kinsman will embroil them in feud or cost them a small fortune in blood money, and they do everything possible to control the actions of their more impetuous relatives. In this way, coresponsibility can guarantee the peace by making everybody accountable to others for their deeds.

Feuding is common in societies in which there is segmentary opposition of the type described in Chapter 5. It may cause fighting between linked patrilineages, but within each opposed segment it produces internal solidarity. That conflict can promote social cohesion was observed early by Machiavelli, but it was raised into a sociological principle by Georg Simmel. For all the violence that warfare entails, it invokes intense feelings of patriotism and unity among the citizenry. Such solidarity is actually essential to the pursuit of war. When it is lacking, as in the case of the Vietnamese War, severe social disruption may result. Controlled conflict is also a way of releasing repressed hostilities and easing social tensions. Competitive sports may serve to act out strife in a kind of athletic psychodrama that can be therapeutic for participants and observers alike. Ceremony may serve the same functions. The anthropologist Max Gluckman noted that ritualized rebellions by central African tribal subjects against their kings served to reinforce authority by challenging it at a specific time and under special, limited circumstances. True rebelliousness was siphoned off, and the royal powers were accented by their symbolic breach. In the same way, court jesters emphasized the majesty of a king by being the only people who could joke about him. The jester was not so much a humorist as a fool. Conflict, then, may be a symptom of social dislocation, but it may also serve to increase solidarity and decrease otherwise dangerous tensions.

The underlying assumption of the feud is that people of a group are equivalent to each other and interchangeable. Their legal status is derived from their kin-group memberships and not from their positions as individuals. This is totally contrary to American and European legal systems, in which the individual is the effective unit before the law, his kinship and other ascribed statuses being considered largely irrelevant. This difference is one of the great watersheds separating complex modern society and the simpler world of ancient societies or modern primitive ones, for the emergence of the legally autonomous individual marks a change in the ways societies are organized. Sir Henry Maine, the great British comparative jurist, contrasted social relationships in primitive societies, which are based upon "status," and social relationships in modern societies, which he characterized as "contractual." In status relations, the person's legal standing is categorical and determined by kin-group membership or by other ascribed criteria. Maine did not infer that the identity or individuality of the primitive person is effaced, or that so-called individualism is undervalued, but only that his legal relations with others are contingent upon his prior social identity. This contrasts with the relationship of contract, which is a wholly depersonalized tie between people, usually individuals, that has no reference to their other social statuses. The essence of the contract is the impersonal legal agreement between individuals, who essentially have no other identity relevant to the contract. If I sign a lease, the conditions of the document ideally should have no relevance to whether I am black or white, male or female, or to whom I am related. Status relations are personal ones; contractual ones are impersonal. An example may set this off more clearly. Two brothers in an African village may help each other and may go into economic ventures jointly, and it is understood that no further conditions have to be set for this tie other than that they are brothers. On the other hand, two American brothers who decide to go into business together will almost always go to a lawyer and have formal partnership papers drawn up, stipulating the share that each has in the enterprise and their responsibilities to each other. The way they conduct business and the way they relate to one another in the commercial context may differ little from the kind of behavior that goes on between unrelated partners. Indeed, our folk wisdom tells us that family affiliates fight more than unrelated ones do; family ties are not very effective in holding businesses together, but business ties sometimes break up families.

Maine's distinction is paralleled by other writers. The German social theorist Ferdinand Tönnies distinguished two kinds of society based on their prevailing types of cohesion. The one corresponding to Maine's status was called *Gemeinschaft*, which infers a system of solidarity based on the likeness of the people and on feelings of loyalty toward each other. It is a brotherhood in which bonds are personal and laced with sentiment, and in which personal statuses are fixed. *Gesellschaft*, the German word for corporation, implies a society in which the principal integrating relations are formal, impersonal, and, as with Maine, contractual. Emile Durkheim, the founder of sociology and one of the great sources of stimulation of social anthropology, distinguished between "organic" and "mechanical solidarity," a typology of social structures. Societies held together by mechanical solidarity have a minimum division of labor and function among individuals and groups. They correspond to the lower end of the scale of social complexity. Since their components are much the same, this similarity is the source of their cohesion. Organic solidarity, on the other hand, is found associated with more complex societies in which there is extensive division of labor and of function among component parts. Being different from each other and specialized in their functions, each part depends upon the others to round out a full existence. The tailor depends upon the textile mills for cloth; the mills depend upon the sheep raisers for wool; the sheep raisers depend upon feed and machinery suppliers, and so on. They are all held together by their unlikeness, which, said Durkheim, is the most powerful form of solidarity.

One of the more influential attempts at isolating the core of modernity was Max Weber's distinction of "traditional" and "rational" societies. Traditional societies are described as those in which there is thorough adherence to customary ways of behaving, and in which these ways of doing things are justified by recall to the past. Rational societies, on the other hand, are those in which the validity of a social usage is found in the logicality of its fit with other usages. Rational social systems are not logically designed and developed, and the logic is usually an ex post facto attempt to make sense out of what evolved without human intent. It might be more appropriate to say that modern society is not so much rational as rationalized. The prototype of rationality is the modern bureaucracy, for it is to a certain extent amenable to deliberate manipulation and creation. Moreover, each part of a bureaucracy derives its rationality from the coherence of its relation to the other parts. The other distinctions between traditional and rational societies are familiar to us from our discussion of status and role. Traditional relations are infused with sentiment, those of rational societies are emotionally neutral. Roles tend to be multiplex and diffuse in traditional societies, but are more specific in a rational regime. Ascribed status is more basic to traditionalism, whereas achievement prevails with rationality. The position of the individual is preset by the circumstances of his birth and is more particularized in traditionalism, but individuals are treated as universal unit-ciphers in the facelessness of rationality.

Weber's types were ideal ones. No societies corresponded exactly to the two extremes, but all could be placed along a line between them. The types are useful for comparative purposes and for analysis. It should be cautioned that rationality does not mean more sensible or absolutely logical. Primitives are every bit as logical as we moderns, and their processes of thought are much of a piece with our own. The difference lies rather in mode of justification, what Weber called "legitimation," of one or another practice or viewpoint. Recalling the section on sex roles in Chapter 3, primitives very commonly legitimize the dominant role of men by recourse to past, mythical events and the example of their ancestors. Moderns are not satisfied with this and seek *the* answer by reference to the logic of the present. Thus, American men arrive at the conclusion that they are intellectually superior to women by biological endowment, a conceit that would be howlingly funny were it not for its unhappy consequences. So much for rationality as a guide to truth. The popularity of Weber's work has led some sociologists and political scientists to regard primitives, of whom Weber had little knowledge, as being totally bound by tradition and slaves to custom, but nothing could be further from the truth. Rather, just like us, they seek to achieve satisfaction of their desires within the broad confines of rules. Values and norms are used by them to justify as well as to guide their conduct, and they are as good as anybody else at manipulating and evading the rules. By the same token, primitive life is not regimented. If it presents little variety, this is only because of its simplicity, for primitive people wander about and do their own chores in their own way and their own time. They do not have clocks and they do not work for bosses; their daily lives are far looser and more uncoordinated than our own. As Maine said, the individual is legally separate from his ascribed statuses in modern society, but this does not mean that thereby individual lives are made richer and more independent.

Weber was one with the other writers reviewed above in seeing a general evolutionary process at work in human society, which, while going from simplicity to complexity, brought about increasing depersonalization of relations, the overlay of a vast number of achieved statuses on the ascribed ones, a growing division of labor, the emergence of the individual as a legal entity, greater specificity of roles, and a loss of solidarity based upon common sentiment—trends in modern culture that will be considered in detail in Chapter 9. Weber's vision of the future was apocalyptic. He saw man becoming increasingly estranged from his own labor and from his fellowman, losing the firm and traditional sources of his identity, and becoming a featureless pawn of life among millions of other identical pawns. Weber could not foresee computers, but if he had known of them, he would have instantly assumed that our Social Security numbers would have become our labels.

In this overall process of differentiation, nothing has split, divided, and riven societies more than the emergence of systematized inequality and the development of social statuses and groups that have the ability to sway or compel the behavior of others. Inequality is not the natural condition of the species, despite recognized differences of strength and intelligence, for the most simple and technologically rude societies are invariably egalitarian. With the exception of the peoples of the Northwest Coast of North America, social hierarchies are found only in farming or herding societies, and by no means in all of these; hierarchy is also universal to industrial societies. There are prestige orders in every society, the outcome of each individual's need for approval and security, but differentials of respect do not automatically bring control over the actions of others. In hunting societies, a successful hunter will generally be accorded considerable esteem, for he shows excellence in a pursuit basic to the group's survival. A brave warrior might also be accorded considerable respect, but this is not universally true. Among some of the Puebloan villages, a man who killed an enemy was considered ritually unclean and had to undergo religious purification to bring him back into society. The most prestigious positions in the community were not military or political offices, but religious ones. On the other hand, the Jívaro of Ecuador, noted for their art of shrinking human heads, place great emphasis on valor, for one captures the supernatural powers of the victim whose head is taken. The Mundurucú took trophy heads too, though they did not shrink them, and the trophies were believed to bring pleasure to the spirits of the forests, benefiting the entire tribe. The successful headhunter was honored for years after, and his person was considered ritually sacrosanct. But the Mundurucú were passionately egalitarian, and the principal trait of the great headhunter was his modesty. Anybody who boasted of his bravery was asked to be the first to enter an enemy village during a raid. Holders of offices, such as chiefs or shamans, were respected by the Mundurucú, but their positions did not entitle them to control over others, however strong their gifts of persuasion may have been.

Power over others is not the issue in egalitarian societies, and ego gratification is the principal reward for those who are proficient in socially valued activities. The privilege of polygyny is accorded chiefs in many South American tribes, a right that may also come with other sources of prestige. Among the Sharinahua Indians of eastern Peru, writes Janet Siskind, successful hunters are given sexual favors by women to whom they bring meat. There is an open quid pro quo here between sex and food, an equivalence that is often expressed in other societies on the symbolic level. When the men go hunting, the women call after them that if they bring back no game "we'll eat penis," and the lucky hunter expects to copulate with any woman he feeds. Egalitarian groups are characterized by a uniformity of living standards and amenities. The great hunter or priest may acquire honor and respect, but he neither lives differently from others, nor does he have significantly more wealth. Indeed, under the reciprocal-exchange systems common in such societies, he may actually be impoverished by demands upon his generosity. In just this way, reciprocity works to level incipient wealth differences and thus eliminates a threat to the rule of equality.

The simple prestige gradients of egalitarian societies are open to anybody qualified. Positions such as chief or shaman are often hereditary and thus not accessible to all members of the group, but fame as a warrior, hunter, or storehouse of myths may come to all having the proper attributes. In many societies, however, valued and sought-after positions are clearly labeled and formalized, and the number of these statuses is less than the number of qualified persons seeking them: this, in brief, is the "ranked society," following the definition given by Morton Fried in *The Evolution of Political Society*. Just as reciprocity is commonly found in association with egalitarianism, redistributive mechanisms are often encountered in societies based on ranking. The most frequently cited examples of ranking are the Northwest Coast tribes, in which nobles accumulated and potlatched valuables as means of validating and increasing rank. As in egalitarian societies, however, titleholders usually lived much as did commoners, for liberality was the basis of success and worth. Office holders in ranked societies may work alongside ordinary folks or they may become partially freed from productive tasks, but resources usually remain in possession of the community or kin groups and are not the property of the high-ranking. Through some degree of control over the exchange system, however, political leaders in ranked societies exercise more authority over their fellows than would be tolerated under egalitarianism.

Ranking produces a hierarchy of individuals and of personal influence, but it entails neither rigid and coercive controls nor extreme differences in wealth. These, instead, are among the attributes of social class. Social class refers to the division of a society into groups or categories within a hierarchical order in which the upper groups control a segment of the lives of those below. The basis of the power of the upper group or groups rests on their control over, or differential access to, the resources of the society. In short, who obtains a grip on agricultural lands, or tools, or the means through which goods are exchanged, or even knowledge exercises a sway over the livelihoods of others and, thereby, over their behavior and their destinies. Class is well established in human history, dating from at least the earliest temple-cities of Mesopotamia in the fifth millennium B.C. It is also pervasive, being an invariant accompaniment of literate civilizations and the state.

One of the remarkable things about class is that the elite get away with it. There have been rebellions, mutinies, and revolutions, to be sure, but one may well be amazed that these are not happening all the time. There is a common acceptance of systematized inequality that persists in the face of resentment toward it; people have a tendency to accept stratification as natural, though they may think that their own position in the system is unfair. Proudhon's cry that property is theft helped let in light upon this murky and opaque aspect of society, as did Marx's later call for the dissolution of class, but it is tenacious and invades even those societies ideologically dedicated to its liquidation.

Karl Marx attributed the emergence of class structure to the development of the idea of private property, which saw an increasing concentration of resources in fewer hands and a concomitant growth of power over others by the wealthy. This is doubtless one way in which class systems have arisen. In the mountains of northern Luzon, for example, there is a clear hierarchy of land ownership and power. Ownership, however, is not the only way in which control can be exerted over resources or over the processes of production. In ancient Mesopotamia, the earliest cities were the hubs of agricultural territories that were owned by the gods and administered by the priesthoods. Extensive private property in land did not appear until the third millennium B.C., when Babylonian rulers awarded tax-farming privileges over certain territories to loyal followers. The land was still under the crown, but part of its wealth went to these de facto owners. In ancient Peru, which had a hierarchy that went from commoners to priests to nobles to the king, private property was equally unimportant. And since the great irrigation areas produced some of the first stratified societies, it is clear that ownership of property is not the critical factor. Rather, both resources and population can be controlled through a ruling class's intervention in some critical phase in production. Thus, the priesthood of Mesopotamia had the knowledge and skills that went into the construction and operation of irrigation systems, and the ruling elite in many traditional African kingdoms held power through their control over trade.

As society grew more complex, its increasingly varied functions required coordination, and elites emerged as the managers of these new regimes. They were the entrepreneurs and regulators of caravan trade, they governed markets, and they served as heads and functionaries of the state types of government—and they are still with us. Socialist revolutions have largely eliminated private property in productive resources in many countries and thus liquidated the elite of land and capital, but they have not been able to dispense with the managerial and technocratic specialists. The Yugoslavian social theorist Milovan Djilas has argued that state socialism has bred an upper class whose positions are not based on ownership of the means of production but on their control. They include political leaders, bureaucrats, scientists, engineers, and others whose education and skills place them at the center of society. They are well paid and rewarded with amenities not available to the ordinary citizen and they live at a significantly higher standard than the mass of the populace. They also use the prerogatives of their positions and their numerous influential associations to guarantee an equally favorable status for their children. In this way, the new classes tend to become hereditary and privilege tends to become entrenched in a narrow group. The so-called "Cultural Revolution" of the 1960s in China was an attempt to fight the growth of bureaucracy and prevent the emergence of a new Mandarin class of technocrats and party cadre, processes which were seen by Mao Tse-tung as contradictory to the goals of the revolution. The technocrats and bureaucrats lack the great wealth of their capitalist peers, but they have no less power over the lives of those below them. It could even be argued that, since the technocrat backs up his economic controls with the authority of the state, his power is greater.

Class has many manifestations and varieties, for it is subject to cultural embellishment and it accommodates itself to different social systems. To take one example, the Tuareg of the southern Sahara desert, breeders of camel, sheep, and goats, are divided into three classes: nobles, vassals, and slaves. Slavery has largely ended in the region, though a scattering of cases may still be found, but the status persists in name and in lowness of hereditary rank. Slaves did much of the housekeeping of the nomadic camps and also served as herders and tenders of the flocks. Some were kept at desert oases, where they cultivated land owned by noble chiefs. Slaves were the individual property of both nobles and vassals, though they were not true chattels in the sense of American slavery. Newly taken captives could be sold in the market, but a slave's children were permanently attached to the owner's family and could only be transferred by mutual consent. Close bonds of camaraderie could develop between masters and slaves, as in the case of one Tuareg who made a practice of selling his slave to humanitarian Europeans, who would promptly manumit him; the slave and the master were splitting the proceeds. The French colonial rulers and the later African governments suppressed trading in slaves and guaranteed their freedom, but one Tuareg assured me that the real reason for the end of slavery was that it had become cheaper to hire a worker than to maintain a slave. Gross materialism, but probably true.

The tie between slave and master was personal and proprietary, but relations between vassals and nobles involved whole tribes. Thus, a noble tribe might have ties to a number of vassal tribes, which paid them tribute and loaned them military support in return for providing for their security. Nobles also guaranteed the security of caravans in their territories, though they seemed to protect the caravans mainly against themselves. The nobles were the military rulers of the desert, the vassals their soldiery, and the grazing lands the joint estates of tribes. Each of the three categories of Tuareg society was endogamous, and neither an individual nor a group could move from one level to another. There was thus a built-in rigidity in the system that caused it to collapse when the French broke the military power of the nobles. Nonetheless, the structure of class and tribe operated well in the integration of the economies of pastoralism and trade, and in maintaining relations with the agrarian sources of much of their food.

American class is of a much different order. As among the Tuareg, elite statuses are based on control of resources and exchange, but the position of the American upper class rests on ownership and management of a vast and diversified industrial apparatus. Capitalist entrepreneurs may exert direct control over labor forces numbering in the tens or even hundreds of thousands, and they exercise additional sway through their connections with government. They influence legislation through lobbying, they choose office holders through campaign financing, they control the mass media that shape public opinion, and they even go into government themselves. Doubters should merely consider the careers of Nelson Rockefeller, Averell Harriman, John Kennedy, and all our other wealthy men of state. If they are still not convinced, they should study the hold of the banks over the City of New York during the fiscal crisis of the 1970s.

However strong the hierarchy, American society is too large and its interests too ramified for class to become monolithic. In contrast to the Tuareg, or to the British for that matter, American class is relatively open and some class mobility is possible. Part of the American creed is that one gets what he deserves in life. The wealthy and the powerful got that way because they were the "best and the brightest," and the indigent are presumed to be unambitious and dull. Supposedly, anybody can be anything he wants to be if he just works hard enough. Even the working poor share the ethic, for they look down upon people on public welfare, most of whom are viewed as too lazy to work and probably dedicated to cheating the government. As for blacks, some scholars who should know better have chosen to regard them as simply the latest wave of urban migrants, following on the heels of the Irish, Jews, and Italians. We are supposed to assume that with a bit of hard work, the resident of Harlem will graduate into middle-class affluence and a split-level in the suburbs, just like grandfather; all of which ignores the intensity of American racism and the heritage of slavery. It is a cruel kind of apologetics, for it continues the American myth that makes all persons responsible for their fortunes; it is an ideological illusion in the service of the status quo, for the poor in America are made to feel guilty rather than angry.

There is some class mobility in America, but not as much as most of us want to believe. The overwhelming majority of people born into a particular class status die in that status, and a lifetime's work by even the most ambitious will usually raise them no more than a half notch. American class offers hope, however, and the progress of technology creates the impression of improvement in life's condition. Increased efficiency of production has filtered down to the worker in some betterment of real wages, and he is a consumer of things that did not exist in his father's or grandfather's day. The fact that the worker has a better car than did Henry Ford I and that he has color TV, which Ford never enjoyed, does not change the worker's position in the system of power and control. It does, however, make him more content with his lot and quicker to fight the upward mobility of those lower in the class hierarchy. The worker has not graduated into the middle class; he simply enjoys some of the things that used to be restricted to people of higher income.

Despite some reluctance to discuss the realities of class, there has been a general consensus in the United States that there are three major classes, upper, middle, and lower, each of which can be again divided into an upper and lower section. Briefly, each class has a certain type membership, sorted out by the criteria of wealth, family connections, occupation, and education. The upper upper class consists of the national elite of "old families," who have great wealth and enormous influence, and who have a sense of identity and cohesion begotten from frequent interaction and intermarriage. They go to the most exclusive private schools, and they occupy commanding positions in the economy. Their education and occupations are not critical to their status, however, for wealth and connections may render these paths to mobility superfluous. The lower uppers are also wealthy, but they are generally not quite as rich, or the money is "new," making them parvenues and climbers in the eyes of the upper uppers. The lower uppers occupy prestigious positions as corporate executives and independent businessmen or investors, and they constitute the elite of local areas. A person may be very wealthy and at the top of the social heap in Des Moines, Iowa, but this will not gain him entry to the social circles that gravitate around New York City and the European capitals.

The upper middle-class American is affluent without being rich; unlike the uppers, he has to work for a living. Upper middles are often better educated than the upper class and number in their ranks professionals, middle-level executives, proprietors of small or medium-sized businesses, higher-ranking government bureaucrats, and the like. They are comfortable, but not in a position to financially endow a similar class status for their children. They seek to provide these guarantees, instead, through educating them well. The lower middle class in America includes white-collar workers, small shopkeepers, highly skilled artisans, and others who have achieved some financial security and respectability. Like the upper middles, they are mobile and look to the education of their children as means of moving the family line into the upper middle class.

Being middle-class places one in a category of stability and respectability, lauded as the backbone of the nation, or jeered for smug mediocrity. The lower classes occasion less ambivalence of attitude. The upper lower-class consists of the great mass of blue-collar workers, lower-level service personnel, and all others who live close to the margin of survival but who have steady employment. They often belong to labor unions and make good wages, but lack of education and the behavioral repertoire of the middle class place them in the lower category. At the very bottom of the social pile are the poor, who work in the lowest-paid service occupations, or are unemployed, or only work sporadically. Their circumstances of life are the meanest in the nation, and they are not accorded the minimal respect that is felt to be a workman's due. Most black Americans fall into this category or into the upper lower class despite the marginal, inflated, and overpublicized gains of recent years.

The six-part hierarchy of American class was first noted by novelists such as Sinclair Lewis and later found lodged in the system of social perceptions of a Massachusetts city studied by the anthropologist W. Lloyd Warner. The categories are not a sociologist's abstraction but part of the popular model of society that people carry around in their heads. The chief criterion of class is patently wealth, for it conditions all the other characteristics. Education is the principal path to mobility in this country, but it costs money; its expenses are within the range of middle-class incomes but may constitute a great burden to the lower classes. Education, we have noted, is not critical to upper-class status, and schools often serve the function of firming up the manners appropriate to the station or widening one's contacts with other upper-class members. Colleges like Princeton serve this purpose, but the Ivy League is no longer the exclusive domain of the rich; more strategic to maintaining status would be a good New England prep school. Occupation is an important avenue of mobility, for it can generate respect as well as income, but it is clearly a variable of wealth, family, and education. The best and most remunerative jobs usually require a college background; moreover, the connections provided by a wealthy family have never been known to hurt one's chances in life. The nebulous category of "family" is, as we have said, based on the existence of a hereditary aristocracy, located mainly in and near the cities of the East. There is a good deal of social cachet in having a notable name, but even more important is the network of friends, relatives, and associates cultivated and utilized by the rich. It is through these connections that influence is wielded and extended, and it is through them that high position and added wealth may be obtained. But behind family is money, the ultimate key to privilege. Others may find roles at the fringes of power, as consultants or advisors, but the center of the system is the yawning and deep abyss of wealth and power that divides our society.

American classes show a strong endogamic tendency, expressed in a pattern in which most people would like to marry up in the hierarchy, but most also do not want to marry down. Interclass marriages are frequent, but they are usually between people in adjacent positions in the hierarchy. If the son of the upper-class banker marries the daughter of the upper-middle lawyer, it remains an acceptable union, but if he weds a girl from an impoverished, uneducated family, then the marriage is considered a social disaster. The family can take some comfort in the fact that, since one gets most of his class status through the father, the children of the union will belong to the upper class. The same principle makes a down-marriage of a woman a greater social misfortune, for unless the upper-class family intervenes to alter the situation, the children will take a lower status. In all of American marital preferences, the taboo against racial intermarriage is the strongest, though the ban is no longer legally enforceable anywhere in the United States. Interracial unions are more frequent today than in the past, but they still constitute only a tiny fraction of all marriages. Race is made into a rigidified and frozen status by forcing each group back upon itself in marriage; it is this kind of radical separation that has led some writers to regard American races as "castes" of a sort.

Properly speaking, the full complex of attitudes, beliefs, and activities that comprise caste are found only in India, although some of the processes inherent in the institution are far more general. Indian caste is based upon the recognition and maintenance of a rigid social hierarchy of caste groups, into which one is born, must marry, and will die. Castes, like class, are found in a stratified order, but whereas class is based on distinctions of control over resources, castes are occupational groupings and more narrowly conceived than class. Moreover, while class may permit some intermarriage, Indian castes are more strictly endogamic. Finally, the social distinctions between castes are also religious distinctions, connecting caste with Hindu doctrine and separating the groups with ritual and symbolic distance.

The institution of caste is weakening today under the pressure of urbanization, industrialization, and egalitarian government policies, and most of the occupations of modern industrial India fall outside its framework. In the past, however, and still in rural districts now, all occupations were the prerogatives of certain castes. There were, and are, castes of sweepers, agriculturalists, priests, goldsmiths, barbers, tailors, and so forth, numbering in the hundreds, and below the level of caste are untouchable groups that handle bodies and skins, and other chores too polluting for a caste Hindu. At the top of the hierarchy are the Brahmins, who in some cases are wealthy landowners or entrepreneurs, but who may also be mendicant priests or cooks. There is a rough congruence between caste and class in modern India, for the two systems exist side by side. Most members of the wealthy and powerful upper class are also members of high-ranking castes, and most low-ranking caste members are poor, but there is no neat overlap and India has both rich untouchables and Brahmin paupers.

The castes depend on each other for their specialized products and services, which in the city are recompensed with money, but in the countryside are exchanged through the *jajmani* system. In the agrarian villages, there may be no more than a half dozen to a dozen castes in residence, all of which carry out some work necessary to the totality of village life. Repayment for goods and services is done through a system of reciprocity, by which people perform work for the farmer throughout the year and are rewarded at harvest time with a traditionally set portion of grain. In the same way, the carpenter and the barber may exchange services with no money passing hands, and all the people of the village are bound together, and to each other, by traditional obligations and rights. The *jajmani* system thus helps to seal over the major cleavages of Indian society and to maintain the peace within the close confines of village life.

Individual rank is fixed by the rank of one's caste, and the only path to mobility is through the acquisition of wealth within the class order or the improvement of the status of one's entire caste. A person cannot change castes, and close scrutiny of people's antecedents by others does much to inhibit attempts to do so. One cannot escape caste through marriage, either, for caste endogamy is the rule except in the case of a marriage between subcastes, in which a man is permitted to take a woman from a group immediately below his own. This practice, called "hypergamy" (up-marriage of the woman; down-marriage is called "hypogamy") is reminiscent of patterns of interclass marriage in the United States.

One of the more striking features of caste is the concept of pollution and the related observance of ritual separation between castes. Pollution involves either the spiritual defilement of sacred people and objects through their contact with the mundane, or the creation of a state of danger through mixing incompatible things. Pollution underlies the Christian practice of barring a woman from church worship until forty days after the birth of a child—a custom now moribund—or the Jewish institution of the mikvah, or ritual bath, which is taken after menstruation or other "contamination." Keeping clear of polluting objects and people is a major preoccupation in India. A man can be contaminated by sexual contact with a lower-caste woman, and a woman is even more defiled by copulation with a lower-caste man. Food is a common source of contamination, and one cannot accept cooked food from a person of lower caste or eat with him. Commensality, or eating together, is an almost universal symbol of solidarity between people, and to break bread with one another is to declare oneness. This is what underlay one of the more curious events of the integration movement in the American South. When black youths demanded service at lunch counters, the owners complied, but only after they had taken out all the seats. To stand next to each other while eating is not quite the same as sharing a meal while seated. Pollution creates anomalous situations in India too. Henry Orenstein reported that in the village he studied the Brahmins took their water from the upstream end of the village, whereas the untouchables filled their containers downstream. Yet, just upstream from the village was another village, in which the lower-caste groups used the downstream end of the village. That the

Brahmins could be contaminated by the other village did not matter, for the separation and distance served to maintain the social hierarchy in one village at a time. By the same reasoning, Africans were served in southern hotels and restaurants long before American blacks were.

Stratification, whether by caste or class, is the invariant accompaniment of the state, for inequality and differences of power are central to political process in complex societies. In simple groups, however, classlessness is commonly found with weakly developed leadership, or none at all. We have seen that among the Shoshoni there were no chiefs, except for the leaders of occasional group endeavors. The function of leadership anywhere is to take part in the formulation of group goals and to direct their implementation; but where the main goals are the pursuit of subsistence by individuals acting singly, there is no cause around which leadership can function. Where there are no clearly delineated groups or group boundaries, potential leadership would lack a subject matter to which it might become attached. Among the equally egalitarian Mundurucú, however, villages are clear-cut, stable social and political units, and well-defined group purposes are a part of the cooperative patterns of warfare and hunting. Each village has a chief, who ideally inherits the office by patrilineal descent; but in keeping with the subdued and even tone of Mundurucú social relations, his authority is subtle and muted. The chief does not issue orders. He neither exhorts people to one or another effort, nor does he formulate plans for joint activity. His principal outward function is to represent the village to outsiders, especially strangers, such as Brazilian traders. Aside from this, he maintains influence by conducting himself with calm and dignity. He takes an active part in the joint planning and discussions that go on in the men's house, but he speaks little until he sees the conversation drift toward a consensus; he then steps in to firm up the agreement and press for unanimity. The chief is the first among equals. His position is much like that of the wily chairperson of a committee or an academic department, who learns early that he has no real power and must be a manager of consensus, a gentle helmsman of discourse.

In his essays on conflict, Georg Simmel wrote that two groups in opposition to each other tend to develop the same forms of leadership as means of mutual coping. This principle can be seen at work throughout the history of white contact with the American Indian, for the need to organize against the European threat or to arrive at agreements with the invaders promoted the development of political institutions and leadership. Thus, some of the Shoshoni of Nevada began to raid wagon trains through their country in the 1850s and 1860s, and the need for coordination of the military effort attracted people to the leadership of certain new chiefs, renowned for their ability as warriors. When the Shoshoni made peace with the whites, the government commissioners sought out chiefs to sign the treaty documents with an X. When they could not find any chiefs, they named them. In this way, millions of acres were ceded to the whites by Indians who did not really know what they were signing, and who represented people who did not even know of them.

Warfare, whether with the whites or with other native groups, did much to strengthen patterns of chieftaincy and widen the size and range of the political unit. The mounted bison hunters of the Great Plains had strong chiefs who led their people in the almost continuous warfare that racked the region. The chiefs were advised by formally constituted tribal councils and their roles supplemented by police and military societies. Among the police-society functions was the forcible restraint of individual buffalo hunting. A lone hunter might kill one or two animals, but in the process he could frighten the herd away, depriving his fellows of the kill. Buffaloes, for this reason, were only hunted collectively, and the violator could be punished by beating, killing his horse, or even ostracism. Collective efforts were, therefore, closely related to the development of collective sanctions, which are the essence of a system of law. Military activity was the principal source of one of the most evolved polities north of Mexico, the League of the Iroquois. The League consisted of six tribes— the Mohawk, Oneida, Onondaga, Cayuga, Seneca, and Tuscarora—inhabiting central and western New York State and adjoining parts of Canada and Pennsylvania. They spoke a common language and were interconnected by membership in matrilineal clans that bridged tribal lines, becoming truly international kin units. The tribes of the League maintained a central council composed of tribal representatives and were permanent allies in both defense and offense. They were expanding rapidly in the northeast at the time of the entry of the Europeans, and their warriors were important military factors in the colonial struggle between the French and the English.

Most of the tribes mentioned thus far had no central political institutions, unlike the Iroquois, and consisted of aggregations of local units— villages or nomadic bands—united by common language and culture and related in a common marriage network. With the evolution of technology and the expansion of human productivity, population increase created pressure on resources, which, in turn, encouraged warfare and the development of political ties that transcended locality, uniting the people of entire districts. The resultant "chieftaincies" heralded the appearance of strong institutions of leadership and hierarchies of authority that linked kin and locality to the political center. The apical figures in these hierarchies reinforced their authority through redistributive mechanisms or some other form of intervention in the economic life. They thus became progressively separated from the rest of the populace by differences of power, if not of wealth. Such chieftaincies were found in the densely populated Amazon shore and Brazilian littoral in precontact times, they were present among Burmese hill groups and they were common in sub-Saharan Africa. Chieftaincies were transitional to the development of a political form that first emerged over five-thousand years ago in the Near East and has grown stronger with each century. This is the state, the Leviathan of Thomas Hobbes, the City of Man of Saint Augustine, and the absolute master of its domains.

The state has been the subject of political thought since man first became interested in studying himself. It presents the anomaly of the cession of freedom and the acceptance of inequality and obedience by its subjects, and it is wrapped in a mystique because the complexities of most states render them unintelligible to their citizenry. The opacity, to use Marx's description of the mysteries of power, numbs our comprehension while exciting our curiosity; it is another peculiar institution. Lewis Henry Morgan attempted to distinguish primitive societies from states by locating the basis of membership in the former in institutions of kinship, whereas the latter were seen as founded upon territoriality. This distinction is acceptable if it is remembered that kinship and territoriality are not mutually exclusive. Territorial propinquity is at the root of much of kinship and all groups must occupy a piece of landscape. In the same way, kinship continues into state forms of government and may even be the basis for the transmission of power, as in the inherited crowns and titles of Europe. The issue between the two criteria rests on their basic premises. In a simple, nonstate society, one is a member of the group and subject to its ways if he was born into it and if his network of kinship lies within it. To the contrary, one is subject to the laws of a state by simple virtue of being within its boundaries, and in most cases one may become a subject of a state without regard to prior affiliations or kin ties. Simple societies are almost always culturally and linguistically homogeneous, but the boundaries of states often encompass people of separate culture and language. This heterogeneity may be an outcome of migrations into a realm, it may be the upshot of trade, or it may result from the conquest by the state of alien peoples. Whatever the reasons, ethnic and linguistic heterogeneity contributes to the complexity of a unit already transected by class and specialization. The state also depersonalizes and universalizes the relation between person and polity. In this sense, it parallels and is one with the shift from status to contract, *Gemeinschaft* to *Gesellschaft*, egalitarianism to stratification.

Most writers on the state have also cited central government as a defining criterion, adding that this center is recognized by the populace to have the legitimate right of forceful coercion over its subjects. The exercise of coercive sanctions against violators of norms is a central element in the development of full-blown legal systems out of the simple rule of custom. It is also an ever-present attribute of the state, for the use or threat of force to compel compliance to a broad range of rules is seldom found in simple societies. The Mundurucú kill sorcerers, as do many other peoples, and the Plains Indians used violence against infractors of the communal hunt, but these are highly specific offenses and the sanctions are not taken by a formally constituted governmental body.

Nowadays laws are usually obeyed by people out of force of habit, deference to others, good citizenship, and all the informal mechanisms of social control that have been discussed. People also tend to look upon laws as just, insofar as they were imposed by a governmental body that in their opinion has the right to rule. Underlying this voluntary compliance, however, is the sure knowledge that if the law is not obeyed, agents of government will apprehend the violator, physically and forcefully, and suspend his liberties. It may not be in the forefront of our minds as we watch our speedometers or file our tax returns, but it is a leitmotif of social life, one of its premises, and a background refrain to our public behavior. The remarkable thing is that we generally accept this coercion as proper, much as we may dislike its application to ourselves. "If you don't like the laws, then go to work to change them," was a common motto of conservatives during the turbulent 1960s, the implication being clear that in the meantime one should obey those laws, no matter how unjust.

The notion of "legitimacy" of rule has loomed large in anthropological writings. It was central to the political theories of Max Weber and a key element in the work of British anthropologists writing on African kingdoms. In Weber's case, I suspect that the emphasis comes out of the Hegelian idea that German freedom would be found in a unified German nation; in the British instance, the national preoccupation with sovereignty and the crown contributed to the idea. Legitimacy infers a set of values or beliefs that endows a rule with rightness. It can come from a sense that it flows from a democratic electorate, as in this country; it may derive from a belief that the reign is divinely recognized, as in monarchical France; it can issue from a regime's position as the heirs of a revolution, as in Mexico and the Soviet Union; or it may be based upon a belief that the rulers are divine, as in ancient Egypt and Peru.

One can grant that authority and legitimacy go together without seeing legitimacy as primary and as a prerequisite to authority. If we have learned one thing in the behavioral sciences, it is that people will generally tend to readjust their attitudes and values to reach congruence with the inevitable or the unavoidable. Part of this process involves "identification with the aggressor," the mechanism that sees the young boy incorporating the values of the threatening father, or concentration-camp inmates adopting the perspectives of their warders. It may seem a craven gambit, but it protects the individual while at the same time reducing a troublesome dissonance between value and reality. Much of legitimacy is begotten by the same process, and, concomitantly, legitimacy may vanish in the wind as soon as the threat of sanction is lifted. Kwame Nkrumah's position as Ghanaian head of state rested upon his identity as father of his country, but a military coup removed him with barely a ripple of protest. The army then became the legitimate governing authority, a position it enjoyed because it already had the monopoly on force. Behind legitimacy there is usually a mailed fist.

One of the commonest forms of legitimation is resort to religion. This is central to the less-evolved states of traditional Africa, Mexico, and South America, but it can also be found in so thoroughly secular a society as our own. "In God We Trust" is emblazoned across our money, and we even pledge allegiance to "one nation under God." These are not archaic holdovers from our early history, for the insertion of God into the pledge of allegiance was done in 1954, one of the few remaining traces of the Eisenhower administration. The state is also swathed in a religious-type mysticism, most neatly expressed in the ways we use and treat the flag. One should never let the flag touch the ground, and it can only be disposed of by burning—though it is sacrilegious to burn it at an antiwar demonstration. You can wear the flag as a shoulder patch, but you cannot use it as a pants patch. Being religious and being patriotic go hand in hand. God watches over us in war and he helps us to victory. Beyond these expressions, there is a cult of the state as a body divorced from one government or another and having a life and powers that transcend those of its subjects. It is a part of contemporary secular religion, to which our discussion of politics has now taken us.

VIII

Religion

Amidst the growing secularism of our time, religion remains an almost universal attribute of cultures, though its expressions sometimes defy classification. At the same time that attendance at established churches continues its progressive decline, there has been a burgeoning of a bewildering variety of movements and phenomena that, for lack of a better term, we label as religion. All of the traditional churches persist, and Americans by the millions are still sorted out as Roman Catholics, Episcopalians, Baptists, Orthodox Jews, Presbyterians, or whatever. But we also have a variety of Asian religions, especially those influenced by Hinduism, and the Guru Maharaj Ji movement alone claims thousands of adherents. There are also a number of West African derived churches in the black areas of our cities, spiritualist congregations practicing possession and trance, rattlesnake-handling cults in the mountains of the southeast United States, and occasional millenarian movements that foresee the imminent end of the world. There are also religions that deal neither with gods nor with spirits, such as the Ethical Culture Society and the Uni-

158

tarian Church, which are founded upon ideals of social morality. All of them, people will agree, are religions, but the same people are usually unable to say what they have in common that makes them so. Religion remains an enigma.

It is this enigmatic nature of religion, its concern with the ineluctable, the ineffable, and the transcendent, that at once is its distinguishing characteristic and the principal obstacle to tidy definitions. Popular opinion may hold it to be centered on a belief in God, but this kind of ethnocentrism would immediately eliminate Confucianism, as well as a host of religions that infest the world with minor spirits, but not with powerful gods. Religion is indeed one of the more active areas of ethnocentric thought, for people who have no trouble believing in virgin birth will deride as ridiculous alien creeds that place no greater strain upon the imagination. Early explorers, finding that God had somehow forgotten to appear before peoples of the non-Western world in approved Judeo-Christian revelation, were wont to describe their new discoveries as "pagan," "godless," and "heathens." Certain European theologian-anthropologists of the 1920s and 1930s tried to explain away the divine oversight by claiming that there had been a primeval revelation to all peoples, which had become overlaid by new beliefs and other forms of error. Their enterprise smacked of Fielding's Parson Thwackum in *Tom Jones:* "When I mention religion, I mean the Christian religion; and not only the Christian religion, but the Protestant religion; and not only the Protestant religion, but the Church of England."

The scope of religion becomes broadened when the definition is expanded to belief in the supernatural, but this meaning falters on two points. First, there are many religions that do not involve belief in gods, spirits, the afterlife, and all the other phenomena lumped under the term "supernatural." And second, the category of supernatural implies that we have a good understanding of what is "natural." The same problem arises when we say that an idea is religious if it cannot be subjected to scientific proof, for this would instantly clutter up religion with every untested, undemonstrated notion that a society ever produced; it would include almost all the society's thought on practically everything. Actually, the realm of what we take to be natural is as much a cultural product as is the supernatural; indeed, they are counterposed to and define each other. Since we may well be approaching the religious life of other societies with our own culture's definitions of nature and supernature, we are in danger of imposing an alien category on the beliefs and actions of others. Most Europeans and Americans do this constantly, in the happy but erroneous certainty that their concept of nature is not only relatively true but absolutely true. They believe that they are guided by science and not by the dictates of a clergy, but they forget that they accept the infallibility of science with as much confidence as most Catholics accord the doctrinal infallibility of the Pope. It may be agreed that we are on much firmer ground when we believe in what scientists say, but the attitudes of faith in both are much alike. Perhaps what is really interesting is the tendency simply to believe.

Religion has long been the subject of scholarly speculation and scientific investigation, for it most tantalizes exactly those people who do not subscribe to it. Lewis Henry Morgan, a good, solid Rochester, New York lawyer, was a nominal Presbyterian, despite his influence on Marx and Engels, and he dismissed most primitive religious belief as "grotesque and to some extent unintelligible." William James was more the rationalist, but the American psychologist's studies of religion led him to postulate a "will to believe"—which is not much of an explanation of why people believe. Anthropologists turned to the subject since the beginnings of the discipline, and all saw the search for a least-common denominator, the very core and nub, of religious experience to be their major chore. In looking for the universal quality of religion, they inevitably were also inquiring into its origins in human history.

The pioneer English anthropologist Edward Tylor found the center and origin of religion to lie in what he termed "animism," or the belief in personalized, often anthropomorphized (modeled on man), spirits. These could include souls, ghosts, angels, gods, demons, or any other incorporeal and invisible creature. The origins of such beliefs, Tylor thought, could probably be found in the life experiences of early man. The idea of a detachable and bodyless part of the self called a soul could have arisen from observing one's reflection in a still pool of water or attributing some special life to one's shadow. This seemed a farfetched derivation to me until I found that the Mundurucú word for shadow or reflection was also the word for soul. A bit of asking, however, revealed that the Mundurucú believe their souls to lie within the spinal column, between the shoulder blades, and not in mirrors or on the ground; the people were not identifying the two as the same, but speaking in metaphor. We do exactly the same when we use the word "shade" for soul; one should never confuse word and reality. A belief in the soul could also have arisen, reasoned Tylor, from vivid and lifelike dreams in which the dreamer seemed to leave his sleeping body and go to distant places where he had strange experiences. Since images of the dead are common in dreaming, early man could also have developed the notion that the soul outlived the body and survived after death. Becoming items of belief, ghosts, souls, and spirits could then provide convenient ways of explaining the otherwise inexplicable.

Tylor's theory has been widely found wanting for its overintellectualization of religion. He first made the mistake of thinking that the chief function of religion is to explain things, and he then proceeded to assume that his own chain of reasoning would be the same as primitive man's. Religion, however, is more than belief. It consists also of activity—physical and verbal events that are found in rite and worship—and these acts cannot be looked on as a simple playing out of beliefs. Moreover, Tylor's personal attitude toward religion was appropriate to a Victorian intellectual and scientist. He looked upon it as an error whose highest expression was Christianity, missing much of its emotional flavor. Religion does more than satisfy curiosity. It stirs our minds with an elaborate imagery of man's condition and fate, it gives comfort and solace, it allays anxieties, it can move to frenzy; it can be a very deeply emotional affair.

There is no doubt that religion tries to explain much, but, significantly, no religion tries to explain everything. There are many primitive societies in which religion makes only passing reference to cosmic phenomena, such as the heavenly bodies, and in which the explanatory function has meaning only in its reference to some other preoccupation, such as the cure of illness. The role of the Judeo-Christian tradition as a popular form of science has been in decline since the time of Copernicus. Many thought that Darwin's writings on evolution would put an end to religion. Biblical fundamentalism, however, still holds sway over the minds of millions, who believe that every word of scripture is God's truth. It is true that not too many educated people take the Book of Genesis seriously anymore, but those who foresaw religion's demise also failed to take account of the resiliency of the theologians, who do not take Genesis literally anymore either. Evolutionary process has replaced divine creation, but it has not replaced religion, which now sees metaphor and symbolism where it used to see the literal and absolute word of God.

One of the early critics of Tylor was R. R. Marrett, who found that animism did not cover the spectrum of truly basic and pervasive religious phenomena, for it omitted reference to supernatural powers. He coined the term "animatism" to refer to belief in impersonalized, disembodied, and transferable forces that may become infused in people, animals, or objects. The ethnographic prototype of such power is the Melanesian and Oceanian concept of mana. A great chief's person may become imbued with mana, making contact with him dangerous to commoners. Anybody who infringes on the halo of space surrounding one of the powerful must reckon not only with his temporal powers but with his supernatural ones too. The chief's person becomes taboo, meaning either forbidden or to be handled only with special care and formality, and people must neither come too close to him nor place their heads at a higher level than his. Gardens are protected from thieves by special spells that place a taboo on their crops, and misfortune or illness is believed to be the lot of the hapless violator. The North American Indians had well developed animatism, as well as animism. The medicine bundles of the Plains Indians contained a number of objects that were believed to be endowed with powers that would protect their owners. Given the focus of Western religions on gods, souls, and the like, the notion of animatism is rather unfamiliar to us, but Catholics will recognize it in the impersonal force latent in holy water or in a relic splinter from the true cross (there are enough such pieces of the true cross in Europe alone to crucify the population of Paris). Jews also will see an element of animatism in the elaborate culinary prescriptions of their religion and the fear of violation of the Ark. Just as there are aspects of animatism in essentially animistic religions, so is also the reverse possible. These are not, then, exclusive categories, and both can be found intertwined with each other to form a single system of belief.

Marrett's minimal definition of religion had the merit of calling attention to one of its main attributes, the sense of awe and power that not only accompanies mana but may be found in attitudes toward the spirit world as well. These were the qualities that Durkheim developed into a theory of religion. Emile Durkheim, in his classic *The Elementary Forms of the Religious Life* (1912), reviewed the various theories on the roots of religion and found them all wanting. Where other scholars focused attention on the objects of religion, he considered instead the subjects of the experience. He reasoned logically enough that there was nothing so remarkable in a dream or reflection that it should generate religious awe, nor were most natural features and phenomena that have become the objects of veneration sufficiently striking or different to evoke such sentiments. In some cultures, stars may be supernaturally important, but not in others, and though some societies may wrap a whole cosmology around the movement of the sun and moon, others might just accept moonrise and sunset as being as natural and ordinary as air.

If the characteristics of the beliefs did not account for religion to Durkheim, then the actions and attitudes of believing did. The things of religion have an almost infinite variety, but the stance of the believer shows greater uniformity. People react toward certain classes of phenomena, activities, objects, and people with a sense of awe, even fear. They are viewed as being different and removed from everyday reality and seen to have an otherness and transcendence that mark them as being of an order different from everyday experience. Durkheim referred to this category of life as the realm of the "sacred," as opposed to the "profane," or mundane, world. Ordinary mortals could deal with the sacred, but only under very special conditions, using diplomacy, formality, and care. On the contrary, the profane world could be handled in a pragmatic and matter-of-fact way, for it was nothing more than the here-and-now realm of everyday life. This division of the experienced world into the sacred and the profane was also the first form of classification, according to Durkheim, and the origin of the dualism that has been a characteristic

of human thought since then. Durkheim thus bypassed all the other binary
divisions that could produce dualistic thought, for he was unswerving in
his adherence to purely sociological explanations.

What is it, then, that makes some things sacred and others profane?
A Mundurucú once showed me, with great solemnity, a five-holed flute
that was used only in certain now defunct ceremonies. When I asked him
to play some of the music of the old rites, he explained that the spirits
would become angry if the flutes were used outside the ceremony. And
when I pointed out to him that the flute was exactly the same as one used
for recreational purposes, he assured me that they just looked the same.
To have played the instrument for me would have been a sacrilege, which,
like pollution, occurs when one mixes up sacred and profane things. In
the same way, a European does not wash his hands in holy water or get
drunk on sacramental wine. Sacred objects may look just like profane
ones, and the attachment of awe and otherness to them is arbitrary. This
should not bother us much, for all meaning is arbitrary and emerges from
the minds and cultures of men rather than from any inherent properties
of the things to which meaning is attached.

Although arbitrary, religious meanings are not random; they make
sense, but only relative to the rest of the culture. Durkheim recognized
this, and after his review of the possible sources of religious sentiments,
he came by a process of reduction to the theory that the sense of the
sacred is generated by human societies. What power is it that we apprehend, however vaguely, in religion that is at once constraining upon our
behavior, remote, and estranged from ordinary experience, but immanent
within it? To Durkheim, only society can be the source of sacredness, and
only society can meet its criteria. Society is within us and among us, but
it is more than anyone of us, or all of us taken together, for it transcends
individuals, outlives them, and has its own imperatives. It also has a
controlling power over our actions and it invades our very sense of identity, processes that humans intuit but cannot objectify. Society thus transcends life, suffuses consciousness, and constrains people, which are also
the main qualities of the sacred. Religion, then, is born of social life, but,
Durkheim added, it also expresses it.

Religious sentiments are born of group life, and it follows that beliefs and rites will, at least in part, reflect the systems of groups and
roles of social units. Durkheim devoted much of his volume on religion
to demonstrating this proposition. Using the Australian aborigines as his
model, he showed that their entire totemic religion was a guide to the
system of localities and kin groups of the native societies. Totemism was
a set of beliefs, but it was also a system of social classification that marked
off every point of social differentiation with appropriate ideas and observances. In much the same way, one can see in a survey of ancient

civilizations that the development of monotheism and the emergence of the centrally governed state went hand in hand. The functions of such expression appear to be twofold. First, by making the major divisions of society into sacred entities, religion reinforces them, adding supernatural and mystical support to society's component units. The totemic clan is more than an overgrown family, it is a communion of believers, a church. The group becomes infused with the awe of the sacred, and the loyalty and devotion of its members is thereby secured. Although this sense of congregational unity is less pronounced in the monotheistic state, the centralization of deity and the omnipotence of the high god bolster and rationalize the centrality and power of the state. In this way, the temporal order appears to the subjects as a replication of the divine order.

The other function of religion, as a projection of social relations, is that it allows those processes of life that are ill comprehended, dimly perceived, barely intuited, and difficult to grasp to be thought about and communicated to others. It is a way of expressing the ineffable and objectifying what is abstract. We thus render the powers and threats of life, the "wee things that go bump in the night," into concepts that we can understand and entities that can be manipulated. Durkheim saw religion as social life written in symbolic language, a metaphorical system of ideas and activities. In a sense, religion is an art form, for it provides an outlet for emotions that cannot be released in ordinary ways. Like poetry and music, it is a nonlinear and elliptical way of saying things that ordinary language cannot communicate. One can go beyond Durkheim's emphasis on social things to say that religion is the poetry of life's loyalties, hopes, afflictions, fears, and uncertainties, as well as a kind of sociological language. It is appropriate, then, that religion should be everywhere so thoroughly integrated with art forms. Sacred music is an almost invariant companion of religion, and painting and sculpture principal means of conveying its major themes. Religion, like art, picks up where ordinary means of comprehension and communication fail.

A constant theme of the French psychology of Durkheim's time was its discovery that the behavior of people in crowds differed from their ordinary deportment. A mob, no matter how inchoate, can produce a unity and fervor of purpose that its component individuals would not ordinarily exhibit, and can impel people to acts that they would not otherwise undertake. Durkheim, we have seen, saw religion to arise from society, but he further believed that its sentiments of awe, excitation, and exaltation would emerge from group participation and thus had an element of crowd behavior. In this way, also, religious sentiments become fixed upon those groups within which the emotions had been stirred, which contributes toward the endowment of the group with sacred qualities. For these reasons, Durkheim saw religion to be an essentially social phenomenon and would not admit private or secret acts such as magic or sorcery under its rubric. Religions are congregations of believers; they are churches in the truest sense of the word.

The collective aspect of religion is eloquently expressed in the physical institution of the church in our own society and the requirement that the principal forms of worship be conducted in groups. There is a manifest purpose for this in sacramental religions, but there are many religions in which the service consists of no more than a sermon or exhortation and prayers. In Islam, the daily round of prayers can be said anywhere, but on Friday, the Sabbath, it is expected that the prayers will be said en masse at a mosque. Similarly, most Americans do not feel that they can fulfill their religious duties by watching a television preacher, and the drive-in churches that flourish by day in California drive-in movies are regarded as but one more instance of the religious eccentricity of what Woody Allen calls "Munchkinland." The group nature of religious devotion is important to Durkheim's functionalist view of religion, which he believed to be one of the most profoundly unifying forces of society. Collective worship draws people together in common devotion and increases the unity and sense of purpose of the communicants. Since the group and the congregation either overlap or are the same, the observances of the church directly express and reinforce the identity and unity of the group. Religion arises from society but then serves to perpetuate it, in circular fashion. Durkheim, then, wrote that people who pray together stay together, but he added that people who stay together pray together.

Bronislaw Malinowski's view of religion had a somewhat psychological slant, for he saw it as man's principal means of coping with anxiety. He noted, for example, that Trobriand Islanders fished in lagoons in a matter-of-fact way, with no special observances, but that deep-sea fishing entailed elaborate magical preparations to assure success and safety. Malinowski was on the right track, but he did not follow it far enough, and much of his psychologizing remained amateurish and slipshod. Religion is certainly a way of coping with fear and uncertainty, but we must recall our remarks on the human situation to appreciate the depths of these anxieties. Man is made free and dominant by his intelligence, but he also labors under certain burdens imposed by it; inherent in his self-awareness and rationality is a lonely terror. Despite the aphorism that elephants never forget, there is no question that man's memory far surpasses that of any other animal, for it is at once the repository of the knowledge by which we survive and a storehouse of much that has happened to us. Among the things stored in the mind are all the dangers, threats, pains, and calamities that have befallen us, and many that have not, but of which we have heard. And what is not imbedded in the active and conscious memory can usually be found below the surface in the unconscious mind.

Experiences so traumatic or socially unacceptable as to warrant repression do not simply lie latent, undisturbed, and undisturbing in the unconscious, for they break through in dreams, slips of the tongue, behavioral aberrations, fears displaced onto other objects, and generalized anxiety. Our memories, both conscious and unconscious, dispose us to anxieties, which are added to and compounded by the knowledge we have of disasters beyond our immediate experience. Religion, then, is not simply a way of coping with one danger or another, but a way of facing a dangerous existence.

When foreknowledge and rough prediction are added to man's memory, it becomes remarkable that our species can take the strain—some, of course, cannot. One fact that we can predict for sure is that we will die, which, as has been noted in Chapter 2, produces a kind of existential fear. Most religions take specific account of the dread of death by depicting an afterlife to which the immortal soul travels. Afterlives are often pleasant places. Popular Moslem opinion inhabits the afterworld with dancing girls, and the Mundurucú soul is said to travel to a land where each person does what he enjoyed most while alive. In the same way, Christians have a heaven, which is supposed to be a pleasurable place, but because most of life's pleasures are frowned upon by most Christians, it is hard to say what one does there. But Christians also have a hell, which has been interpreted as either a place of fire and brimstone or an exclusion from the presence of God, and we might well ask what comfort this notion could possibly give the average sinner. The answer is simple: even hell is preferable to the total extinction and elimination of consciousness and identity. Our very category of "death" implies an altered state of existence and is therefore a kinder word than "nonlife," or "nonexistence." Religion denies the end of life and makes it palatable to the survivors; it gives a triumph of the imagination over an old enemy and constant companion. In the words of First Corinthians: "Oh death, where is thy sting? Oh grave, where is thy victory?"

Death is a premise of life and the subject of all man's immortality projects, whether they be belief in paradise, child rearing, the Oedipal desire to be one's own father by mating with the mother, or the tenacity of our clutch on the stable and familiar symbols of culture as life draws to a close. Death also is a constant reminder of the finite limits of life and our persons, a limitation that may conjure up the opposed concept of infinitude, making appropriate the modern theological opinion that religion is founded upon man's contemplation of the infinite. One might alter the tenet, however, to say that it is preoccupation with finitude and an unarticulated wish to return to the expansiveness and indivision of our early infancy that generates the sense of the infinite. Religion is always born of human experience. It is grounded in a reality that is human, not divine, and even the most chimerical of its beliefs, as Durkheim told us, has a reality that derives from the fact that they influence social life. It is a good bet that there is neither heaven nor hell, but to the extent that a belief in these places influences behavior, perhaps they might just as well exist. Voltaire had reached the same conclusion when he said that if God did not exist, then man would have had to invent him. Man did.

Sigmund Freud's contribution to the study of religion found its origins in the extirpation of guilt for the primal crime of parricide. The course of human culture since that time has seen, Freud thought, a continual and normal recurrence of the parricidal urge in the Oedipal episode, along with its repression and the identification of the son with his father. Instead of physically ingesting the father's powers through cannibalism, the boy adopts the father's attributes, including the rules and values he bears. This process is important in the enculturation of the child, and it is also a key to the development of the superego, or conscience, and the means whereby public duty becomes individual compulsion. Both the superego and the ego, that part of the psyche that copes with reality, act as repressive agents, thrusting into the unconscious the unspeakable and the unthinkable. But, as we have seen, the repressed always revisits us, and its pressures are relieved by its expressions in the veiled language of the dream, and by its reliving in the compulsive act. The repressed works its way through culture too, providing reenactment and catharsis, or purgation, of the traumata of life. Just as people project their private fantasies and fears onto other people and objects, so also are some of the symbols of culture public fantasies of a sort. Religion, in the Freudian world view, is a system of projections of unconscious, repressed experiences that are characteristic of a people; they are expressions of the wishes of the soul.

There is much more going on in religion than just psychological processes, for it functions in social control and cohesion, it has economic roles, and it is expressive of conscious aspiration and perception as well as of repressed impulse and experience. But the hidden activity of the mind permeates and colors all of these eminently practical uses. Indeed, the work of the mind is most evident in exactly those areas that seem least responsive to utilitarian ends, such as mythology. Most peoples have a body of myths, a collection of sacred or semisacred stories from an imagined remote past, which are handed down by word of mouth or in writing. The story of Oedipus, the Greek king who unknowingly killed his father and married his mother, came down to us in the form of a play by Sophocles, but it originated much earlier in Greek mythology. I discovered a similar story among the Brazilian Mundurucú, the full text of of which is published in my book *Mundurucú Religion*, but which I will briefly recapitulate. There was once a man called Wakörömpö, who was so ugly that he ran away to the forest in shame. The Sun—that is, the spirit of the sun—took pity on him, put him into his wife's uterus, and when he was reborn molded him into a strikingly handsome man. He went back to his village, where an envious man named Karuetaouibö wheedled from him the secret of his transformation. Karuetaouibö tried to repeat the same events, but copulated with Sun's wife, whereas Wakörömpö had not. The angry Sun placed him in the wife's uterus but, when he was reborn, warped and twisted his features into grotesqueness. When he went back to his village, Wakörömpö sang to him a song that said "you were curious for your mother's vagina." Later, the two men were killed by an enemy war party and their heads taken as trophies. The heads rose toward the sky one day and their captors shot arrows at them. Wakörömpö's head escaped injury, but that of Karuetaouibö had its eyes put out. The latter is, of course, the punishment that the Fates had inflicted upon Oedipus after his incestuous crime became known. This parallelism is not an accident nor is it due to diffusion of the story from ancient Greece. Rather, it expresses the universality of the Oedipal experience and the need of peoples everwhere to speak about it and release its tensions in the Aesopian language of myth and dream.

Claude Lévi-Strauss, who has developed a method for the investigation of the logical structure of myth, found that the hidden meaning of the Oedipus tale was man's desire to be father of himself, to be self-sufficient, to be autochthonous. This is essentially what the Freudian version told us, though the same conclusion was reached by radically different paths. Freud saw the story as arising from the tribulations of libido, and Lévi-Strauss from its appeal to our inner logic and the desire to overcome the contradictions of the world. One does not have to choose between the two perspectives, for mythology, and all of religion, may follow a pleasure principle of the mind as well as of the body.

We can find a similar overlap in the theories of Freud and Durkheim. In his monograph *Moses and Monotheism,* Freud traced the Hebrew idea of an omnipotent high god to the patriarchal role of the Jewish father in ancient times. Supernatural figures are often temporal roles projected into another dimension, an idea that fits well with Durkheim's work, and the obedience and awe felt toward the Hebrew god mirrored the austere authority of the father. The conjunction of divine and human roles is manifest in the cult of the Virgin Mary in Catholicism, a devotion so widespread in Europe and the New World that one can wonder which spirit, Christ or his mother, is the focal point of popular worship. It is particularly well developed in Mexico, where millions of people have made their way to the shrine of Our Lady of Guadalupe. People seeking supernatural help in Mexico generally pray to Mary, and not to God the Father, or Jesus, or that most enigmatic member of the Trinity, the Holy Spirit. The

ultimate authority of God is recognized, but he is too powerful and remote to be approached by the average person. Instead, they go to a less-
forbidding figure, the motherly and tender Mary, who is asked to intervene with God on the appellant's behalf. For this reason, the Virgin is
sometimes referred to as the *abogada de Dios*, or "the lawyer of God."

The anthropologists May Diaz and Cynthia Nelson find the roots
of Mexican supplication and worship in the role system of the Mexican
family. One does not bother his father, for he is an important man and
cannot be worried with the trifling troubles of children and the household.
His place is on the avenue, in the plaza, or in the local bar, where, in the
company of other men, he discusses affairs of importance. The children
go instead to the mother with their problems and requests, and she tells
them that she will ask the father. But since the mother can present the
child's petition in any light she wishes, she effectively makes the decisions
herself. Despite, or because of, the remoteness of the father role, the
mother is the de facto authority in the household. When male prestige
and power are pushed far enough, they became self-liquidating, a dialectical process that runs throughout social life. In Mexico and other lands,
the family of God is really the family of man.

The variety of religious practices found in human cultures is extensive, but there are certain recurrent beliefs and activities that have a
broad and general appeal. One of these is the practice of magic, or the
use of certain spells, objects, or actions that are believed to compel a desired result. Some anthropologists exclude magic from the sphere of religion because of its practicality and the individualism of its practice. It
is included here because it also concerns awesome and dangerous acts
and objects and thus shares the qualities of the sacred. Magic deals with
supernatural, or at least nonnatural, forces and has the curious characteristics of being automatic in its operation, unspecified in the sources of
its power, and lacking in spirits or other intermediary agents. One can
incur a magical result accidentally, for example by breaking a mirror, by
seeing a black cat cross one's path, or by any of the other events that bring
bad luck; but the magical result is usually due to a private, perhaps secret,
and very deliberate act. Anthropologists generally recognize two kinds of
magic, imitative and contagious. The former operates on the principle that
like produces like. A rainmaker will sprinkle water in the air in the belief
that nature must then do the same. One can also make a doll in the image
of his enemy and proceed to inflict injuries upon it, which will be, it is
hoped, automatically visited upon the foe. Contagious magic is predicated
upon the premise that something pertaining to a person, animal, or object
may keep some of the qualities of the original and may exert power over it.
Many cultures, for example, have beliefs that one can inflict harm upon
an enemy through manipulations performed on body products. Members

of these societies must take care to bury their feces, carefully gather up and dispose of nail and hair clippings, and refrain from spitting. Like most of our categories, contagion and imitation are not mutually exclusive, and a magical act may use both principles.

As in the case of avoiding black cats and leaning ladders, there are many magiclike beliefs that do not involve spells, incantations, or objects. One of the more common of these is the mechanism of the "evil eye." Common throughout the Middle East and southern Europe is the notion that there are some people whose gaze is dangerous and who must, therefore, be avoided. The evil eye can inflict bad luck or make its victim ill, and these things may happen without any intent whatsoever on the part of the perpetrator. Much like the evil eye in its results and its geographic distribution is a fear that praise of a person or open comment upon his good fortune will bring bad luck to that individual. To tell an Arab mother that her baby is beautiful may seem a small politeness to a northern European, but, to Arabs, it subjects the child to risk of illness or accident. This is not at all a localized phenomenon, for we do much the same thing in the United States. When an actor or performer goes out on stage, especially on opening night, his fellow cast members say to him, "Break a leg." The magical logic of this curious phrase is that if I wish you well, it will attract misfortune. If I wish you ill, the forces of chance will not be tempted to select you for harm. In the same way, students tell their fellow students, when they enter examinations, that they are totally unprepared and sure to flunk. Or youngsters go to the plate to bat, muttering to themselves that they are going to strike out. The same kind of logic makes it absolutely taboo to comment upon the fact that a baseball pitcher has a nohit game going, for this will surely invite a hit.

By its anticipation of bad luck, the logic of the evil eye sometimes has the effect of lowering self-confidence and bringing poor performance. The little boy who says that he will strike out often does, and the incantation has the negative effect of preconditioning him to defeat. And by muting good fortune or one's natural endowments, by connecting the threat of the evil eye with envy, the belief also acts to level out differences within society. Magic usually promotes self-confidence, however, and has a more optimistic slant, and it is for this reason that it often works. Magic produces the illusion that people are masters of their fate, controllers of their environment and not its pawns. Rainmaking may not work, but the participants in rain magic, both the professionals and their clients, are at least doing something in a situation that would leave them otherwise dispirited and helpless. Perhaps this bit of activity, and its accompanying feeling of mastery and accomplishment, better enable them to cope with the realities of the drought; it is at least more satisfying than sitting around wringing one's hands. Another reason why magic works is because its practice is often deferred until it looks as if nature might accomplish the desired end. Rain magicians become active in West Africa just around the start of the annual rainy season, for rain is neither missed nor expected before then. Besides, even the rainmakers know that they will never be able to produce any rain in January.

The combination of a sense of mastery with a rote, formulated procedure makes magic a singularly compulsive practice—a quality that did not escape Freud's attention. Magic is different from prayer, as the latter involves worship and supplication, whereas the former is impersonalized and automatic and must precisely follow an exact formula. In prayer, one asks a deity or ancestral spirit for some benefit and, though men in some societies threaten the spirits with revenge for noncompliance, the supplicant usually tries to please the gods to gain their favor. Magic makes no such appeals to intermediaries. It simply says: "do X and Y will follow". This immediacy of cause and effect led Malinowski to call magic the primitive man's science, a generalization that revealed a deep knowledge of magic but none at all of science. Science is not concerned with finding little series of cause-and-effect chains, for it does not even talk in the language of causality anymore. Science is a way of combining controlled observations with human rationality in such a way that intelligibility and order may be discovered. Magic does none of these things. Actually, most primitive peoples have good pragmatic grasps of how things work and do not resort to magic for ordinary, recurrent matters. Rather, they will make magic in situations where there is high indeterminacy requiring much luck, such as a love affair or hunting. Magical thought cannot simply be equated with primitivity. In the Brazilian tropics, the peasants have an elaborate system for planting certain crops at certain phases of the moon. When I asked the Mundurucú whether they do this, they laughed. The men added that they were aware of the Brazilian beliefs but regarded them as idle superstitions. "All the plants need is rain and sunshine," they said. We may grant that there is something mechanical about magic, but primitives have no monopoly on this mode of thought, nor are they lacking in common-sense, scientifically sound knowledge of how nature works. The similarity of magic and science is based upon a faulty analogy.

One can control supernatural forces through magical coercion, but this may also be done through direct contact with and control over the spirit world. This is one of the most pervasive religious practices, for it can be found on every continent, and it thrives as well in the spiritist churches of New York City's Caribbean population as in the shamanism of Siberian reindeer herders and native South American hunters. The shaman, popularly known as a medicine man, is a religious practitioner whose supernatural powers derive from his contact with the world of spirits and his ability to cajole or force them into cooperation with man. Shamanism was present throughout the New World, and the practices and beliefs were undoubtedly brought by the Indians across the Bering Strait some forty-thousand years ago, for much the same customs are found among Siberian tribes. The shaman uses his powers for a number of social ends. He cures illness, finds lost people and objects, foretells the future, casts spells and counterspells on others, and is the general custodian of the unseen forces of good and evil in society.

The role of shaman differs from that of the priest, for the latter is usually part of a larger religious establishment, is more concerned with the conduct of group ritual, and derives his relation with supernatural powers by virtue of his office within a church. The shaman, on the contrary, is usually an individual practitioner, and his contact with the supernatural is personal and immediate. In most societies, both shamans and priests are male roles, but there are several groups in which females are admitted to practice. In certain spiritist religions of Brazil and the Caribbean in which African and Catholic themes have been syncretized, or blended, the principal practitioners and trance-adepts are usually women.

There are a number of routes to the shamanistic vocation. Perhaps the most spectacular is among the Chukchee, a tribe of nomadic reindeer herders in Siberia, where the potential shaman is recognized by his unstable behavior. The novices actually display symptoms that Western clinicians would diagnose as psychotic, but which are interpreted by the Chukchee as the work of the spirits, who are calling on the young men to "take up the drum." The call of the spirits cannot be refused, though many men dread the profession, for they can drive mad or kill those who do not heed them. The young men undergo a period of training under the tutelage of older shamans before they become independent practitioners. According to the ethnographic accounts, the aberrant symptoms usually disappear with the assumption of the profession. There are elements of seemingly schizophrenic behavior in the performances of the Chukchee shaman, but these are culturally patterned and approved acts, and we may assume that shamanism provides a socially useful outlet for what would otherwise be disruptive personalities.

In the New World, shamanism is usually either an inherited power or voluntarily followed, although the most powerful and respected shamans among the Mohave Indians are male transvestites. And among the Indians of the Plains, a man engaged in the "vision quest"—an attempt to gain contact with the spirit world—undertook self-torture in order to induce the extraordinary state of consciousness that brings receptivity to visions. Some sat on isolated buttes for days without food and water, and others cut off a finger joint to attract the sympathy of the spirits. In his suffering, the seeker would usually lapse into a trancelike state, and it was then that a spirit would speak to him and identify himself as the man's guardian. During the trances, the spirits also instructed the visionary in the preparation of a medicine bundle and other fetish objects that were believed to have an intrinsic force and identity. The quest for a guardian spirit was undertaken by most young men among the Plains tribes, and not just by shamans, though contact with benevolent spirits was central to the latters' profession as well.

The trance seems a highly individualized state of consciousness, removed from social reality almost by definition. The dreamers and visionaries come out of these episodes, however, with experiences that fit the patterns of their religions and are consistent with the trance experiences of their fellows. This takes place through advance conditioning in what the subject expects or wishes to encounter. Moreover, at the conclusion of the altered mental state, novices are usually helped to interpret their visions by more experienced people; the content of the trance experience is made into a cultural thing. Possession states in religious practice transcend social frontiers and can be found in societies at every level of complexity. Epileptics were thought to be holy people in medieval Europe, and the trance state is believed to be a pathway to divinity in many cultures, but this does not explain its appeal to the individual. For the person, trance provides an occasion for an escape from the self and a shift out of a naturalistic frame of reference. It offers surcease from everyday lives and environs and opens up a new reality, for the passage to a sacred state is a transformation of personal identity.

Trance, frenzy, and possession are recurrent features of religions around the world, from the "speaking in tongues" phenomenon of Pentecostalism to the vision quest. Among the Chukchee, the shaman's séances are always done at night by a flickering fire and to the constant accompaniment of steady, rhythmic drumming. The shaman goes into trance during the performance, but he is sufficiently aware of his surroundings to be able to engage in very deft sleight of hand and ventriloquism, producing the illusion that unnatural and unexplainable events are taking place. His audience's susceptibility to the illusions is probably heightened by a semihypnotic state induced by the fire and the drumming. As the drumming becomes faster and the shaman's behavior more frenetic, voices are heard to issue from above, from outside the tent, and from the ground, and at times the tent itself is believed to rise and shake, all the voices and work of the spirits. It is during these times that the spirits do the bidding of the shaman, telling him of distant or future events, healing ills, or remedying whatever else is troubling the shaman's clients.

North and South American Indians often induce trance states with psychoactive substances. A wide variety of drugs and hallucinogens were and are used, but the most common of all the narcotics is tobacco. The average smoker does not think of tobacco in this way, but it *is* a narcotic as well as a carcinogen. Puffed lightly in cigarettes, tobacco has little effect upon consciousness, except for satisfying a craving, but when smoked in large cigars and swallowed and inhaled in great quantities, tobacco smoke can send a person into trance. Most American Indian groups believe that tobacco has a manalike power, and Mundurucú shamans, who seldom go into trance, smoke studiously and intently while performing cures. They say that it helps them to "see" better and that it increases their diagnostic and curing abilities. The only time Mundurucú shamans go into deep trance is during a trip to the spirit underworld. For this, the shaman wraps himself inside a hammock, and a group of other shamans blow large quantities of tobacco smoke into the cocoon. The shaman then enters the world of possession in which he can see and communicate with spirits, leaps from the hammock, and dashes off into the bush, where it is believed he enters a tunnel to the underworld. Charles Wagley observed that shamans among the Tapirapé Indians of Brazil go into tobacco-induced trance during all of their cures. North American Indians also used tobacco for this purpose. One famous northern California shaman was noted by people to prefer Lucky Strike, and every shaman in the state soon switched to the brand.

William James laid great emphasis on the use of identity-transforming substances in religion, though the limited ethnographic knowledge of his time led him to direct most of his attention to alcohol and its use in the Christian communion. Far more widespread, and potent, are the various psychoactive natural substances taken in ritual. The religious use of marijuana has been noted in Asia and Africa, and peyote is used by Indians in Mexico and the United States in both rituals and shamanism. The widely read books of Carlos Castaneda on a Yaqui shaman named Don Juan have introduced an entire American generation to the full pharmacopeia of the Indians of the Southwest. Not as well known is the use of the root called *ayahuasca,* or *yahé,* by South American Indians living along the western and northern headwaters of the Amazon. Andean Indians have chewed coca leaves—from which cocaine is derived—for centuries as a restorative or sedative, but ayahuasca is generally taken only in connection with ritual and shamanism. The impact, though not the specific effect, of ayahuasca is of the same order as that of the synthetic LSD. But although some recreational LSD users in the United States are known to have developed severe psychosis or other mental impairment after prolonged use of the drug, the South American users do not suffer such effects on a pronounced scale. The drug produces visions of terrifying brilliance and realism, and it is understandable that the user feels that he has entered another world, one populated by spirits and other wondrous beings.

The standard shamanistic cure among the Munducurú follows much the same pattern as among other South American tribes. The shaman talks to the ill person about his symptoms and makes a diagnosis; this is done by palping parts of the body and staring at it intently while smoking, as if the shaman could see through the skin. Disease is believed to be always due to the activity of sorcerers, who make small, invisible objects that float through the air and enter the body of anybody who is unfortunate enough to be touched by them. It is much like the germ theory of disease, except that it has the satisfying feature of fixing the blame on people. The malignant objects make people ill through causing internal damage, and the shaman must remove the cause and give medicines to repair the injury. To do this, he smokes deeply, so that he can see the object's location, and he blows smoke over the patient's body to loosen its hold. He next manipulates the afflicted part to work the evil object toward the surface, applies his mouth to the locale of the pain and sucks out the source of the illness. He then rushes to the fire and spits the object into it. Usually this is a pebble or a pit that he had stored in the side of his cheek and into which the invisible object supposedly went. After this is done, the shaman prescribes the application by ingestion, rubbing, or vapors of any of a number of herbal remedies, depending upon the disease. The shaman receives no compensation for his work, and he even courts the risk of being accused of sorcery. As far as could be determined, Mundurucú shamans are altruistic people who are motivated by a sense of pride in their work and the esteem in which they are held. Of an entirely different order are some Jívaro shamans, who are paid for their cures. Michael Harner found one cabal of shamans in which some of the practitioners were making people sick, while the others cured them; they then split the fees.

Shamanistic cures often work, just as people can also become sick from supernatural afflictions. Some years ago Australian newspapers gave extensive coverage to the case of an aborigine who had fallen ill after learning that he had been bewitched. Convinced that he would die, the man lost hope and interest in life, stopped eating, and began to show a rapid decline in his vital functions. The doctors monitored his deterioration but could find no physical cause for it. They tried all the strategies for sustaining life, but to no avail. The patient died. There is a deep and still largely unknown relationship between the mind and the body that forms the subject matter of psychosomatic medicine. Persons experiencing depression, anxiety, or other psychic stress often exhibit dramatic and serious physical symptoms, which respond more readily to psychotherapy than to treatment of the manifest ailment. In the same way, people who live under fear of witchcraft may develop real physical afflictions, and the shaman's ministrations may be just as effective in alleviating the symptoms as are the psychoanalyst's. People do improve after shamanistic cures, for most diseases are self-limiting—that is, like colds, one just gets over them—and many others are of psychosomatic origin and respond to the sense of healing and renewal that the shaman gives. Some of the herbal cures are also medically sound. We owe the discovery of the usefulness of quinine bark in treating malaria to South American Indians, and ginger-root infusions are used throughout the area for colds. I even found that the Mundurucú thought highly of chicken soup for the treatment of colds, a discovery that boggled my mind until I found out that they had learned this from German missionaries. The shaman is a general practitioner in the highest sense of the word, for he treats ailments of the soul and not just of the body; indeed, he often regards them as the same thing. Thus, the modern medical specialist treats a disease, but the shaman treats a patient. Ironically, this has become a new and advanced form of wisdom in medical circles.

The practice of shamanism is generally an individual affair in which audiences, if present, take no active part in the proceedings. In religious ritual or ceremony, however, group participation is a central part of the religious events taking place and a key element in placing the congregants in contact with sacred forces. There are several kinds of ritual. Some, called calendrical rites, take place each year at approximately the same time; Christmas and Easter are examples from our own culture. Others, called rites of passage, center upon individuals and changes in their social statuses; these include weddings, confirmations, bar mitzvahs, and the like. Still other rituals are of a situational nature and are staged because of some special need or circumstance. All are collective affairs, and all place the congregation and the officiants in a special, sacred setting and condition.

Rituals are staged events that follow a standard protocol every time they are performed, for the participants are engaged in the dangerous act of approaching the sacred and must be themselves in a transformed and sacred state to do this. For example, the person receiving Christian Eucharist, or Communion, must be without major sin at the time of the sacrament, a state he can reach either by confession or by proper conduct. Moreover, it is forbidden for the communicant to have eaten or drunk in the morning of the ritual, for he must be in a condition of fasting as well. The process by which the celebrants of a rite attain the ritual state was called "sacralization" by the French sociologist-anthropologists Henri Hubert and Marcel Mauss and was regarded by them as one of the common features of all ritual. The shift in state of ritual purity is but one aspect of the identity changes that are a recurrent trait of much religious practice, whether it be the trance of the shaman or the anointment of the priest. The ritual state can be reached by systematic fasting, as in Lent or in observance of Yom Kippur; it can be attained by washing, or lavation, a practice followed by Moslems, who wash before their prayers; it may be reached by abstaining from sex, which underlies the chastity vows of some clerics; or it may be gained, as was noted, by the taking of identity transforming substances. All involve either an abasement or an effacement of the self and transition into an altered, sacred condition.

Identity change may be religiously expressed in the new names that a nun takes upon ordination or in the Christian notion of being "reborn." But nowhere is the shift more dramatically illustrated than in the rites of passage. There are many such rituals in American and European culture, some of them religious and others secular. The pervasiveness of ritualization of status change is, in fact, at the root of secular rites, for even where religious belief has been dropped, certain events in the lives of individuals call for a gathering of friends and relatives. Despite the declining participation in organized religion of the American public, it is estimated that 80 percent of marriages in this country take place in churches. Others are presided over by public officials, but it is still common in these cases for familiar formulas to be invoked and for an audience to attend. No matter how militantly secular, most Americans feel that "it just doesn't seem right" for a couple to go to City Hall by themselves and have the clerk simply ratify their wedding license.

The pressure toward ritualization is social in nature. Any change in status, whether a normal part of the aging process or not, occasions a period of anxiety and uncertainty for the subject of the change and for all those around him. The shift brings with it a corresponding change in role, and the web of expectations between the person and those close to him is disturbed and altered. This is most evident in the dramatic changes that take place in the social relationships surrounding a person who has died, but it is manifest in lesser degree in the minor shifts of behavior observed toward a person who has moved from childhood into the teens, a transition that may have been marked by a confirmation ritual or perhaps just a grade-school graduation ceremony. An old status and all the role behavior that goes with it must be expunged, and the person brought into his new one. This is a delicate process for all concerned, for the change leaves the individual in a transitional—or "liminal," in the usage of Victor Turner—state in which conduct toward him is necessarily indeterminate. Ritual structures the transition, provides markers for bringing the person into his new status, and gathers all those close to him in a congregation, lending psychological reinforcement to the initiate and to all the participants.

The classic study of the so-called life-crisis rites is *The Rites of Passage*, by the anthropologist Arnold Van Gennep. Van Gennep found the rites to fall into three separate parts. The individual is first separated from the rest of the group for a period of time during which he undergoes certain trials, is given instruction, or simply remains isolated. This is followed by a period of merger, which sees the initiate undergoing a public ritual that formally inducts him into the new status. The final phase is one of reincorporation into the society as a new and changed person. In effect, the old social person has died, and a new one is born.

Most societies center a series of religious observances around birth, for the new life that is brought into the group must be given a social identity and become a member of the society. This commonly takes the form of a naming ceremony, which can take place soon after birth, as in baptism. In societies in which there are especially high infant-mortality rates, however, the naming ceremony, and the induction of the child into society, may be deferred for a year or longer, until it becomes more certain that the child will survive. Christian birth ceremonies usually entail the symbolic washing of the child as means of relieving it of "original sin," and perhaps to free it of the ritual contamination of birth. Contemporary Judaism preserves the ancient Semitic custom of circumcision, the removal of the foreskin of the penis. This practice has, interestingly, spread to the non-Jewish population of the United States, due to a widespread belief that circumcision inhibits venereal contagion. This is another How-the-Leopard-Got-Its-Spots story, for circumcision gives no protection whatsoever against gonorrhea and was instituted in the Near East, and in Africa, New Guinea, and Australia, before syphilis spread through the Old World. In any event, the only protection against the latter illness offered by circumcision is through removing a flap of skin under which germs can breed. This can be corrected by a bit of extra care in washing oneself; however, as everybody knows, or should know, washing gives small protection against any venereal disease; but neither does circumcision.

A likelier interpretation of circumcision is that it is the first of the ordeals that are visited upon people as they pass through the social stages of life, and it sets the indelible stamp of human culture on a squalling, grasping, suckling creature born of nature, which must be made into a bearer of culture and a member of society. Circumcision has also been given various psychological interpretations, including Freud's view that it is symbolic castration of the son and a preview of the Oedipal drama, and Bruno Bettelheim's reading of it as a male emulation of uterine bleeding and, thus, of female fertility. Whereas Jewish circumcision occurs shortly after birth, other Semitic peoples perform the rite when the child is about seven years old. Being done at this age, it is one of the first of the ordeals to which the boy will be exposed on the road to manhood, and a marker of his progressive liberation from the world of women.

A striking form of female genital mutilation, also done before biological puberty, is clitoridectomy, which involves partial or total excision of the clitoris. The more radical forms of the operation also remove the labia majora; some Arab and Sudanic groups cap off the operation by in-fibulation, or suture and partial closing of the mouth of the vagina. Clitoridectomy is practiced among the people of the Nile valley, a scatter-ing of Arab groups, Somalis, and various Sudanic peoples from the Horn of Africa westward to the Atlantic coast. The only occurrence in the New World is among a few Panoan-speaking tribes of the Peruvian jungle. How and why it started there is anybody's guess, but the Indian women believe that it enhances their attractiveness. In Africa and the Near East, clitori-dectomy is often associated with a belief that the natural sexuality of women is so strong that it must be culturally inhibited if male dominance and the stability of the family is to be maintained. The operation, then, is part of an underlying fear of female sexuality and potency, the kind of ambivalence that makes the Mundurucú refer to the vagina as "the croco-dile's mouth."

Male circumcision and female clitoridectomy constitute, where they are practiced, the early phase of puberty rituals, but the full round of puberty ceremonies in most societies takes place a few years later, at from about ten to fourteen years of age. The three-stage process of these ceremonies is vividly evident in the puberty rites of the Mehinaku people of the upper Xingú River, in Brazil. The first stage, separation, is marked by the physical seclusion of girls at their first menses and of boys at about twelve years of age. A child entering seclusion is placed by him or herself in a section of the longhouse that has been walled off. He cannot have visitors, nor can he take part in the round of life of the village. Secluded youngsters come out at night to bathe and carry out their body functions, but they must avoid others. Girls are secluded continually for three years and boys for the same time, reports anthropologist Thomas Gregor, except that boys are allowed out for periods of a few months at a time. While in seclusion, the children are given instruction in their cul-ture, and boys are expected to go through a number of ritual ordeals to build up and try their strength and courage. In one of these, long gashes are made in the skin, leaving scars that mark the individual's social ident-ity for life. In another, the boys must wrestle with anacondas, a rather terrifying experience despite the choice of only medium-sized snakes. The climax of the rites of merging comes in intervillage ear-piercing ceremon-ies, after which the former juveniles are reincorporated into village life as young men and women.

The use of ordeal in puberty rites is widespread. The Australian aborigines subincise their young men, an operation in which the bottom of the penis is opened to the urethra with a stone knife, producing a curiously flat and splayed organ. All kinds of explanations for this prac-tice have been advanced, including one which sees it as an imitation of the kangaroo's penis and another that views it as a primitive method of birth control. Both strain credulity, for they would constitute ritual over-kill of the most flagrant sort; subincision would seem the hard way to emulate a kangaroo. The Mundurucú place the tribal stamp on their people by a painful tattooing process that covers the body with geometrical designs from head to feet. And the Maué Indians of Brazil have a puberty ceremony in which young male initiates dance with their hands in gloves that have been filled with fire ants. Courage and fortitude are developed by these tests, and they often alter the individual's natural appearance, lifting the animal creature to cultural human. The Dogon of West Africa circumcise their boys and perform clitoridectomies on their girls. As they explain it, the duality of the sexes is left incomplete by nature, and it is through these operations that culture completes the process.

Our own puberty rites are tame by comparison, despite the efforts of the occasional sadistic teacher or parent. The child preparing for bar mitzvah or confirmation is often required to attend religious instruction that takes him away from his friends, a trifling form of separation. But puberty rites are often episodes of degradation and depersonalization. They are painful and altering, and the only comparable institution in middle-class American society is orthodontia, which ranks with the "training bra" as the hallmark of adolescence. Depersonalization is effected in other ways in our rites of passage. One of these is through cutting the hair, which destroyed Samson's identity as a strong man and which marks many of our radical status shifts, especially those that involve a total change of social personage. Nuns formerly had most of their hair removed when entering their novitiates, just as convicts do when entering prison, another kind of all-committing and all-encompassing setting that Erving Goffman lists as a "total institution." And beyond the inhabitants of jails and convents, millions of male inductees into the armed forces can remember that their initial ultrashort haircut was given at the same time they were assigned a number, jabbed with hypodermic needles, and issued uniforms, the clothing of the anonymous man. All previous marks of identity were suppressed, and all ties severed during the confinement to camp of the basic-training period; the homesick were told that "if the Army wanted you to have a wife, they would have issued you one." In this way, civilians were expunged and soldiers born.

Marriage in our society entails a rather curious inversion of separation, for the honeymoon seclusion comes after the marital rite. A similar mechanism can be found among the Mundurucú, who have no wedding rituals at all, for marriage is marked merely by public knowledge of the union and a three-day period during which the bride and groom avoid the company of others. They are "ashamed," say the people, who explain all avoidance behavior in this way. Liminal, or transitional, individuals pose a problem in social relations, for one does not know quite how to act toward them, and ritual avoidance is one way out. Even the dead enter liminality, a phase that often begins while the person is still dying, and which make the final visitations to the ill socially difficult as well as emotionally distressing. The terminally ill themselves slowly let go of life and often show decreasing interest in the world about them and even in their close relatives and friends.

The onset of death is universally the subject of ritual, and there is not a single human society that simply throws the body out as a mass of decaying protoplasm, which it really is. Many societies practice cremation of the dead, whereas others dispose of the corpse differently. Several Plains Indian tribes placed the dead on platforms in the branches of trees, and certain West African groups inter theirs in hollow tree trunks. Interment in the ground is the most common custom, though place of burial, position of the body, adornment, preparation and dressing of the corpse, and time of burial may vary. The mourning period usually starts a short time after death. Jews bury the dead on the day after death, and then observe a week-long mourning period. Most Christian denominations bury the body about three days after death, and the official mourning period usually falls between death and interment. There are some groups that bury the dead and observe a year or two of mourning, after which they disinter the bones and have a final burial ceremony in which the soul is believed to be put to rest. During these prolonged mourning periods, certain acts of self-abnegation, such as haircutting and self-inflicted injury, are common, and form an effective way for the survivors to purge themselves of a sense of guilt, born of the ambivalence felt toward the deceased.

There is an old saw that funerals are for the living, but, unlike most popular wisdom, this one is true. The funeral is a time for release of sorrow and guilt under controlled conditions, the community of believers comforting and strengthening each other in a time of stress and need. All the passages of life leave little rips in the fabric of society, death most of all. The coming together of the mourners reestablishes social relations between them, places the deceased in the social status of "dead," and restates the theme that life can now continue. Some think it curious that a Jewish shiva consists largely of sitting together, talking and perhaps laughing, and eating cake. Or that people drink at an Irish wake, and get together after the burial for food and more drinks. The behavior seems anomalous to the occasion, but the sharing of food and drink is sacramental in nature, and the often cheery gatherings are a reknitting of the social fabric, the final phase of reincorporation.

Modern man thinks of time as a linear affair, progressing inexorably by seconds, minutes, weeks, and years, without return or repetition. Time can also be viewed as a cyclical matter, in which the round of seasons closes upon itself, and each year becomes an image of the one before. Calendrical religious rites are stable markers in this endless circle, for they may highlight the winter solstice, as does Christmas, or they may signal the reawakening of the world in spring, like Easter and Passover. The institution of holy seasons introduces periods of sacredness in the mundane round of the seasons, heightens social solidarity through congregation, and celebrates important social, economic, and political aspects of life. Sacredness and solemnity are often counterpointed and stressed, as Edmund Leach has written, by closely associated periods of ritual license. We celebrate New Year's Eve shortly after Christmas, carnival ushers in the forty-day Lenten holy season before Easter, and the Australian aborigines' annual totemic rites are followed by a period of corroboree, a time of revelry during which even the incest taboos are suspended.

The calendrical rites provide the occasion for periodic sacralization of time and populace through close approach to the forces of sacredness. Australian totemic rituals, which often have the purpose of increasing the fertility of the totemic animals, are occasions on which the ancestral surrogate is consumed by the clan members in a group meal, and the power of its spirits ingested. It has been suggested by some early anthropologists that these totemic meals were the evolutionary forerunners of human sacrifice and ritual cannibalism, which, in turn, were the precursors of the Christian Eucharist and other sacramental means of absorbing the powers of deity. This is strongly suggested by the fact that Communion is almost invariably taken in groups in a ritual setting, and by the metaphor that the people are ingesting the body and blood of their god.

Ritual may also be staged for special occasions, such as a severe climatic threat or some natural or social disaster, but these may be the harbingers of new religious movements, born of new social circumstances. Christianity came into being in this way, for it offered the oppressed lower classes of the Roman Empire hope of a hereafter and of a justice dispensed by a god before whom all men were equal. It promised a millennium in which God would appear before man and the meek would inherit the earth; it was deliverance. Christianity is but one among scores of millenarian religious movements that have appeared in the past and continue to do so to this day. Usually lumped under the anthropological rubric of "revitalization movements," they serve to reinfuse the society with a new sense of purpose and solidarity in the face of threat. Max Weber saw revitalization movements as common sources of new religions, arising from an incremental accumulation of social change that renders obsolete the world view and interpretation of society of the old religion. There follows a period of experimentation with alternate religious forms, often preached by prophets, and a subsequent institutionalization of the new beliefs as standard worship. In the case of Christianity, the stirrings of a number of millenary movements were felt at the time of Christ among the lower classes and subject peoples of the Roman hinterland. The Christian prophecy was, for a number of historical reasons, the only one that succeeded, and in less than four centuries it became the official religion of the empire. It thus went from revolutionary credo to doctrinal upholder of the established order, which is often the way of political ideology as well as of religious belief.

The spread of Western society and its penetration into the remotest reaches of the world was a trauma and catastrophe for the hapless native peoples who felt its brunt. Many resisted by force of arms and were defeated, others were absorbed into its mercantile structure in a kind of osmosis, and others simply collapsed in its face. Defeat and despair were mitigated in several areas by religious movements that at once explained the new situation in which the people found themselves and offered spiritual surcease from its dangers and deprivations. The native peoples of the American West had been mostly subjugated and confined to reservations by the 1870s; their entire economic base had collapsed with the destruction of the buffalo herds and the occupation of their lands by the whites; their political systems had been smashed and outside coercive authority imposed upon them, and their religions seemed largely irrelevant to their new way of life. In this atmosphere of total defeat and numbing discouragement, the preachings of a Nevada Paiute shaman named Jack Wovoka offered hope, spreading rapidly across the Rocky Mountains and into the Great Plains. Wovoka's message was that if a certain ritual dance, which became known as the "Ghost Dance," were held, in time all of the dead Indians would return to life, the bison herds would come back, and the whites would disappear. It was a thoroughly nonviolent form of protest, but the whites were contemptuous of Indian religion and suspicious of any gatherings of large numbers of people. In this atmosphere the U.S. Army attacked a Ghost-Dance meeting on the Sioux reservation in South Dakota on December 29, 1890, murdering over two-hundred children, women and men, and even managing to hit a few of their own in the cross fire.

Among the better-known revitalization movements are the so-called "cargo cults" of Melanesia. These have been recurrent in the region since the early part of this century, but increased in frequency and intensity with the Japanese and American occupations of World War II. Overwhelmed and awed by the enormous show of materiel of the American forces especially, many peoples developed the belief that if certain rites were performed, they would become wealthy too. They first believed that cargoes of goods would come in ships, and they built piers into the sea; but in more recent years, cultists have been building landing strips. One of the latest expressions of cargo cults was the President Johnson movement of the 1960s, which saw the American leader coming to live in New Guinea, bringing with him all the wonders of American society. Cargo cults and other millenarian movements disappear more often than they succeed in becoming established religions, and most of those of primitive peoples have either been crushed or rendered meaningless by the total destruction of what was left of native society. The American Indian today knows that Ghost Dances and all the rest do not work, and revitalization has taken the more pragmatic direction of political activism. Fittingly, their major confrontation thus far with the government authorities took place on the Pine Ridge Reservation in South Dakota, where the Wounded Knee Massacre took place.

We have surveyed only a small part of the religious phenomena of human cultures, but even this sample shows a bewildering variety and is a testimonial to the richness of the human imagination. At the outset, the difficulties of definition were noted, and the range of functions found to be so varied that it was difficult to find the essence of the religious experience. Whatever our definition of religion, we have learned that the subject must be approached pragmatically and scientifically. Judgments about the relative truth or falsehood of one religion as opposed to another are irrelevant to anthropological inquiry, for the religions of primitive peoples have the same truth (*for them*) as the more elaborated sects of our own civilization. Beliefs, Durkheim told us, are socially true to the extent that people believe they are and adjust their behavior to these beliefs. Religions express cultural truths, for they symbolize social relationships and reflect our anxieties and our hopes.

The truth of religion is a relative matter, not an absolute one, but the world's religions are consistent in their projection of a dimension of the wonderful and the mystical. Religions do explain the inexplicable, but they more often render the explicable unexplainable. They seize on what is remarkable in nature, but they also *create* out of whole cloth beings and forces that are beyond everyday experience and common-sense understanding; religions invent mysteries. One attribute of religious tenets is supposedly the intensity of belief we accord them—an intensity which I would suggest is an overprotest arising from an unarticulated doubt. We *believe* in God, but we do not *believe* that the earth revolves around the sun. We *know* that. There is always surrounding the things of the sacred a special quality that strains credulity and evokes assertive belief, rather than simple acceptance of them as among the phenomena of nature.

This brings me to a final speculation on religion. Reality, we have said, is in good part a cultural construct, and the preconceptions of culture plus the consensus of our fellows allow us to naturalize and routinely accept the everyday "profane" world. But this profane world is always counterpointed and set off by the sacred realm. Reality is made "real" by the positing of the unreal, and the category of the "natural" rendered so by a dimension of the "supernatural." Reality is neither cut and dried nor readily acceptable, and much of what we view as natural is as unprovable and chimerical as the most fanciful religious notions. We live in a world of invented symbolism, selective perceptions, shifting images, and transient feelings, and an abyss of unreality lies just below the surface of everyday experience. Perhaps, then, the major purpose of religion is to explain ordinary life, and, indeed, to make it ordinary by contrasting it to the extraordinary. Our grasp of the world is contingent upon our apprehension of phantoms.

The Unfolding World

The eighteenth century used primitive cultures as exemplars of what man was like in a state of nature, that pristine condition that was supposed to have preceded the corruption, or edification, of organized society. The nineteenth-century scholars attributed a rather different significance to primitives, for though they too considered primitive society to represent a condition of early man, they also believed that the varieties of such groups would reveal the steppingstones that humanity had scaled on the way toward civilization. The shift of emphasis appears slight, but it is of great importance in the evolution of social thought, for it represents a change from the Enlightenment concern for human rationality to the historicism of nineteenth-century romanticism. It was a step too in the direction of modern social science in that it moved us from the search for a rational and just society to consideration of society as it is. It led also to a scientific study of cultural change and transformation, and of the unfolding of human institutions through the ill-perceived reaches of remote time.

The assumption that primitive societies are vestigial remains of early human history—of phases that Western society had passed through on its course toward civilization—has a great deal of merit. Common sense and firm evidence from prehistoric archeology show that mankind foraged for a living for hundreds of millennia before learning the arts of animal and plant domestication. Societies based solely upon hunting, fishing, and wild-vegetable collecting gave way to simple hoe horticulture at least twelve-thousand years ago in Asia and almost ten-thousand years ago in Mexico and Peru. Animal domestication must have appeared after the invention of farming, and a merger of the two economies in early Asia ultimately gave rise to plow agriculture. A good deal of human history from that time until the recent past revolved around the development of these arts and their uneven spread through most parts of the world. The primitive societies encountered and studied since the age of exploration began were indeed enclaves into which more advanced technologies had not yet been extended; they were relics of times past as well as varieties of contemporary humanity.

The world's primitives are not exact replicas of past human societies, nor are they crystallized and unchanging museum pieces. They have been, however, subject to the limitations of their technologies, and the study and analysis of these limitations have revealed the overall outlines of social life in archaic periods. We know that there were neither cities nor states before the emergence of agriculture, and that such social forms presuppose high productivity and a fairly dense population. The archeological residue of the past consists of material artifacts, and we can learn of the social and intellectual lives of remote ages only through inference from these clues, a process of deduction based on ethnographic knowledge. Thus, we find no traces of social norms as such, but we can tell from the size, design, and distribution of house types a good deal about family life. Moreover, we know from all the social anthropological research that has ever been done that if the technology of the people was rude, then their society was largely structured by kinship. In this way, the present variety of human cultures can be seen as roughly representative of the order of their emergence. This order is clear in the area of economic activity, but it is not so evident in the spheres of social, political, and religious life. Inquiry into this process of unfolding of human culture in all its forms and sequences—the issue of cultural evolution—has been one of anthropology's most persistent quests.

The theme of cultural evolution dominated nineteenth-century anthropology and persists as a more muted interest to the present day. Most of the early evolutionary theories were characterized by grand sweep and vision, a splendor of conceptualization that often hid loose and fragile generalizations and insufficient evidence. Research at the time was rustic and our information scanty, but this seemed to encourage rather than deter theory. A feature of this school of thought was the premise, almost an axiom, that all societies tend to go through the same phases, each typified by certain institutions that every group would, or should, develop in proper order. A corollary of this belief was the assumption that those societies that had not yet evolved civilization would have to go through all the intermediate stages before reaching it. There were exceptions, but each required a special explanation. It was a congenial theory for a Europe bent on reducing all the non-Western world to colonialism and an America still busy subjugating the Indian, for it provided a pseudoscientific basis for the argument that the native peoples were not yet ready for autonomy. "Perhaps in a century or two, but surely not in our time," was a comment that could be heard in Africa until only a few years before the colonies achieved independence in 1960 and thereabouts. Implicit in the remark was the creed that there are no shortcuts to the future, and that the experience of each stage of evolution is necessary to the attainment of the next.

The positing of a set sequence in social and cultural evolution through which all societies would pass has been called "unilinear" (single-line) evolution. It was allowed by some that special circumstances might cause a society to deviate from the line, but the order of evolution was thought to have a logical basis as well as a historic one. This is especially clear in the work of Lewis Henry Morgan, whose position as a founder of kinship studies is matched by his stature as a student of the Iroquois and as an evolutionary theorist. In his book *Ancient Society* (1877), Morgan outlined a threefold scheme of evolutionary stages termed savagery, barbarism, and civilization, each of which was marked by an item of technology and organized according to a certain set of institutions. The three major stages corresponded roughly to hunting and gathering societies, horticultural and pastoral groups, and the literate state. The sequence was complex and the correlates of each stage many, but Morgan's treatment of marriage was central to his evolutionary scheme. He saw the earliest period to be one of primitive promiscuity, or a phase of no marriage, followed by group marriage. The institution then passed on to polygamy, and finally to monogamy, a progression which at once saw an increased particularization of the relationship and a development toward the Christian, middle-class American family that Morgan saw as marriage's highest development.

The forms of mating were determinant of other institutions in Morgan's scheme. The monogamous nuclear family was its latest and most-evolved result, whereas early family forms were more communalized. Group marriage, he theorized, led to extended family aggregates in which paternity could not be determined due to the multiple nature of mating. For this reason, he believed that matrilineal descent and the matrilineal clan were the earliest social forms. Later in human history, the development of plow agriculture brought about patrilineality; the conjugal family of one man and wife came to primacy with private property.

Morgan was a solid middle-class lawyer from Rochester, New York, and it is ironic that one of his lasting claims to fame is that he was read avidly by Karl Marx and ultimately inspired Friedrich Engels's *Origin of the Family, Private Property, and the State*, published in 1884. The great socialist theoreticians found substantiation of some of their ideas in Morgan's contention, which I outlined in Chapter 6, that there was no private property in primitive societies, and that its development was a condition for the emergence of class stratification and the state. Morgan was not, however, a materialist, for his overall scheme, especially in the earlier stages of evolution, made little systematic argument for economic or ecological causality. He did not set out the material conditions for group marriage, and one must presume that he formulated this stage, for which there is no ethnographic evidence other than certain kin terms, solely because it came close to primal promiscuity and was a far cry from modern marriage. As for the presumed priority of the matrilineal clan, this rested on little more than ignorance of paternity, which he assumed was universal in those benighted times. Morgan also explained the spread of institutions of exogamy as being due to the evident biological superiority of the offspring of outbreeding; he neglected the fact that exogamy entails outbreeding only with regard to certain relatives and often is accompanied by inbreeding with other types of kin. In actuality Morgan, and most of the other evolutionists of the period, did not have a coherent general theory for cultural evolution, but had instead erected a vast typology to which they attached temporal significance.

By the first decades of the twentieth century, evolutionary theory was coming under strong criticism from a new breed of full-time professional anthropologists—the place of the gentleman-scholar had been taken by empirically oriented social scientists. One element of the attack came from Great Britain and the writings of A. R. Radcliffe-Brown and Bronislaw Malinowski. Both dismissed the use of supposed vestigial traits, or "survivals," as clues to past human history as simple "conjectural history," maintaining that items of culture persist because they have current functions and not because they are the dead residue of a distant past. Radcliffe-Brown's study of the role of the mother's brother in Africa, referred to in Chapter 4, was actually written to refute the evolutionary notion that special ties of warmth and closeness between a man and his mother's brother in patrilineal societies are a relic of a former matrilineal phase. Radcliffe-Brown demonstrated convincingly that the avunculate fits in very well with both the logic and operation of patrilineal systems and that the attribution of prior matrilineality was gratuitous and without empirical basis. The critique was totally successful in Great Britain, but one of the more unfortunate aspects of the functionalist emphasis on the present was a disinterest in history that persisted until the 1960s.

The American criticism of evolutionism was, on the other hand, historically oriented from the outset. Much of the antievolutionary writing of the early twentieth century came from the researches of Franz Boas and his students at Columbia University. Boas had been deeply influenced by the German scientist and philosopher Ernst Mach, who advocated a strict empiricism and a theoretical caution that did not permit much straying beyond the facts. Armed with an increasing inventory of data collected by themselves and others, the Boasians riddled the evolutionary schemes with exceptions to the grander generalizations, substituting rigorous description and analysis for the broad syntheses of the evolutionists. The "totemic complex," believed by Sir James Frazer and others to be a universal stage in the evolution of religion, was shown by Alexander Goldenweiser and others to consist of a series of distinct culture elements that only occasionally came together to fit the standard definition of the complex. Totemism was seen, then, as a catchall term. In this sense, it should be noted that animal names are common in our own culture as well as in simpler ones. For some reason, we do not think it especially totemic when we meet Mr. Wolf, Miss Fox, or Mrs. Badger, who may be members of the Elks or Moose clubs and root for the Columbia Lions and the Chicago Bears. But it is totemism of a sort and should serve as warning that conceptual schemes built upon typologies—whether called totemism, matrilineality, exogamy, or whatever—rest upon shaky grounds. One of the errors of evolutionism was to attribute a solid and concrete reality to what were at best handy typological pigeonholes.

The publication in 1920 of Robert H. Lowie's book *Primitive Society* dealt what appeared to be a final blow to evolutionism. Lowie, a student of Boas, demolished the notion of group marriage and showed that monogamy is not the creation of civilization but is found as the predominant marriage norm in some of the world's most technologically simple societies. In the process, he demonstrated that the nuclear family was found in all societies and was the major kin group among the Shoshoni and other peoples living near the margins of bare subsistence. Lowie also argued against the priority in time of matrilineality over patrilineality and, more important, arrayed evidence to show that clanship was not typical of peoples having the rudest technologies. Rather, he concluded, the clan is generally found in societies at the middle level of social complexity and technological efficiency, a finding that has been corroborated by the recent research of the anthropologist Michael J. Harner. Lowie's contribution to evolutionary theory was not, then, entirely critical and negative, for he laid the foundations for a more cautious social evolutionism that would be more closely tied to the development of technology and would at the same time deny the unilinear character of the early schemes; we will come back to modern evolutionism later in this chapter.

The sharpest attacks of the American group were leveled at the idea that evolution goes through a quite fixed progression of stages, throughout the world. This would assume that each society generated its next stage out of the knowledge and institutions of its past phases, a kind of self-contained growth process. The critics of this viewpoint stressed, however, that the principal way by which societies develop and change is not through internal and autonomous means but by outside influences. This occurs through the process of "diffusion," or the passing of items of culture from one society to another. Even were the stages of the evolutionists granted to exist, it was argued, entire phases could be leapfrogged through the intrusion of some new technology or by heavy contact with a more advanced society. Thus, archeological evidence shows that humanity made some of its earliest tools out of flaked stone, followed by a period in which the stone tools were ground and polished. The subsequent period of metallurgy started with copper and went on through bronze and iron ages to steel and all the new metals and alloys of our time. This whole process took millennia, but many societies have made the transition from stone to steel tools in a few years. Usually obtained through trade, the steel artifacts displace the stone ones immediately and almost completely, with repercussions throughout the culture. Similarly, after Japan opened itself to the West in the nineteenth century, it moved in but a few decades from feudalism to a modern industrial state. There are indeed shortcuts to the future.

The question of whether an item of culture was diffused into a society or came about through independent invention became a critical issue for those who emphasized the fortunes of history over rigid evolutionary sequences, just as it remains an important problem for those using the comparative method. It would be safe to say that over 90 percent of the content of almost all cultures was derived in the first place through diffusion. Nonetheless, there are important examples of independent and parallel inventions, which show that culture is often produced by its own antecedents. G. W. Leibniz (1646–1716) and Isaac Newton (1642–1727) invented the calculus independently of each other, though both were working from the common background of the mathematics of their time. Charles Darwin and Alfred Wallace hit upon the idea of natural selection at about the same time and without consultation. Again, it must be remembered that there was a great deal of speculation about biological evolution in the mid-nineteenth century, and this particular theory was well-nigh inevitable. Among the most important independent inventions in human history was the domestication of plants, which happened at least once in the New World and had two or more independent recurrences in the Old World. One can speculate that it came about when wild-vegetable collecting peoples began to save some of their harvest for re-planting in favored places. It would be only a small step to prepare the ground for sowing the wild seeds and to keep it weed-free during the growing period. If only the best seed specimens were saved for planting, then the group would be well on its way to developing domestic plants and the achievement of full agriculture. It was a remarkable and revolutionary development, which probably came about in small and simple increments.

In agriculture, as in calculus and the theory of natural selection, innovations appear—and more important, are accepted—because preceding cultural conditions provided the raw material and the incentives. The automobile is a wonderful invention, but every part of the early cars incorporated principles and mechanisms already invented. The most important of these was the wheel, some six-thousand years old. The car was not invented out of thin air but was rather a rearrangement of pre-existing parts, as are most innovations. Invention may be based on human genius, of which there is a store in all societies, but this genius must operate within the framework and with the materials set by culture. It is also true that although necessity is the mother of invention, need is a cultural thing. That necessity and prior background lead to innovation may also explain why some elements of culture diffuse into certain societies, whereas others are rejected. Societies are not mindless sponges that sop up bits and pieces of culture from their neighbors, for the process of diffusion is highly selective, depending on both the culture in question and the trait being diffused. Utilitarian objects, such as steel axes and knives are usually adopted immediately, for they replace stone tools with similar implements of superior material. This process has affected a good deal of the material culture of primitive peoples throughout the world. Pottery making is a dying art among the Mundurucú, and most of their cookware now consists of aluminum and steel pots and pans and five-gallon gasoline cans with the tops cut off. Firearms are common and would be universally used in the group were it not for their expense and the cost of ammunition. Even hammocks are being bought from traders and it seems but a question of time before the arts of spinning and weaving will disappear as well.

Many items diffuse rapidly because of some intrinsic attraction. The spread of alcohol use among North American Indians was matched by an even speedier diffusion of tobacco from the Americas to the rest of the world. First introduced into Europe in 1556, the Indian practice of tobacco cultivation and smoking traveled completely around the world in less than a century, finally reaching to the Alaskan Indians through Siberia.

There are a variety of circumstances that account for the diffusion or rejection of cultural traits aside from utility and addiction. Some elements are accepted because they come from a culture that is considered more prestigious. This has been an important source of the diffusion of Western culture to the non-Western world. European haircutting styles and dress have tended to become worldwide in scope, and our popular music has taken hold on every continent. The travels of musical style show some of the intricacies of the diffusion process. Our rhythmic musical traditions such as jazz, blues, and certain kinds of rock derived from music brought by African slaves to the plantations of the New World. This modified African music spread to the white population during the twentieth century, a reversal of the drift of culture from the more to the less prestigious group, and the Afro-American music has finally been readopted by Africans.

The ultimate key to whether a diffused culture element will be accepted or rejected is its compatibility with the culture of the recipient society. The religious use of the peyote button, a mild hallucinogen, has spread from Mexico northward to the Indian tribes of the Southwest United States and to those of the Great Plains. Quests for visions and direct communication of people with the spirit world while in a state of trance formed a standard part of traditional Plains cultures, and the hallucinogenic experience fitted into this preexistent pattern. In Africa, Christianity has been losing ground to Islam, a religion that permits polygyny and that requires little more from its members than a statement of faith, participation in prayer, and a few minor observances such as the Semitic-derived injunction against eating pork. Christianity, on the other hand, is laden with an insistence upon monogamy, an emphasis on guilt and sin that is at variance with traditional African forms of social control, an overburden of clergy, and an injunction to adopt a life-style that is at heart European. The churches achieved early successes through providing school facilities and training the young for a new era that was being imposed upon them. The new national governments, however, have established public schools and now exercise tight central control over education, all of which has further weakened the missionary effort. Finally, Christianity is a European religion to the average African and is identified with colonialism, whereas Islam set its roots in Africa over one thousand years ago. Christianity is thus seen as alien both in content and in origin.

Resistance to culture change and technical innovation has been especially noted among peasant groups and is often attributed to a general innate conservatism. Distrust of the outside by peasant farmers, who cultivate land for subsistence and sell small amounts through markets, is not at all a result of ignorance and irrationality but manifests a keen understanding, based upon long and bitter experience, that they can expect little good from the cities and from government. When the much publicized "Green Revolution" was exported by American agricultural experts, many peasants rejected outright the new seed strains and cultivation methods, despite clear promise of higher yields. The experience of some peasant farmers showed that the holdouts might have been right all along. Many of the new plant strains proved to have little resistance to local blight and disease or depended upon a set of climatic conditions that occurred only in the best years. There were some spectacular successes, but there were also spectacular failures. To complicate matters, most of the agricultural innovations required capital investments in machinery and fertilizer. This favored the prosperous farmers, who also sought to extend their holdings to make more efficient use of the new technology. The lot of the small holder correspondingly worsened. The Green Revolution has been a social disaster, and increased crop yields have been bought at the expense of rural poverty and landlessness and growing inequality.

New items of culture, whether arising from within or outside a society, must find acceptance in terms of the prior meanings of the culture. If these meanings are totally foreign or repugnant, the proffered item of culture, be it an idea, an artifact, a belief, or a style, may well be rejected outright. It is also common that the item will be accepted, but that in the acceptance process it will be interpreted and reworked to fit into the recipient culture. Three examples from Mundurucú folklore will illustrate the process by which diffused items become modified during their integration. The Mundurucú tell a story of two lost children that is so close in content to the Hansel-and-Gretel tale that independent invention can be ruled out. There are, however, two significant differences between the Mundurucú tale and the European one. First, the stepmother role is not considered malign among the Mundurucú, and this part of the story made no sense to them. It was changed accordingly, and the children are simply abandoned by their natural parents. Second, at the end of the story, the children push the wicked witch into the fire, but an element is added. As the flame consumes the witch, her eyeballs explode and out of each erupts a hunting dog. These were the first dogs and the ancestors of those kept by the Mundurucú today. The tale in this way becomes one more episode in the Mundurucú cycle of creation legends.

The Mundurucú have been in contact with Brazilian Christianity for over a century, and several Bible tales have entered their oral literature. The influence of Genesis is evident in the story of Adjung and Eva, who lived in a beautiful land where there was no work, but in which sex was equally unknown. A snake came and told Adjung what he should be doing with Eva, but he rejected the suggestion, saying that it would hurt her. The snake pursued his advice, Adjung gave in, and people have been having sexual relations ever since. In a third tale, the Mundurucú recount the African-derived story of the tortoise and the hare, though a deer is substituted for the hare, which is not found in the area. The tortoise conspires with his fellow tortoises, each posting himself along the line of the race, leading the deer into thinking that the original tortoise has kept up with him. The deer finally runs himself to death, and the tortoises sit down and eat him. This is a far cry from the African moral "to the slow and steady goes the race," but it fits perfectly well into a cycle of tales in which the tortoise is a trickster. Unless one knew the African story, it would seem to be a typical Mundurucú folk tale.

The process by which the new and old become fused in the spread of culture is known as syncretism. Christianity, for example, is a syncretistic religion derived from Greek rationalism and mystical Judaism, just as Islam syncretized traditional seventh-century Arab religion with elements of Christianity and Judaism. The process is still at work in almost all situations of culture change. In the northeast part of Brazil, there is a form of religious sect known as candomblé, which is dedicated to a cult of spirits named after Catholic saints, but which have alternate names and the behavioral characteristics of West African gods. Prominent in the ritual is ecstatic possession by the saint-gods, another West African trait, which has in turn influenced Brazilian Christianity through the growing popularity of Pentecostal movements.

The incorporation of new traits through reinterpretation and syncretism has allowed societies to draw upon the cultures of their neighbors while maintaining the individuality, distinctiveness, and integrity of their own. The dimensions of the change are thereby lessened and the possibilities of discordance with the recipient culture reduced, but over a period of time there is nevertheless a progressive tendency for the cultures of neighboring societies to become increasingly alike because of diffusion. The trend toward convergence of the cultures of adjoining or nearby societies has resulted in regions of cultural similarity, called "culture areas." Within the limits of the culture area, the component societies, although by no means identical, have a number of distinguishing traits in common. The delineation of culture areas shows that there is much more involved in their growth than the simple mechanics of diffusion. The anthropologist Clark Wissler found in 1922 nine culture areas in North America north of Mexico: the Eastern Woodlands, Southeastern, Southwestern, California, Plateau, North Pacific Coast or simply Northwest Coast, Plains, Eskimo, and Mackenzie (interior northern Canada and Alaska). These areas showed close correspondence to the environmental zones of North America, and Wissler noted an intimate association between culture area and dominant subsistence pursuit. The California area, which included most of Nevada, was a seed-gathering zone; the Plains area was typified by bison hunting from horseback; the North Pacific Coast and Plateau societies relied greatly on salmon fishing; the Eskimo and the people of the Mackenzie area hunted caribou, among other pursuits; and the tribes of the Southeast, the Eastern Woodlands, and the Southwest depended heavily upon maize cultivation. A good deal of the similarity of the cultures was a result of similar accommodations to the environment, as discussed in Chapter 6. Moreover, traits were passed from one group to another more readily because of the likeness of their ecological adjustment; in this way, equestrianism spread rapidly among the Plains bison hunters, and the fishing technologies of all the North Pacific Coast groups were much the same. As geographic entities, the culture areas were also regions of intensive communication. There was extensive travel by horse throughout the Plains, and the peoples of the Northwest Coast traveled to each other's communities by canoe through the inland waterways of the Canadian Pacific. Some culture areas were separated from each other by natural barriers, further inhibiting diffusion. The Rocky Mountains walled off the Plains from the Plateau and Great Basin areas of Utah, Idaho, and Nevada, and the North Pacific Coast was cut off from the interior Mackenzie area by the Canadian Cascades and Rockies. These barriers were not impassable, but they did serve to dampen contact.

The phenomena of diffusion and the historical influence that cultures exert on each other seem at first glance to introduce an adventitious factor, an element of caprice and accident, into the analysis of social and cultural change. In the hands of some of the early critics of evolutionism, diffusion was indeed used in this way. The neat and orderly evolutionary systems were replaced by narratives that explained the development of one or another culture by inventories of where its various traits had come from. It was a particularistic and antitheoretical approach that rebutted the evolutionary order by a denial of all order. In actuality, the operation of diffusion is not radically different from that of independent invention, and an accommodation between the processes of diffusion and evolution is inherent in our data.

The term cultural evolution, if it means anything at all, must refer to historic processes that are orderly and have a direction. One of these directions will be toward increased social complexity and another will be toward ever more superior technology; the latter two characteristics are not, of course, independent but feed upon each other. Everything we have learned about diffusion suggests that it is an orderly affair. More effective technology usually replaces the less-efficient, leading to a general tendency for societies to develop more productive means of exploiting the environment by capturing ever greater amounts of energy. The short-term choices involved in the diffusion of a better kind of axe, a superior bow, or a new crop lead to long-term changes that we can term evolutionary. Diffusion occasionally results in radical and disruptive breaks with the past, but it is more common that a trait that has no place, function, or meaning in the preexistent patterns of a society will be either rejected or modified. The idea of the state will not diffuse to societies that lack any germs of the institution, except when imposed deliberately from the outside. And agricultural technology will not diffuse to desert areas, except when accompanied by the knowledge and techniques of irrigation; diffusion and ecological process follow a common course. Diffusion occurs when a culture is receptive to an innovation, and in this sense the conditions for the acceptance of both independent inventions and diffused items are much the same. In both, the future must be accommodated to the present, just as the present is an outcome of the past. The vagaries of history fit into the loose framework of cultural evolution in a manner that renders cultural and social change orderly and predictable.

Diffusion is important to our understanding of evolution in another way. This is the lesson that the evolution of mankind's knowledge of its surroundings and its ability to control them were not accomplished by one or another society or nation, for each social group owes most of its culture to other groups. The flow of tools, knowledge, belief, art, and all the rest of culture from one society to another is a vast, restless, and continual movement that pools the genius of every society into a body of common talent. One can speak of the evolution of a particular society, but it is also possible to speak of the evolution of human culture.

The distinction between the evolution of human cultures seen as a totality and that of individual cultures became a prominent theoretical issue during a revival of evolutionary thought that began in the 1930s, picked up momentum in the forties, and declined in the sixties. The principal architects of this so-called "neo-evolutionism" were the anthropologists Leslie White and Julian H. Steward. The theories of each were characterized by a heavy stress on economic, especially technological, factors, and both were therefore important figures in the growth of a materialistic school that has become significant in anthropology during the past decade.

Leslie White was drawn to the work of Lewis Henry Morgan through an interest in the Iroquois. Instead of finding in Morgan the grossly wrong theorization that his earlier studies had led him to expect, White discovered a germinal thinker whose work, in his opinion, had been maligned and shamefully neglected. He embarked on a series of papers defending Morgan, but in the process he advanced a theory of evolution that was more distinctly his own. White hypothesized—and often stated as fact— that the evolution of human society is caused, promoted, and determined by growing technological effectiveness, measured in units of energy harnessed per capita by a society. The earliest and least-evolved groups utilized manpower only, although certain technological innovations such as the axe or the bow and arrow enabled humans to deliver this power more effectively. The arrow is propelled by human strength only, but the pull of the arm muscles on the bowstring is converted into the forward thrust of the arrow. This constitutes a distinct step in cultural evolution, although not of the same magnitude as the development of agriculture, the use of animal power, the invention of the steam engine, or the birth of the atomic age. These all represent phases in which man captured sources of energy outside his body, and began to spend the resources of the planet in a profligate way.

Despite White's admiration for Morgan, he was not a unilinear evolutionist of the type that sees human society going through fixed stages. Rather, though he saw a universal sequence on the path from the simplest societies to the most complex, it was a sequence for all of human history and not the history of one or another culture. He recognized that any catalogue of technological advances would take one on a bewildering tour back and forth between continents and from society to society. Europeans and Americans may have discovered atomic energy, but they surely did not invent agriculture, wind power, or the wheel. Technology did more than mark phases of human progress in White's writings; it was the prime cause of progress. In a division parallel to a Marxian distinction, White saw every culture to consist of a technologically based economic infrastructure, a social system, and an ideological system. The first of these, technology, was determinant in his scheme of the latter two. It was a one-way causality, and White made no allowance for the possibility that social institutions, religions, and philosophies could affect technology.

White's concern with a universal scheme of cultural evolution lifted his theory to such a high level of generality that it was difficult to apply it to particular cases. He thereby stressed technology without corresponding attention to the applications of the technology in concrete settings. Unable to deal with the particular, the theory could not cope with the special circumstances posed by physical environment, and he was left with a technological determinism that did not tell us how the tools were used. An alternative theory that would take local ecological factors into account was offered by Julian Steward in 1948. Steward's evolutionary theory emerged naturally from his ideas on cultural ecology, discussed in Chapter 6. As we learned, Steward found that similar combinations of tools and resources, or products exploited, resulted in quite similar social structures throughout the world. He assumed that since the parallels had resulted from similar forces acting over time, history should reveal that these societies had taken somewhat parallel paths. This was proved to him conclusively by the aforementioned parallel development of the state in five separate areas in conjunction with the practice of irrigation agriculture. Not all complex societies used irrigation, of course, and the state could evolve in other ways. The "irrigation state" was, however, one line that

social evolution could follow, whereas other groups in different environmental circumstances and with a different technology might follow other
lines. Steward called his theory "multilinear (several lines) evolution" in
recognition of this pluralism of history.

White's theory was universalized to provide an explanation of the
evolution of all human culture, whereas Steward's explained the orderly
emergence of social institutions in limited numbers of societies that had
like historical experiences. In another sense, Steward's theory was a
method for determining and verifying the causes of culture change. Following the comparative method, he explained cross-cultural similarities
or recurrences of social institutions by reference to ecological likenesses
in their settings. After using the comparative method as the first proof of
his hypothesis, he then went back into history to provide a second proof.
His conclusions were that the cultural ecological nexus of activity is a
principal determinant of social change and evolution.

Steward and White found common ground in an aspect of evolutionary theory that had never been refuted, not even by the Boasians. This is
the proposition, expressed in the works of Emile Durkheim and Herbert
Spencer, the nineteenth-century English social philosopher, that the evolution of society and culture is characterized by growth in scope and scale
of social-political units and by a progression from simple to complex social
organisms, or from homogeneity to heterogeneity. The increase in scope
and scale can be illustrated by comparing the small hunting bands of the
African Bushmen to modern nation-states. And the growth of complexity
is evident in the proliferation of criteria for distinguishing groups and
statuses, by the growth of the division of labor, and by the elaborate interdependencies of people in modern society. Steward referred to these
gradients of scope and complexity as "levels of sociocultural integration," a jawbreaker of a term, though descriptive enough. The simplest
and smallest type of social unit is exemplified by the almost autonomous
Shoshoni family, followed by the more stable local groups of hunting
bands or village-dwelling horticulturalists. The most complex and comprehensive of all social units in this sequence is the state. A similar series of
evolutionary stages was formulated by Elman Service, a student of White,
who saw a progressive growth from bands to tribes to chiefdoms to the
state, each larger in size and with more developed political controls.

Anthropology's interest in the transformations of society over time
led to the study of social and cultural changes resulting from the contact
of societies, a process called "acculturation" in anthropology. The earlier
phases of anthropological research aimed at the cataloguing and description of the remaining primitive cultures, and the study of cultural change
was confined mostly to evolutionary schemes or histories of trait diffusion.
By the 1920s it was becoming clear that little more could be learned about

"aboriginal" North American Indian cultures, and increasing attention was given to the changing circumstances of the reservation dwellers.

It was manifest that everywhere that Western culture had penetrated the territories of simple societies—which was indeed almost everywhere—vast changes had occurred in the ways of life of the primitives. Some groups were almost instantly decimated by diseases and others by the superior military technology of the Europeans. Interbreeding with the whites had leached off population, and many drifted off to life in the towns and settlements of the frontiers. The remaining American Indians were forced into reservations, whereas the people of South Africa were dragooned into work in the mines and on the farms of the white colonists; the Australian aborigines became dependents of mission stations, and the surviving Brazilian Indians were pushed far into the South American interior. Change was inevitable, and chaos common.

Acculturation is said to take place when two or more societies have firsthand and continuing contact with each other. One of the more important phenomena of acculturation is large-scale diffusion, brought about by emulation of the politically superior group, utilitarian motives, and sometimes by duress. The Spaniards forced Christianity on the Indians in their colonial domain, just as they forced them into work in the mines under the encomienda system and into agricultural labor on Spanish haciendas. In the process, the Indians often assimilated the customs of their conquerors, and today the "native" garb of many Mexican and Guatemalan Indians is really the dress style of sixteenth-century Spain. A good deal of syncretism resulted also, and one can still find blends of Catholic and Mayan ritual in the highlands of southern Mexico. The net flow of culture went in almost all cases from the stronger to the weaker group, but this was not a completely one-way movement. The Europeans borrowed tobacco, which has not done them very much good, but they also adopted Indian potatoes and maize, which did. Both societies in contact became transformed in the process, although not to the same degree.

Societies and their cultures form systems, and any disturbance in a part of a system may affect the others. This can happen through the introduction of a new item, as when steel axes allowed certain South American Indians enough new leisure time to embellish and intensify their ritual life, or when the Spanish-derived horse revolutionized Plains Indian cultures. More happens, however, than diffusion and its consequences. The groups in contact form a structure of ties with each other, which in turn modify and alter relations within each society. Moreover, the ecological adjustments of the groups may be radically modified. Culture contact commonly takes place through the intermediary of persons acting as agents of their respective societies. Government administrators and missionaries have in that sense played important "boundary roles," but the most pervasive and strongest ties are often established through trade and labor. The nonindustrialized people of the world have been, as we have noted, avid consumers of the manufactured goods of the West. The utilitarian lure of the steel axe in a past period is matched by the charms of transistor radios today. One Tuareg blacksmith, reports anthropologist Candelario Saenz, even has a television set; reception is possible in the deep Sahara desert through beaming by satellite.

All of these new things must be bought, and acculturation is in large part the story of how this is done and what are its social and ecological consequences. North American Indians were drawn into the fur trade, and their Amazonian cousins collect wild rubber. Pacific Islanders work on copra plantations, and West Africans grow cocoa. They have obtained manufactured goods in this way, but they also established close ties of dependency on white traders and changed their work patterns to accommodate the new activities. The search for marketable commodities had the effect of modifying rather delicate ecological relationships. Canadian Algonquian and Athapascan Indians trapped fur for the Hudson's Bay Company, developing proprietary rights in districts where they laid traplines. In time, Indian life and the focus of community came to center on the trading posts, and the band organizations of aboriginal times were correspondingly weakened. In South America, many Amazonian Indians became so enmeshed in debt to traders that the additional time spent in the individualized labor of rubber collection interfered with the agricultural cycle. Ecological readjustments have drastically modified primitive social systems, and trade by individuals has had the net effect of loosening communal interdependencies and sapping the functions of corporate groups. In the final analysis, the acculturation process will soon bring primitive culture to a close, as all the peoples of the world become increasingly drawn into the maw of mass, industrial society.

The study of acculturation joined with the expansion in scope and size of the anthropological discipline to draw the field away from absorption in the primitive world toward a concern with complex societies. American anthropologists such as Elsie Clews Parsons and Ruth Bunzel began working among Middle American Indians who, though primarily subsistence farmers, also produced a small surplus for sale in markets and were incorporated in the political systems of their nations. The study of such "peasant" societies took anthropology into confrontation with the problems of the modern world. Like primitive societies, peasant populations are being so heavily drawn into the world market economy and the political orbits of modern states that they are losing their semiautonomous status. The peasant is a disappearing type in France, Germany, and other European countries, where farming operations have become increasingly mechanized, requiring capital and bank loans, and numbers of farms have decreased with concurrent increases in farm sizes. The modern French peasant may well have a tractor, drive a car, consult with agricultural extension service specialists, and keep a close eye on Common Market agricultural policies. His life is a far cry from that of the simple tiller of the soil of less than a half century past.

The production of cash crops for a market has tended to make agriculture become less diversified, and the peasant who once supplied almost all of his family's food needs has become the contemporary farmer who raises a single crop and buys the bulk of his food at the supermarket. Farm specialization has meant greater vulnerability to outside forces. In bad times, the peasant was able to fall back on his own resources, but today's soybean or sugar beet farmer is at the mercy of government price supports and world market prices. The peasant is being torn out of his semiisolation by forces beyond his ken or control, ending forever his self-sufficiency and making him willy-nilly an integral part of national economies and political systems.

The process of modernization, as it is often called, has been almost as traumatic for peasants as for primitives. Some attempts have been made to ease the transition. International programs of aid to non-industrial countries have dispatched agronomists armed with new plants and techniques, animal husbandry specialists, medical people and sanitarians, road builders, and even anthropologists. The latter, or "applied anthropologists," are usually charged with giving advice on how to make proffered changes more acceptable. Applied anthropologists have had some success in introducing public health and other programs, but their general effectiveness is limited by the policies of governments. They are seldom asked whether the introduction of some innovation is desirable in the first place, and by the time they are called in to study the consequences of programs, it is usually too late to correct them. Anthropology has, however, a very important message for planners and policy makers: this is the dictum repeated so often in this book that human actions inevitably bring a train of consequences that were in no way anticipated, planned, or foreseen by those responsible for the decisions. We are all indeed the victims as well as the unwitting creators of history.

Aid programs and applied anthropology are being overwhelmed and lost in the great changes happening throughout the world today. The rural universe of the peasantry has been opened up by new roads and airports, its visions broadened and its disappointments made more acute by education, its culture brought closer to that of the nation by mass media. Anthropologists started to study peasant communities as if they were as removed from the outer world as those of primitives—very few of whom are completely isolated—but they soon learned that the structure of community life and the directions of social change were in part determined by actions and policies emanating from cities and national governments. The study of the peasant community became a part of a more general inquiry into the nature of social transformation and a steppingstone in an attempt to understand national cultures.

The city has come to the country, but the countrymen have also gone to the city. A combination of the lure of wage labor in monetary economies, high rural birthrates in the underdeveloped world, and increasing consolidation and mechanization of farms have sent migrants streaming into the cities from lands that could no longer support them. Anthropologists had been occasional students of the city since the 1940s, but more concerted research came about through tracing the tribulations of rural migrants to the cities. The late Oscar Lewis studied the Mexican peasant village of Tepoztlan and later followed many Tepoztecans to the Mexico City barrio where they had settled. In recent years, anthropologists have worked among American Indians relocated in the cities, and with various ethnic minorities and urbanites of all stripes. Research in large-scale societies having huge populations and great internal diversity has forced the adoption of many sociological methods for insuring accuracy and representativeness of data. The urban anthropologist still uses traditional interviews and observations, but he also goes armed with questionnaires and computer programs. Methodology and theory have yielded to the circumstances and subjects of research among British anthropologists as well. The neat social system boundaries of functionalism did not fit analyses of copper miners in the Katanga or wage laborers in Zambian cities, leading to a profound loosening of what had been a tight methodology. Attention shifted away from stable and bounded social systems to "social fields" or "social arenas," open-ended concepts that dealt less with corporate groupings than with networks of interpersonal relations. Such "network analysis" attempts description of social relations through following out the bonds between individuals until the various strands encompass the population under study, or at least that part necessary to resolve a problem. There are no neat limits in the methodology, just as there are none in the groups being studied.

One finding of urban anthropology is that formerly rural people often form enclaves within cities, preserving the values, language, and customs of their origins. The sociologist Herbert Gans has coined the felicitous term "urban villagers" to describe the extent to which city neighborhoods can become turned inward and parochialized. There is nothing in all this that any New Yorker—or Chicagoan or Bostonian—did not already know from personal experience. People in large and alien cities create within the mass of population little islands of people whom they know, whose language and values they understand, and with whom they can form little communities. They thus find love, companionship, and the reassurances of the familiar.

Neighborhoods and barrios ease the shift to urban life by minimizing changes in attitude and behavior, but they can only slow down, and not arrest, the urbanization of city dwellers. The phenomena of urbanization are in large part processes that are occurring in industrial society at large. They are first and best exemplified by the cities but not peculiar to them, for in the most technologically advanced societies the gap between the culture of the cities and that of the countryside is narrowing rapidly. The nature of this transformation is basic and affects the entire fabric and quality of social life. It is described in Karl Marx's ideas on alienation and Max Weber's theory of the growth of rational society. Variations on these themes are presented, recalling Chapter 7, in Maine's notions on the move from status to contract, in Tönnies's concept of the shift from *Gemeinschaft* to *Gesellschaft* and in Durkheim's ideas on the transition from mechanical to organic solidarity. Out of the work of these founders, and from the perspective of modern social research, we can see the broad outlines of the future.

Fueled by a technology whose expansion is explosive, accelerated by soaring populations, and marked by growing internal complexity and differentiation, modern society is evolving toward a future that leaves most people troubled and uncertain. Social systems and the very tone and quality of social life have been altered in ways that leave the individual progressively more alone and with less social definition. There has been a wide tendency for ascription of status to give way to achievement. The particularism of the past is yielding to a kind of universalism that sees all humans to be distinguished only by their individual abilities and attainments. This is, from one perspective, a realization of aspirations for freedom and equality of opportunity, but, from another point of view, it is an end product of the reduction of people and their labor to commodities, one of Marx's major themes. In a fully rationalized industrial bureaucracy, a worker's kin, sex or skin color should make little difference, for the interest of those who use his or her labor lies only in the ability to carry out the role. The legitimate aspirations of the oppressed may thus be realized through the evolution of the postindustrial society of the future, and time will tell if this can be achieved while avoiding the facelessness of an anthill society.

One problem in the decades to come will be the maintenance of a value upon the individual at a time when many of the traditional criteria of personal identity are being erased. Superficially, it would appear that the growing isolation of the individual and the weakening solidarity of social groups in general may contribute to the strengthening of individuality as a positive personal attribute, but it is not so simple. The erosion of extended bonds of kinship has moved apace with decline of church participation, the swallowing of small economic units by large conglomerates, and the growing anonymity of city life. What appears to be individualism is really aloneness, and, since personal identity is in good part derived from one's social relations, their infrequency and amorphousness can result in loss of a clear definition of the self.

Universalism and individuation are closely linked to the decline of diffuse social roles and the growth of significance in our lives of functionally specific ones. And inasmuch as the former roles are generally suffused with emotional tone, whereas the latter ones are neutral, relations are correspondingly more shallow and entail less individual commitment. They are also less rewarding. These are the ingredients of a new kind of culture in which individuals are set adrift in a social world lacking depth or love, engaged in activities that have little inherent meaning, and turned in on themselves in private narcissism. Industrial man long ago became estranged from the products of his labor, and he is now increasingly estranged from his fellows, and himself. These are the contours of a future that has not fully arrived but whose vanguard is already here.

Another direction of our modern age is the decline of a form of social life that was infused with the aura of sacredness and the emergence in its place of a thoroughgoing secularism. There is far more involved here than the fortunes of churches, which seem to go up and down these days in keeping with the whims of fashion. What is really happening is that the magic is going out of life, and with it the sense of wonder, awe, and otherness that in simpler times charged all aspects of culture. The methods and results of the sciences have invaded our everyday thinking, and this may be all to the good, but it has been at the expense of charm and in the direction of a further flattening of the landscape of the imagination.

These transformations are not peculiar to American culture, or even to capitalistic societies, but are a direction of industrial societies everywhere. One result of these grinding processes is that cultural differences are decreasing among the more technologically advanced countries, whereas the primitive and peasant populations of the world are being acculturated to our norms. It is questionable that all cultural differences will be submerged by these convergences, but there is no doubt that similarities will increase and the more riotously colorful forms of diversity will disappear. We are heading for a worldwide culture of a sort, but there are too many imponderables to allow a prediction of exactly what it will be like. We do not know how or if the energy crisis will be resolved, we cannot predict new technology accurately, and we do not know whether nuclear warfare can be avoided. We only know that we are on the frontiers of unknown country, a time when the institutions of the past will be nullified by the future. This is a period of great indeterminacy and peril, and even greater possibilities.

Epilogue

The narrative is ended, the scope and vision of social anthropology set forth, its findings presented. We have answered the question of *what* social anthropology is, and there remains only the issue of *why?* What use is it? Which human needs does it satisfy? What are its purposes beyond ethnic voyeurism and curio hunting? These seem to be the truly difficult issues.

Questions of so fundamental a nature can only be answered by posing another, more basic, question—the dialectical method of discourse of ancient Greek philosophers and New York delicatessen clerks. The counter-question that must first be considered is: why man? What are humanity's purposes? What is mankind's goal? All persons will have different answers to these questions, depending on their culture, their creed, their position in life; but unless these questions can be answered, there is no use considering the value of anthropology or of almost anything else. The anthropological answer is, however, transparently simple: mankind has no purpose at all in any absolute or final sense.

Life had its beginnings in certain accidental events that befell carbon molecules over three billion years ago. These were accidents that could happen elsewhere in the universe wherever a similarly propitious situation existed, and they probably did, again and again. The subsequent career of life on our planet during all the intervening eons has been toward differentiation and multiplication of bioforms. The direction of evolution, and the only absolute purpose of life, is to fill every available niche of the environment with protoplasm. Nothing more. Lest this be considered an austere, even nihilistic, viewpoint, it should be recalled that this was a latent premise of the entire book. Life does have purpose and values, but these are humanly bestowed. We are meaningful, then, only because we believe we are, and our meanings are arbitrary. This is one of the great lessons of anthropology and sufficient justification for its existence.

The social uses of the discipline, as distinguished from its broad goals, have been many. On the barest utilitarian level, anthropologists have introduced outhouses and new tools and seeds in undeveloped areas, they have advised on the relocation of migrants, and they have, alas, even taken part in intelligence operations. It is this kind of usefulness that seems reasonable to most Americans, who might ask whether anthropology is worthwhile without ever doubting the common sense of paying a million dollars a year to grown men for playing children's games or questioning the absolute value of electric can openers, roll-on deodorants, aerosol douches, and every other gewgaw and gimcrack purveyed in our society.

Applied anthropology can be a powerful tool if used properly, but the true practical usefulness of anthropology lies in its educational functions. From the time of Franz Boas, anthropology has been the single most effective voice against racist theories. The fight against racist practices must, in the final analysis, be waged by its victims, for the struggle itself is the condition of their liberation. Racist ideas, however, must be displaced by other ideas, and anthropology has had singular success in disproving and discrediting the ideology of prejudice. It is a battle that must be fought in every generation, for racism serves important political and economic interests, but it is a struggle in which all the facts are with the anthropological perspective. The latter is very simply that the differences between the customs and attainments of different peoples are not the product of dark biological forces but are due to culture.

The idea of culture was revolutionary in other ways. It represented an important step in the objectification and demystification of society. In doing so, it robbed social life of some of its enchantment, but it also made it more accessible to reason. Whereas humans once limned the dimensions of their societies in the symbolism of the sacred, they now do so in the language of science. And where they once found awe and transcendent power in society, they now find an object of criticism, a thing that can be transformed. This gives birth to the hope that having understood the forces of culture, we can contain and control them. In the process of understanding society, then, we have separated ourselves from it. The dimensions of this change in our way of thinking about ourselves remain to be charted, but they are vast. In a very real—and perhaps terrifying—sense, we are becoming self-conscious to a degree beyond anything in past experience.

The uses and results of anthropology are great, but its true goal, the one that it sets for itself, is nothing less than to describe and explain the ways of man. We are brief and temporal creatures, our lives finished in a blink of the eye of human history, which in itself may be only a short flash in interstellar time, and our purpose is a fiction of our own devising. If man's ultimate goals are his own creation, then he should also be their subject matter. What else is there for us to do but contemplate our surroundings and ourselves? What other purposes could mankind have? Many sciences study the human situation, but only anthropology tries to see the full panorama, in time and space, of the career of our species. There was a time when seers, mythmakers, and theologians were charged with explaining humanity to itself, but their age is passing. In their place, the secular students of man have assumed the responsibility for understanding humanity's position in the cosmos. The results of the anthropological enterprise lack the poetry of its predecessors, but its curiosity has laid bare a world that is no less remarkable.

Suggested Readings

Dates in parentheses indicate year of first publication, where different from issue cited.

I Prologue to Anthropology

FIRTH, RAYMOND. *Human Types*. New York: New American Library, 1956.

FRIED, MORTON. *The Study of Anthropology*. New York: Thomas Crowell Co., 1972.

LÉVI-STRAUSS, CLAUDE. *Tristes Tropiques*. New York: Atheneum, 1974 (1955).

WHITE, LESLIE. *The Science of Culture*. New York: Farrar, Straus, & Giroux, 1949.

II The Human Situation

ALLAND, ALEXANDER. *The Human Imperative*. New York: Columbia University Press, 1972.

FREUD, SIGMUND. *Civilization and its Discontents*. New York: W. W. Norton & Co., 1962 (1930).

LaBarre, Weston. *The Human Animal.* Chicago: University of Chicago Press, 1954.

Lévi-Strauss, Claude. *Structural Anthropology I.* New York: Basic Books, Inc., 1963.

Murphy, Robert F. *The Dialectics of Social Life.* New York: Basic Books, Inc., 1971.

Simmel, Georg. *The Sociology of Georg Simmel* (K. Wolff, ed.). New York: The Free Press, 1964.

III Social Systems

Banton, Michael. *Roles.* New York: Basic Books, Inc., 1965.

Benedict, Ruth. *Patterns of Culture.* New York: Houghton-Mifflin Co., 1961 (1934).

Firth, Raymond. *Elements of Social Organization.* Boston: Beacon Press, 1963 (1951).

Linton, Ralph. *The Study of Man.* Englewood Cliffs, N.J.: Prentice-Hall, Inc., 1964 (1936).

Mead, Margaret. *Sex and Temperament in Three Primitive Societies.* New York: Mentor, 1950.

Mead, Margaret. *Male and Female.* New York: William Morrow & Co., Inc., 1975 (1949).

Merton, Robert. *Social Theory and Social Structure.* New York: Free Press, 1968 (1949).

Murphy, Yolanda, and Robert F. Murphy. *Women of the Forest.* New York: Columbia University Press, 1974.

Radcliffe-Brown, A. R. *Structure and Function in Primitive Society.* New York: The Free Press, 1965 (1952).

IV Marriage and Family

Fox, Robin. *Kinship and Marriage.* New York: Penguin Books, Inc., 1968.

Freud, Sigmund. *Totem and Taboo.* New York: Random House, 1960 (1913).

Lévi-Strauss, Claude. *The Elementary Structures of Kinship.* Boston: Beacon Press, 1969 (1949).

Schneider, David M. *American Kinship.* Englewood Cliffs, N.J.: Prentice-Hall, Inc., 1968.

Willmott, Peter, and Michael Young. *Family and Kinship in East London.* Baltimore: Penguin Books, 1962.

V The Net of Kinship

EVANS-PRITCHARD, E. E. *The Nuer.* New York: Oxford University Press, 1969 (1940).

GRABURN, NELSON (ed.). *Readings in Kinship and Social Structure.* New York: Harper & Row, 1971.

LOWIE, ROBERT. *Primitive Society.* New York: Liveright Publishing Corp., 1970 (1920).

MORGAN, LEWIS HENRY. *Systems of Consanguinity and Affinity of the Human Family.* Atlantic Highlands, N.J.: Humanities Press, Inc., 1966 (1870).

MURDOCK, G. P. *Social Structure.* New York: Free Press, 1965 (1949).

RIVERS, W.H.R. *Kinship and Social Organization.* London: Constable, 1914.

SAHLINS, MARSHALL. *Tribesmen.* Englewood Cliffs, N.J.: Prentice-Hall, Inc., 1968.

SCHUSKY, ERNEST. *Manual for Kinship Analysis* (2nd ed.). New York: Holt, Rinehart and Winston, 1965.

SERVICE, ELMAN. *Primitive Social Organization* (2nd ed.). New York: Random House, 1971.

VI Ecology and Economy

MALINOWSKI, BRONISLAW. *Argonauts of the Western Pacific.* New York: Dutton & Co., Inc., 1961 (1922).

NASH, MANNING. *Primitive and Peasant Economic Systems.* San Francisco: Chandler Publishing Co., 1966.

POLANYI, KARL, CONRAD ARENSBERG AND HARRY PEARSON (eds.). *Trade and Market in the Early Empires.* Glencoe, Ill.: Free Press, 1957.

SAHLINS, MARSHALL. *Stone Age Economics.* Chicago: Aldine, 1972.

STEWARD, JULIAN H. *Theory of Culture Change.* Urbana: University of Illinois Press, 1976 (1955).

VII Order and Authority

ENGELS, FRIEDRICH. *Origin of the Family, Private Property and the State.* New York: International Publishers, 1972 (1884).

FORTES, MEYER AND E. E. EVANS-PRITCHARD (eds.). *African Political Systems.* New York: Oxford University Press, 1958 (1940).

FRIED, MORTON. *The Evolution of Political Society.* New York: Random House, 1967.

VIII Religion

DURKHEIM, EMILE. *The Elementary Forms of the Religious Life.* Glencoe, Ill.: Free Press, 1954 (1912).

FREUD, SIGMUND. *Moses and Monotheism.* New York: Random House, 1955 (1937).

HARNER, MICHAEL (ed.). *Hallucinogens and Shamanism.* New York: Oxford University Press, 1973.

LaBARRE, WESTON. *The Ghost Dance.* New York: Delta Publishing Co., Inc., 1970.

MALINOWSKI, BRONISLAW. *Magic, Science and Religion.* Garden City, N.Y.: Doubleday & Co., Inc., 1954 (1948).

MAUSS, MARCEL AND HENRI HUBERT. *Sacrifice.* Chicago: University of Chicago Press, 1964 (1897–1898).

RADIN, PAUL. *Primitive Religion.* New York: Dover Publications, 1937.

TYLOR, E. B. *Religion in Primitive Culture.* New York: Harper & Row, 1958 (1871).

VAN GENNEP, A. *The Rites of Passage.* Chicago: University of Chicago Press, 1960 (1909).

WALLACE, ANTHONY. *Religion.* New York: Random House, 1966.

WEBER, MAX. *The Protestant Ethic and the Spirit of Capitalism.* New York: Charles Scribner & Sons, 1958 (1904–5).

WORSLEY, PETER. *The Trumpet Shall Sound.* New York: Schocken Books, 1968 (1957).

IX The Unfolding World

HARRIS, MARVIN. *Cannibals and Kings.* New York: Random House, 1977.

MORGAN, LEWIS HENRY. *Ancient Society.* New York: Meridian Books, 1963 (1877).

REDFIELD, ROBERT. *The Primitive World and its Transformations.* Ithaca, N.Y.: Cornell University Press, 1957.

STEWARD, JULIAN H. *Evolution and Ecology: Essays on Social Transformation* (Jane C. Steward and Robert F. Murphy, eds.). Urbana: University of Illinois Press, 1977.

WHITE, LESLIE. *The Evolution of Culture.* New York: McGraw-Hill Book Co., 1959.

WISSLER, CLARK. *The American Indian.* New York: D.C. McMurtie, 1917.

INDEX

Page numbers in *italics* stand for figures.

213